DRAWING MEN TO GOD

MEN'S MINISTRY MANUAL

Compiled by Sid Woodruff

LifeWay Press
Nashville, Tennessee

ISBN 0-7673-9077-6

Dewey Decimal Classification: 267.2
Subject Heading: MEN'S MINISTRY

This book is the text for course LS-0034 in the Adult Leadership and Skill Development diploma plan in the Christian Growth Study Plan.

Scripture quotations identified as GNB are from the *Good News Bible*, the Bible in Today's English Version. Old Testament: Copyright © American Bible Society 1976; New Testament: Copyright © American Bible Society 1966, 1971, 1976. Used by permission.

Scripture quotations identified as NASB are taken from the NEW AMERICAN STANDARD BIBLE, © Copyright The Lockman Foundation, 1960, 1962, 1963, 1968, 1971, 1972, 1973, 1975, 1977. Used by permission.

Scripture quotations identified as NIV are from the Holy Bible, *New International Version*, copyright © 1973, 1978, 1984 by International Bible Society.

Scripture quotations identified as CEV are taken from the *Contemporary English Version*. Copyright © 1991, 1992, 1995 American Bible Society. Used by permission.

Scripture quotations identified as KJV are from the *King James Version* of the Bible.

Order additional copies of this book by writing to Customer Service Center, MSN 113; 127 Ninth Avenue, North; Nashville, TN 37234-0113; by calling toll free (800) 458-2772; by faxing (615) 251-5933; by ordering online at *www.lifeway.com*; by emailing *customerservice@lifeway.com*; or by visiting a LifeWay Christian Store.

For information about adult discipleship and family resources, training, and events, visit our Web site at *www.lifeway.com/discipleplus*.

Cover Illustration: Edward Crawford
Design: Stephen Phanco

Printed in the United States of America

LifeWay.

LifeWay Press
127 Ninth Avenue, North
Nashville, Tennessee 37234-0151

As God works through us, we will help people and churches know Jesus Christ and seek His kingdom by providing biblical solutions that spiritually transform individuals and cultures.

CONTENTS

THE WRITERS

The Compiler

Sid Woodruff, the compiler of *Drawing Men to God: Men's Ministry Manual*, is the men's ministry specialist in the Adult Discipleship and Family Department at LifeWay Christian Resources of the Southern Baptist Convention. Sid is a graduate of Baylor University, where he played on the football team. He holds a master of divinity degree from Southwestern Baptist Theological Seminary in Fort Worth, Texas, where he has also done doctoral study. Prior to joining LifeWay in September 1997, Sid served several churches in a variety of staff positions and was the pastor of West Conroe Baptist Church in Conroe, Texas, where he saw the church grow from 58 to 1,500 members in 13 years.

Sid is also the editor-in-chief of *Stand Firm*, a monthly devotional magazine for men. He has spoken to men's groups all over the United States. He currently serves on the steering committee of the National Coalition of Men's Ministries, a network of men's ministry leaders from more than 20 denominations, representing more than 200,000 churches and most parachurch men's ministries in America.

The Contributors

Nate Adams	Vice-President, Mobilization and Mission Education The North American Mission Board of the Southern Baptist Convention Alpharetta, Georgia
Jim Brown	Consultant, Human Needs and Crisis Management The International Mission Board of the Southern Baptist Convention Richmond, Virginia
Richard Brunson	Executive Director/Treasurer, North Carolina Baptist Men Cary, North Carolina
Phil Downer	President, Christian Business Men's Committee Chattanooga, Tennessee
Toby Frost	Event Evangelism Manager The North American Mission Board of the Southern Baptist Convention Alpharetta, Georgia
Don Gibson	Assistant Executive Director, Texas Baptist Men Dallas, Texas
Bobby Jackson	Director of Men's Ministries, South Carolina Baptist Convention Columbia, South Carolina
Patrick Morley	President, Man in the Mirror, Inc. Casselberry, Florida
Joseph Northcut	Team Leader, Field Service, Adult Discipleship and Family Department LifeWay Christian Resources of the Southern Baptist Convention Nashville, Tennessee
Jerry Pipes	Director, Ministry Evangelism Team The North American Mission Board of the Southern Baptist Convention Alpharetta, Georgia
Steve Sonderman	Associate Pastor of Men's Ministries, Elmbrook Church Brookfield, Wisconsin
Sid Woodruff	Men's Ministry Specialist, Adult Discipleship and Family Department LifeWay Christian Resources of the Southern Baptist Convention Nashville, Tennessee

INTRODUCTION

◆

Sid Woodruff

hen it comes to assembling things, I don't always take time to read the directions. I would rather try to put it together first and then resort to reading the instructions only if I can't figure it out on my own. But writing and compiling this book was different. From the beginning I knew that I needed help, and I did not hesitate to ask for it. I sought help from God and from others who specialize in men's ministry. With all of this help available, I thought this manual would come together easily. It didn't.

From the beginning the writing was slow and difficult. This mystified and frustrated me, because I felt that I had done much to prepare myself for this assignment. I had devoted hours to prayer, Bible study, and ministry in the local church. I had conducted numerous interviews with pastors, laymen, and men's ministry specialists around the country. I had also done extensive reading on the subject. But after weeks of laboring over an incomplete manuscript, it seemed as if none of this advance preparation mattered.

Fear overtook me as publishing deadlines approached. I feared failing those who were relying on me to complete this assignment on time. In hopes of quickly getting something down on paper, I tried to restate what others had already written on men's ministry. But there was a noticeable absence of God's peace and blessing on everything I attempted to rewrite. I soon recognized this as God's way of getting my attention.

I vividly remember a Wednesday morning when I hit rock bottom. In desperation for a movement of God, I bowed my head in front of the computer in my office. Tears fell on the keyboard as I cried: "Lord, I'm relying on You. Why aren't You helping me complete this men's ministry manual?"

Immediately, God revealed to me why the book had been placed on hold. Although I had been telling God how much I needed Him, my actions had actually indicated that I had more confidence in what others had written on the subject. That morning I apologized to the Heavenly Father for doubting what He wanted to say to me personally about men's ministry.

Other church leaders may have made the same mistake. They may have asked God for direction, but rather than waiting on the Lord for His answer, they turned away to see what someone else was doing. The result is that many of God's servants are missing the fresh, unique things the Lord wants to do through them. This breaks the heart of the Heavenly Father, who delights in revealing Himself to the world through His activity in the lives of His children.

In John 15:4-5 Jesus taught that God not only gives life but also produces fruit in believers' lives. The secret to this productivity is in the relationship between the branch and the Vine. Unfortunately, many of God's servants today elect to master someone else's method rather than develop their own daily walk with the Master. When the people of Israel were making their journey from Egypt to the Promised Land, they did not know where God was leading them. He faithfully led them "in a pillar of cloud by day ... and in a pillar of fire by night" (Ex. 13:21-22, NASB). Similarly, God has a unique route for each church to take in men's ministry, and He will faithfully guide those who keep their eyes on Him.

> *"I am the vine,*
> *you are the branches;*
> *he who abides in Me,*
> *and I in him,*
> *he bears much fruit;*
> *for apart from Me*
> *you can do nothing."*
>
> John 15:5, NASB

✳ **Before you read any further, stop here and prayerfully answer the following questions.**

What evidence exists that you are trusting God for the direction of your men's ministry?

_____

_____

_____

What has God said to you personally about your needs as a man?

_____

_____

As you read this manual, frequently returning to those two questions will help you remain reliant on God for your ministry and relevant with men in your ministry.

A CLEAR VIEW OF MEN'S MINISTRY

In Deuteronomy 34:1-3 the Lord brought Moses to the "top of Pisgah" (NASB) so that he could look into Canaan. From the top of the mountain Moses could clearly see the land. Many churches want to see what lies ahead in men's ministry. This manual was written to help bring pastors, church staff, and laymen to the top of the mountain so that they can give visionary leadership to men's ministry, seamlessly integrating and implementing evangelism, discipleship, ministry, and missions. The manual provides a biblically based model for reaching men and practical tools for starting and evaluating men's ministry in a local church.

The diagram on the inside front cover of the manual illustrates how an integrated men's ministry connects men to God and to one another. It features men working together in the local church to reach a common goal: for every Christian man to discover how he is uniquely called and shaped by God to live the Great Commandment (see Mark 12:30-31) and to fulfill the Great Commission (see Matt. 28:19-20) in every aspect of his life—personal, home, church, workplace, community, and world.

AN EFFECTIVE MEN'S MINISTRY IN EVERY CHURCH

A church of any size and location can have an effective men's ministry if it follows several basic biblical guidelines. These guidelines are depicted on a diagram to illustrate how they work together to move men toward the common goal. As you examine the diagram, bear in mind that all illustrations have their limitations, and this diagram is no exception. Keep your eyes focused on the goal and do not become distracted by the diagram itself.

The points (chapters) in this manual were written to teach and apply each of the following guidelines. Effective men's ministries are careful to score each of the following winning points.

Point 1. *Partner with God, the pastor, and other men and surround the ministry with prayer.* Connecting men to God, the pastor, and one another is vital. The highest compliment that can be paid to a men's ministry is that it is led by men of prayer who are surrendered to hearing and obeying God in every area of life.

Point 2. *Propose a written, biblically based purpose statement.* Search the Scriptures together to define the goal for your men's ministry. Develop a statement that is clear and concise. Publicize this statement frequently and in a variety of ways so that the men remember it and take ownership of it.

Point 3. *Prepare leaders.* As the leaders go, so goes the ministry. Healthy men's ministries have a leader-training process and do not launch new ministries until they have godly leaders who are called and prepared to direct them.

Point 4. *Plan a balanced ministry that meets needs and develops disciples.* This point ensures that you understand your men's needs and plan a course of action that helps them work and move together toward the goal.

Point 5. *Provide multiple entry points and pursue participants through relationships.* The men of each church and community have different interests, pressures, schedules, and incomes. They also vary in spiritual maturity. Draw men and keep them involved through common interests and relationships with one another.

Point 6. *Promote times to celebrate God's victories and to kick off new ministries together.* Throughout the Bible God's people prayed for one another and celebrated God's victories together. Men's ministries should do the same.

✴ **How did you feel when you read the six points involved in launching a men's ministry? Check all that apply.**

❑ Excited   ❑ Overwhelmed
❑ Inadequate   ❑ Worried
❑ Thankful   ❑ Frustrated
❑ Other: _____

As you evaluate your ministry to and with men, remember that God takes only a few days to grow a squash plant but years to grow a mighty oak tree. Likewise, there are no shortcuts to growing a mighty men's ministry. It takes time to grow a disciple. Trust God to start with you where you are and rely on Him to score each point.

Genesis 5:24 tells us that "Enoch walked with God" (NASB). He was a man of integrity who stood tall in his faith. Men's ministry seeks to produce men like Enoch. Men's ministry seeks to develop men who, like John the Baptist, walk before the Lord " 'in the spirit and power of Elijah, to turn the hearts of the fathers back to the children, and the disobedient to the attitude of the righteous; so as to make ready a people prepared for the Lord' " (Luke 1:17, NASB). *Drawing Men to God* has been written with the prayer that God will use it as a tool to help churches develop not just better methods but also better men. It will take you and God working together to make that happen.

POINT 1

◆

Partner and Pray

1. Partner and pray

Imagine that you are seated in a sports arena prior to a huge sporting event. Before the contestants are introduced, the lights in the arena are dimmed, and the enthusiastic voice of an announcer is heard over the public-address system: "Ladies and gentlemen, welcome to the main event!" The crowd comes to its feet. The darkness is broken by a spotlight that strikes dead center on the floor of the arena. Something big is about to happen.

Every ministry has a focal point, a main event to which the audience is directed. An examination of Jesus' ministry reveals that the main event for Him was " 'to seek and to save that which was lost' " (Luke 19:10, NASB). By His sinless life and substitutionary death on the cross, Jesus paid the penalty for the sins of humankind. He gave His life so that we could have eternal and abundant life by trusting in Him for salvation. But this main event had another aspect. Jesus made advance preparations for spreading His message. During His 3½-year ministry He devoted a majority of His time to the spiritual development of the men He called to be His disciples. By openly living His life before them, Jesus was able to teach these men lessons from life. He modeled for them what it means to be a man of integrity, how to respect and treat women and

children with dignity and honor, and how to be a servant leader. The Book of Acts shows that the time Jesus invested in the lives of His disciples paid huge dividends. With the power of the indwelling Holy Spirit these men became faithful, bold witnesses for Jesus Christ, bringing hope to a world that was consumed by sin and wallowing in despair.

Wise churches will follow Christ's example by investing in the spiritual development of men. In Matthew 4:19 Andrew and Peter heard Jesus say, " 'Follow Me, and I will make you fishers of men' " (NASB). Jesus implied that fishing for men involves a learning process. By following Jesus' example, we learn how to be good fishers of men. Like a good fisherman who studies the fish—how and where to catch them, what and when they eat, and the kind of equipment needed to catch them—churches that want to be effective in making disciples of all men must use the right approach when fishing for men. Each church must develop an intentional strategy for reaching men for Christ.

"Follow Me, and I will make you fishers of men."

Matthew 4:19, NASB

WHY HAVE A MEN'S MINISTRY?

A great spiritual hunger exists in our world today. For years we have witnessed a significant, life-changing movement in and through men. Some, labeling it a

men's movement, have evaluated it from social, politi-
cal, and spiritual perspectives. Others have judged it as
a reaction to the women's movement. Actually, it is
something very different. Rather than a movement of
men, it is a movement of God's Spirit in and through
the hearts of men.

Not long ago it was almost impossible to gather men
for any kind of event, let alone for a Christian conference at a football stadium. This movement of God's
Spirit has little to do with any one men's ministry but
everything to do with His sovereignty. This work points
to a deep spiritual hunger. Men are discovering that
they have a God-shaped void that only He can fill. They
want lives that count for something, that really make a
difference. Men want their lives to be productive, to
have real meaning and purpose.[1]

In men God has given us a tremendous, untapped
resource to assist in changing and influencing our world,
our cities, our workplaces, our families, our neighborhoods, and our relationships for Christ. In this manual
you will discover how to mobilize this great force to do
God's work in the world today. The first step is to
examine men's needs and the challenges they face.

The Needs Are Great

Alexander Mitserlisch once wrote: "Society has torn the
soul of the male, and into this tear the demons have
fled—the demons of insecurity, selfishness and despair.
Consequently, men do not know who they are as men.
Rather, they define themselves by what they do, who
they know, or by what they own."[2] The following facts
illustrate the spiritual state of American men today.
These statistics are from a nationwide survey of a ran-
dom sampling of two thousand men.

- Approximately 94 million males are 18 or older.
- On a typical weekend about 26 million men
  attend church services; 68 million do not.
- During a typical week roughly 27 million men
  read the Bible; 67 million do not.
- One of three men embraces Jesus Christ as Savior
  and Lord; 60 million rely on other means for
  "salvation."
- Eighty-five percent of all unchurched men were
  previously churched.
- Since 1991 church attendance, Bible reading, Sunday School attendance, volunteering at church, and
  contributions to church have all decreased among
  men. The proportion of born-again men has
  remained unchanged.
- From 1992 to 1996 the average church attendance
  among men has declined.[3]

What do these statistics say about men and about our
need to connect them with God's life-changing power?
God's heart is broken over men who—

- are spiritually lost;
- are caught in cycles of pain, addiction, and sin;
- are confused about masculinity;
- have rejected their commitment to marriage;
- abuse their spouses and children;
- have abandoned their families physically or
  emotionally;
- have been captured by pornography;
- have been deluded by the pursuit of worldly
  success;
- have been disillusioned by the false promises of
  wealth and power.

✳ **As you reread the previous list, think about the
men you know. Write beside each category the
initials or names of men who fit that category.**

Sixty-eight million men do not attend church.
Unchurched men today have the following needs.

Unchurched men need understanding. They want a
church that helps them truly understand the Bible.
They want a church that seeks to understand them.

Unchurched men need relationship. Most men feel
lonely, isolated, and disconnected. They would appreciate a church that brings them in contact with like-
minded peers in a nonthreatening setting.

Unchurched men need instruction for kids. Millions of
men want their kids to have positive Christian learning
experiences.

Unchurched men need solutions. Men are staggered by
the pressures they carry. Most men require that the
church provide practical, tangible solutions to the difficult problems they face daily. They want to know spiritual principles that make life "work." The church must
answer the questions men are asking.

Unchurched men need to know God. Many unchurched
men have given up on organized religion but not on
God. They want to know God but don't know how.[4]

It's becoming clear to men that activities, professions,
hobbies, sex, addictions, sports, and traditional church
programs cannot fill the void in their lives. Their hunger
finds ultimate fulfillment in a pure, right, and intimate
relationship with the Heavenly Father, accessed through
the life and work of His Son, Jesus Christ. Men are discovering that without this relationship their church
attendance, commitments, promises, and good inten-
tions lead to little personal satisfaction. These men need
to be confronted with the life-changing grace of Jesus
Christ. They need to hear the good news that His
power is greater than any problems they face. And they
need to understand how they can gain the fulfillment
they long for by living and working for His purposes.

What about men who have already accepted Jesus
Christ as their personal Savior and Lord? They have
daily opportunities to become involved in what He is
doing; yet many are hindered by great problems and

challenges. A survey of Promise Keepers attendees conducted by the National Center for Fathering, an independent research foundation, revealed that Christian men have a number of deep needs in their lives.

Christian men are not satisfied with themselves. Forty-four percent would like to change the way they feel about themselves. Forty-three percent feel a deep sense of failure when they think about their pasts.

Christian men are not satisfied with their marriages and family lives. Only 25 percent indicate satisfaction with themselves as fathers, while only 62 percent are satisfied with their relationships with their wives.

Christian men experience stress on the job. Eighty-one percent describe their jobs as highly stressful, while 63 percent are concerned about the future health of their careers.

Christian men struggle with sexual matters. Fifty-three percent admit fantasizing about sex with other women. Fifty-four percent state that they feel shame about past sexual experiences.

Christian men need relationships with other men with whom they can be open and honest. Seventy-five percent in the survey have feelings they do not share with anyone. Only 35 percent have others to hold them accountable for their sexual thoughts and behavior.[5]

✳ **What other needs would you identify for the men in your church?**

_____

_____

Men want to be successful, to feel significant, and to have meaning in life. Men want to be good husbands, good fathers, and the spiritual leaders of their families. But many of them do not know how to accomplish these goals. The programs the church has used to reach lost men and to meet the needs of redeemed men are not sufficient. George Barna states: "The explosive growth of Promise Keepers in the past several years is clear evidence of a turn in American churches: men are finding freedom and renewal in the name of Christ. But outside the church, the battle for the hearts of male America is just beginning to take shape. The stage is set for a dramatic awakening of our nation's men."[6]

A men's ministry can provide the spiritual direction men need to join God's work in every area of their lives. A men's ministry that draws men to Christ and mobilizes them for ministry must be based on a thorough knowledge of their specific needs and characteristics.

✳ **Use "Men's Ministry Questionnaire" on pages 10–11 to gather information about the men in your locale.**

The Benefits Are Life-Changing

Today is a new day in men's ministry, a day full of new opportunities. Your church can lead men to assume more responsibility and to become more intentional in their personal spiritual pilgrimages and in the ministry of their local church. Let's look at some benefits your church can expect from such a men's ministry.

Men's ministry helps reach men who have been unreached through the church's other ministries. Men who have rejected traditional ministries, like choir, Sunday School, and worship services, may be more willing to become involved in an athletic league or a ministry project. The male context provides an atmosphere to address male life issues that cannot be addressed effectively in a coed environment. A variety of entry points offers acceptance at men's comfort levels.

Men's ministry develops leaders. For years many men have abdicated their leadership responsibilities in the church. The result has been that women have been forced to fill positions that ought to be filled by men, such as boys' mission-group leaders. A nucleus of men can become the future leaders of your ministry. Men's ministry is a great tool for a pastor to use to develop leaders in the congregation.

Men's ministry moves men out of the pews and onto the field. For many years the only place you would see men serving was ushering or mowing the church lawn. A men's ministry helps men appreciate the true nature of servanthood and then realize that they have gifts they can use in and through the church.

Men's ministry starts men growing in Christ. Many men are tired of just getting together with other men over breakfast and talking about sports. They want to grow in Christ but don't know how. Therefore, men need discipleship to learn the basics of Christianity and to be grounded in the disciplines of prayer, Bible study, Scripture memorization, service, and fellowship.

Men's ministry provides the next step for men after national conferences. After attending soul-stirring men's conferences, many men have been discouraged to find that nothing was provided to help them take the next steps in their commitments.

Men's ministry starts new small groups. Men can meet each week to complete a discipleship study.[7]

Men's ministry develops mentors. Christian wives want their spouses to be spiritual leaders at home, but many men are unable to fulfill this role because they were reared in homes without the influence of godly fathers. Men's ministry is designed to link men with spiritual role models. Through a safe, loving relationship, men are provided an example to follow and someone to hold them accountable.[8]

Men's ministry strengthens families. For children to continue worshiping in church as adults, it is important that they have strong father involvement during child-

MEN'S MINISTRY QUESTIONNAIRE

Date: _____

1. Age: ❏ 18–24 ❏ 25–29 ❏ 30–39 ❏ 40–49 ❏ 50–64 ❏ 65+

2. Marital status: ❏ Single ❏ Married ❏ Formerly married ❏ Widowed

3. What is the highest level of education you have completed?
   ❏ Less than high school   ❏ Some college
   ❏ High-school graduate or GED ❏ College graduate
   ❏ Trade school   ❏ Postgraduate degree

4. Family information:
   a. Number of persons living in your household (including yourself): _____
      Number of sons: _____ Age range of sons: ❏ Preschool ❏ Preteen ❏ Teenage ❏ Young adult
      Number of daughters: _____ Age range of daughters: ❏ Preschool ❏ Preteen ❏ Teenage ❏ Young adult

      Others in your household: _____

      _____

   b. Number of grandchildren: _____
   c. How many years have you been married? _____

5. Occupation: _____

6. Which of these life issues are most important to you? Check three.
   ❏ Job security/changing careers   ❏ Family finances   ❏ Relationship with wife
   ❏ Relationship with parents   ❏ Parenting skills   ❏ Handling conflict
   ❏ Planning retirement   ❏ Spiritual life/growth ❏ Job advancement
   ❏ Balancing work, home, and personal needs

7. How long have you lived in this community?
   ❏ 1 year or less   ❏ 6–10 years
   ❏ 2–3 years   ❏ More than 10 years
   ❏ 4–5 years

8. What clubs or organizations do you belong to? _____

   _____

9. Name two activities or hobbies you enjoy participating in.

   _____

   _____

10. How frequently do you attend a church meeting?
    ❏ Rarely   ❏ Once a week   ❏ Twice a week
    ❏ More than twice a week ❏ Once a month   ❏ Once a year

11. Does your wife and/or family attend church meetings regularly? ❏ Yes ❏ No

12. Would you be interested in joining an effective and creative men's ministry in our church? ❑ Yes ❑ No

13. What would you personally like to accomplish through your involvement in men's ministry?
    Check two.
    ❑ Enjoy a closer walk with God   ❑ Have fellowship with Christian men
    ❑ Find a way to serve God more productively ❑ Enhance my Bible knowledge
    ❑ Discuss/deal with problems, frustrations, or ❑ Other: _____
      temptations related to the home, church, and/or
      workplace

14. For meetings and/or projects, when are you most likely to be available?
    ❑ Weekends   ❑ Early morning
    ❑ Lunchtime   ❑ Evenings—which ones? _____

15. If we have retreats as a part of this ministry, would you be interested in participating? ❑ Yes ❑ No

16. What type of retreat would most interest you?
    ❑ Adventure (canoeing, camping, fishing, etc.) ❑ Teaching, including discussion of relevant, practical issues
    ❑ Spiritual and personal renewal   ❑ Some combination of the above

17. Would a short-term mission trip interest you? ❑ Yes ❑ No ❑ Maybe
    If yes, what type of mission projects or activities would you be most interested in? Check at least two.
    ❑ Disaster relief   ❑ Construction projects
    ❑ Helping underprivileged   ❑ Evangelism projects (tract/Scripture distribution, revivals, etc.)
    ❑ International mission projects ❑ Youth activities (VBS, True Love Waits, camps, etc.)
    ❑ Sports evangelism   ❑ Training in practical skills
    ❑ Medical/dental projects   ❑ Other: _____

18. In your opinion, how does a person get into heaven?
    ❑ Church membership   ❑ Church contributions
    ❑ Benevolence   ❑ Belief in a Supreme Being
    ❑ Daily prayer   ❑ Personal relationship with Jesus Christ
    ❑ Regular Bible study   ❑ All of the above

19. When the men's ministry emphasis begins, I would appreciate a contact so that I can become involved
    and/or receive further information.

    Name: _____

    Address: _____

    State: _____ ZIP: _____

    Home number: _____ Work number: _____

    Church affiliation (if applicable): _____

hood. Note the significant influence a father has on a child's spiritual life.

- When Mom and Dad both attend regularly, 72 percent of their children remain faithful later in life.
- When only Dad attends, 55 percent remain faithful.
- When only Mom attends, 15 percent remain faithful.
- When neither parent attends, 6 percent remain faithful.[9]

✳ **Beside each benefit of a men's ministry write the names of two men you know who would benefit in that way.**

Reaches unreached men: _____

Develops leaders: _____

Involves men in service: _____

Starts men growing in Christ: _____

Provides the next step after a national conference:

_____

Starts new small groups: _____

Develops mentors: _____

Strengthens families: _____

Now that you understand some of the challenges men face today and some of the ways men's ministry can meet their needs, let's consider the foundational ideas necessary to build a strong men's ministry.

PARTNER WITH GOD

Effective men's ministries make listening to and obeying God their top priority. They understand that it is God who takes the initiative in revealing Himself to people. They watch to see where God is at work in men's lives. They understand that God is always working and that He invites men to join Him in His activity. They view men's ministry as a partnership with God. In this partnership the Heavenly Father speaks to His children by the Holy Spirit through His Word, prayer, the church, and circumstances.[10]

In Psalm 81:8 the writer captures the heart of God:

*"Hear, O My people, and I will admonish you;
O Israel, if you would listen to Me!" (NASB).*

In the next verse the Lord communicated what He expected from His people:

*"Let there be no strange god among you;
Nor shall you worship any foreign god"
(Ps. 81:9, NASB).*

Then the Lord told the people what they could expect from Him if they would obey His command. He would " 'subdue their enemies' " (Ps. 81:14, NASB) and " 'satisfy' " their needs (Ps. 81:16, NASB). But in verse 11 God told the people why they had failed to receive His choicest blessings. He lamented,

*"My people did not listen to My voice;
And Israel did not obey Me" (NASB).*

As the Lord longed for Israel to lend a responsive ear to Him, our Heavenly Father wants to converse with His people today. This passage can be brought up-to-date by replacing the name of Israel in Psalm 81:8 with your name and your men's group. God is still speaking. He is calling men to listen to Him.

One New Testament example of God's communicating His plans to His people is described in Acts 13:2: "While they were worshiping the Lord and fasting, the Holy Spirit said, 'Set apart for me Barnabas and Saul for the work to which I have called them' " (NIV). The Spirit of God communicated His plans to the believers in Antioch. As they were praying and fasting, God gave this church a vision for sending Paul and Barnabas on a church-planting mission beyond Antioch. Why? Because they were willing to listen to and obey God. From the beginning this group of believers fully understood that ministry is a partnership with God.

Follow Jesus' Example

Jesus had His eyes on the Heavenly Father and was able to recognize the Father's activity in the world. He said: " 'My Father is working until now, and I Myself am working. The Son can do nothing of Himself, unless it is something He sees the Father doing; for whatever the Father does, these things the Son also does in like manner. For the Father loves the Son, and shows Him all things that He Himself is doing; and greater works than these will He show Him, that you may marvel' " (John 5:17,19-20, NASB). Jesus was aware of God's activity in the world and sought to join God in what He was doing in the lives of those around Him.

In *The Mind of Christ* T. W. Hunt wrote about this partnership between God and people:

> Jesus was sensitive and responsive in the utmost degree to His Father. Jesus said, "I do nothing on My own initiative, but I speak these things as the Father taught Me" (John 8:28, NASB). He claimed to see what the Father was doing, to hear what the Father was saying, to do noth-

ing independently of the Father, and to be taught by the Father. Jesus devoted Himself to reflecting the mind of the Father, and His reflection was exact. As the Father is to the Son, so Christ is to you.[11]

Men are to follow Christ's example in partnering with God. Just as Jesus saw the Father's activity, men must pay close attention to Jesus' known earthly activity, including His present activity.

Those who partner with God acknowledge the Holy Spirit's role in drawing men to God. Jesus said, " 'He [the Holy Spirit], when He comes, will convict the world concerning sin, and righteousness, and judgment' " (John 16:8, NASB). In other words, the Holy Spirit leads people to seek God.

The Holy Spirit is also responsible for imparting spiritual truth. In John 16:13-14 Christ announced that the Spirit " 'will guide you into all the truth; for He will not speak on His own initiative, but whatever He hears, He will speak; and He will disclose to you what is to come' " (NASB). The Lord added, " 'He shall glorify Me; for He shall take of mine and disclose it to you' " (NASB). Therefore, whenever someone talks about turning from his sinful lifestyle or applying biblical truth to his personal life, it is the Spirit of God who has brought this to pass.

✳ **Identify where you think God is already at work among men in your church and community.**

_____

_____

Develop a Practical Approach
What practical steps can men follow to develop a ministry that flows from their partnership with God? In *Experiencing God* Henry T. Blackaby offers the following helpful insights.
1. "When you want to know what God is doing around you, pray." Start by fasting and praying with your pastor and a group of men on a regular basis. Pay close attention to their prayer requests.
2. "Get up off your knees and watch to see what God does next. Watch to see what people are saying when they come to you."
3. "Make the connection between your prayer and what happens." Rethink your prayer and ask yourself how others' comments to you relate to your prayer.
4. Ask probing questions:
   • "How can I pray for you?
   • What can I pray for you?
   • Do you want to talk?
   • What is the greatest challenge in your life?

   • What is the most significant thing happening in your life right now?
   • Would you tell me what God is doing in your life?
   • What is God bringing to the surface of your life?
   • What particular burden has God given you?"
5. "Listen." The answers to the above questions are God's way of alerting you to His activity in a man's life. On a larger scale if several men are talking and praying about the same praises, burdens, or needs, this is the Lord's invitation for you to join Him in His activity in those areas.[12]

✳ **Reread the five previous steps and place a check beside the ones you are already following. Bracket the ones you need to initiate with your men's ministry leadership team, if you have one, or with a group of men who might be interested in beginning a men's ministry.**

Someone might ask, Why is God still speaking today? The answer is simple. He is motivated to do so. He loves each individual today as much as He loved those He addressed in the pages of the Bible. He speaks to people and churches individually, because every person and church is unique. God wants to help believers make the right choices among the good, better, and best. Of course, the most important reason God speaks to men today is that He wants them to get to know Him. A love relationship with God was never intended to be a monologue. After all, not much of a relationship exists if one person does all the talking.

By developing a partnership with God, you will counter the worldly approach that plans first and seeks God's blessing second. That approach most often leads to minimal results and maximal frustration. However, when men discover where God is already working, they can serve with the certainty that "what God initiates, He completes."[13] While partnering with God may lead to planning fewer activities for men, it is more likely to result in the need to devote more time to equipping men so that they are prepared to join God in the many opportunities He presents.

PARTNER WITH YOUR PASTOR
God has established order for the church. In a local church, pastors are charged to "shepherd the flock of God among you, exercising oversight" (1 Pet. 5:2, NASB). In Ephesians 4:11-13 Paul stated that the pastor's role is to equip the laity for doing the ministry. The writer of Hebrews admonished members of the body of Christ to respect and honor their leaders: "Obey your leaders, and submit to them; for they keep watch over your souls, as those who will give an account. Let them do this with joy and not with grief, for this would be unprofitable for you" (Heb. 13:17, NASB). Ministry is a

partnership between church members and their pastor.

In addition to partnering with God, anyone initiating men's ministry should partner with the pastor. Many pastors have a love-hate relationship with new ministry ideas. Pastors are excited—someone else is grabbing hold of ministry! The best ministries are those started at the grass-roots level. But pastors are also nervous: where is this thing headed? Pastors look at the big picture of the whole church and wonder what additional demands they will face to keep one more ministry going. They can also interpret a ministry start-up as criticism that they aren't doing an adequate job to meet needs.

Here are some steps you can take to help.

Include your pastor. The time you spend with your pastor and other church-staff members can be highly profitable. Before you begin your men's ministry, make an appointment with him to share your vision and ideas. Explain that a men's ministry is not a separate program but a part of the church's discipleship ministry. Ask whether he already has plans for starting a men's ministry and what they are. Ask him the best time to begin.

Your pastor may ask you to speak to the church or may place you under the supervision of a deacon. If he does, work hard to include that man in your planning in the same way you would include your pastor.

Inform your pastor. Send the pastor copies of the minutes from your meetings as well as the results of your survey if you take one. Keep him involved in the process by scheduling your planning meetings when he can attend, if he wants to be there. Ask him whether he wants to attend or just be informed. Don't pressure him to attend.

Intercede for your pastor. You can give your pastor no greater gift than your prayer support. One church has a group of men who meet in the pastor's office each Sunday morning to pray for the pastor before he goes into the pulpit. What an encouragement! Call your pastor and ask him how you can pray for him and his family.

Invite your pastor. Invite him to the events you sponsor. Ask him to speak at some of your events, as well. Pastors enjoy the opportunity to get out with the guys, talk with them, hang out with them, and teach them. Don't take it personally, though, if your pastor doesn't show up for every event. He could easily be at meetings every evening if he said yes to everything.

Encourage your pastor. Make sure men encourage your pastor in the work he is already doing. Drop him a note or call him to let him know how much he means to you and the church. It is a great feeling for a pastor to know that the men of the church stand with him.

✳ **If you haven't already done so, schedule a meeting with your pastor to discuss the need for a men's ministry. Write the date of your meeting: _____**

✳ **Begin praying for this meeting and for your pastor's openness to God's work in this area.**

PARTNER WITH MEN IN PRAYER

The foundation of ministry with men is built on a prayer foundation with God. E. M. Bounds wrote:

> We are constantly on a stretch if not a strain, to devise new methods, new plans, new organizations to advance the Church and secure enlargement and efficiency for the gospel. … Men are God's method. The Church is looking for better methods; God is looking for better men. … The Holy Ghost does not flow through methods, but through men. He does not come on machinery, but men. He does not anoint plans, but men—men of prayer.[14]

Spiritual goals can be achieved only through spiritual methods. The greatest tool God has given to man is prayer. Throughout the Scriptures believers are admonished to pray. Passages such as Jeremiah 29:11-13; 33:3; Matthew 7:7-11; and John 15:5,7 promise that God hears and responds to the prayers of His children. Almighty God reveals His plans to men who search for Him with all their hearts. Yet many ministries do not place the same importance on prayer that the Lord has attached to it.

The possibilities of group prayer are phenomenal. Our Lord has promised to be present in a unique way when we join our hearts together in prayer: " 'If two of you on earth agree about anything you ask for, it will be done for you by my Father in heaven. For where two or three come together in my name, there am I with them' " (Matt. 18:19-20, NIV). He promises special guidance and power when Christians gather to pray as a group. If several agree in prayer, the Holy Spirit has led them to pray that way. Jesus promised that the Father will answer the requests we agree on in group prayer.

In the New Testament believers can be observed praying together frequently. On the Day of Pentecost the church was gathered in prayer (see Acts 1:12-14). The next chapter describes the regularity of their prayer meetings. The early church was "continually devoting themselves … to prayer" (Acts 2:42, NASB). When there was a need, such as in a time of crisis, the church body met together to intercede for one another (see Acts 12:1-16). Effective men's ministry depends on men who are committed to pray consistently for one another and the needs of the men's ministry.

Seek God's plan for your men's ministry. In men's ministry you need to be certain that God is the supreme Head over all you do. You can make your plans and ask God for His rubber-stamp approval, or you can invite Him to guide and empower all He wants you to do.

How do you know that God is leading your ministry? Prayer. It undergirds your entire ministry. Ask God for help. Express your dependence on Him. Humbly invite Him to act. Prayer is the real work of men's ministry. Service is gathering all God has done through prayer.

✳ **Describe the role prayer has played so far in your planning for men's ministry.**

_____

_____

Pray for the men in your men's ministry. A godly men's ministry leader prays for the men God gives him. Paul gave us a prayer model to follow in Colossians 1:3,9-12:

> We always thank God, the Father of our Lord Jesus Christ, when we pray for you. … For this reason, since the day we heard about you, we have not stopped praying for you and asking God to fill you with the knowledge of his will through all spiritual wisdom and understanding. And we pray this in order that you may live a life worthy of the Lord and may please him in every way: bearing fruit in every good work, growing in the knowledge of God, being strengthened with all power according to his glorious might so that you may have great endurance and patience, and joyfully giving thanks to the Father, who has qualified you to share in the inheritance of the saints in the kingdom of light (NIV).

Notice the depth of Paul's prayer. He prayed about things of eternal consequence. He did not pray trite clichés devoid of sincerity. An intercessory prayer for men could include—

- thanksgiving for perfecting their faith and changing their lives;
- asking God to give them spiritual wisdom and understanding;
- asking God to perfect their lifestyles to bring Him glory;
- asking God to perfect their spiritual strength and endurance;
- asking God to perfect their joy, their strength, and their love relationship with Him.

Jesus prayed for His disciples (see John 17:9,11, 17-19). No one ever modeled prayer like Jesus. Throughout the Gospels we find Him alone over and over again as He spent time with the Father. Before He called His disciples, He prayed all night.

Make prayer a priority in your men's ministry. A men's ministry leader has great influence with other men in many areas in which men need help. None is more important than prayer. Help men realize that in prayer a man can—

- have uninterrupted quality time with God;
- evaluate what God has been doing in his life;
- hear what God would like to say to him;
- nail down Christ's lordship over all aspects of life;
- receive guidance for future plans or ministry;
- work out major problem areas in his life and in his family;
- intercede for others, the pastor, and the church;
- develop a prayer list of concerns for all areas of life;
- advance beyond self-centered prayer;
- keep a current prayer journal, record answers and remember what was prayed for, and discern where God may be leading him;
- get to know God better;
- express his deepest feelings to God;
- grow spiritually though quality time with God.

Encourage prayer for your men's ministry. For men's ministry to move forward and bear lasting fruit, it must move forward on its knees. The only way you should be willing to do men's ministry is if other men regularly pray for the ministry and its leaders. It is vital to start a prayer ministry first. Here are four ways to utilize prayer to support your men's ministry.

- Find a small group of men who will commit to pray regularly for the ministry and its leaders. You can find these men through a number of means. Make a list of 15 to 20 men and send each a letter and a commitment card to return to you. Publish a bulletin announcement letting the men of your church know that you are developing a prayer team. Ask the men to pray for the ministry on a given day at noon. They do not need to gather to pray; each man may pray wherever he is.

✳ **If you do not already have a group of men who are praying for your men's ministry, follow the previous step to enlist them. List their names here.**

_____

_____

- Regularly send the men requests for your ministry. You might send a prayer card before the first day of the month so that men can pray specifically. These cards usually have new requests, both personal and ministry, as well as answers to prayer.
- Get the men together. During the year have a breakfast for the entire prayer team. The men can get to know one another, and a couple of them can share testimonies about how things are going. They should share struggles as well as joys.

• Keep the men informed. You might publish a monthly newsletter to instruct the men on prayer. Encourage them to read about and grow in prayer. Let them know ways God is answering prayer. There is no greater motivation for prayer than to see and hear about answers to prayer.

CHARACTERISTICS OF AN EFFECTIVE MEN'S MINISTRY

You have seen the importance of discovering men's needs and have been introduced to three principles for planning men's ministry: partnering with God, with your pastor, and with men in prayer. From these foundational understandings grow the following biblical characteristics of an effective men's ministry.

God-centered rather than program-centered. The greatest need in men's ministry is to teach men to hear and obey God. Keeping your eye on the ball is a requirement for being a good hitter. Spiritually speaking, it is easy to take your eye off the ball by relying on a program rather than on a Person, Jesus Christ. Effective men's ministries develop men who are radically in love with Jesus Christ and are committed to knowing and doing God's will. The Heavenly Father reveals Himself to those who love Him, seek Him, and obey Him (see John 14:23).

Founded on and fueled by prayer. Jesus modeled a prayer life for His followers. He must have felt that He was making progress with His disciples when He heard them say, " 'Lord, teach us to pray' " (Luke 11:1, NIV). So from the beginning, a group of men must gather for prayer weekly to pray for the needs of their church and especially for the needs of their men's ministry. Jesus taught that " 'at all times' " His disciples " 'ought to pray and not to lose heart' " (Luke 18:1, NASB). Men grow weary without the supernatural power of the Spirit of God, who grants wisdom, encouragement, and power for ministry to those who call on Him. The need for a men's prayer team remains constant even though other aspects of men's ministry constantly change.

Led by men who model what they want to see multiplied. As the leaders go, so goes the ministry. John 1:14 says, "The Word became flesh, and dwelt among us, and we beheld His glory, glory as of the only begotten from the Father, full of grace and truth" (NASB). Jesus modeled what He wanted to see multiplied. Each men's group needs leaders who do the same. Healthy men's groups establish a leader-training process and do not initiate new ministries until they have men prepared to lead them. Through the leader-training process men are equipped for service (see Eph. 4:11-12) so that they can carry out the ministry themselves.

Balanced. A written purpose statement for men's ministry should be composed to reflect a balance among helping men come to God, grow in Christ, serve

through the church, and go to the world. Thriving men's ministries lead men to discover how they are uniquely called and shaped by God to live the Great Commandment (see Mark 12:30-31) and to fulfill the Great Commission (see Matt. 28:19-20) in every aspect of their lives. Effective men's ministries keep the various aspects of their ministry interdependent and mutually supportive, providing a variety of entry points that make it easy for men to get involved.

Culturally relevant. Paul declared, "I have become all things to all men, that I may by all means save some" (1 Cor. 9:22, NASB). Though his presentation of the gospel never changed, Paul's methods for delivering the message constantly changed. In Iconium he entered the synagogue to share the gospel (see Acts 14:1). In Philippi he went to the riverside to fish for souls (see Acts 16:13). In Athens he initiated conversation about religion with the men gathered on the town square (see Acts 17:16-34). Effective men's ministries find ways to connect with men on their turf. In addition to being at different levels of spiritual maturity, the men of each church and community have different interests, pressures, schedules, and incomes, and different methods are required to reach them.

Sustained by relationships. Believers are not "Lone Rangers." The many one-another passages in the Bible tell us that men need one another for encouragement, accountability, and spiritual growth (see Prov. 27:17; Rom. 15:14; 1 Thess. 5:11; Heb. 10:24). A Christian man needs to surround himself with trusted friends who will be honest, transparent, and confidential as weaknesses and burdens are shared. Relationships are crucial to building and maintaining an effective men's ministry, because men are far more interested in relationships than in programs.

✳ Match each characteristic of an effective men's ministry with an appropriate implication for your ministry.

___ 1. God-centered

___ 2. Founded on and fueled by prayer

___ 3. Led by men who model what they want to see multiplied

___ 4. Balanced

___ 5. Culturally relevant

___ 6. Sustained by relationships

a. Provide a variety of entry points.

b. Organize a prayer team.

c. Organize small groups for sharing and accountability.

d. Teach men to hear and obey God.

e. Find ways to connect with men where they are.

f. Establish a leader-training process.

Check your answers on page 17.

HOW TO GET STARTED

You are ready to begin a men's ministry when God places a desire in the heart of at least one layman to reach and develop men for Christ. This is the real starting point—one man's passion and willingness to be used by God. At that point you can take these practical steps.

1. Share your vision for men's ministry with the church staff and ask the pastor and other staff members to join you and other men in an informal prayer meeting. Resist the temptation to talk about programs. Pray for God to meet men's needs. This will establish the ministry as one that is focused on God and men. Continue meeting for prayer weekly.

2. Assess the needs of men in your church. With the support of your church staff, develop and administer a needs survey or use "Men's Ministry Questionnaire" on pages 10–11. The questions can be tailored to fit your church and community.

3. Form a diverse men's ministry leadership team to evaluate the surveys and to develop a written purpose statement for your men's ministry. Point 2 in this manual will give you guidance for writing your purpose statement.

4. Develop a timeline for beginning a ministry that will address men's needs. Refuse to start too much too fast. Devote time and energy to establishing leadership requirements and a leader-training process (see point 3 in this manual). Building a Christ-honoring men's ministry takes time. Wait on God and do not begin a new ministry or group without having prepared leaders in place. Points 5 and 6 in this manual provide more information on developing a timeline for your men's ministry.

The remainder of this manual will help you build a men's ministry that will draw men to God and motivate them to minister in His name.

✳ **What is your church already doing to reach and disciple men?**

_____

_____

✳ **Rate the effectiveness of what your church has been doing to reach and disciple men:** ❏ **Ineffective** ❏ **Somewhat effective** ❏ **Very effective**

✳ **Describe the next step you need to take to begin a men's ministry or to improve what your church has been doing.**

_____

_____

Resources
Blackaby, Henry. *The Power of the Call.* Nashville: Broadman & Holman, 1997.
Blackaby, Henry, and Tom Blackaby. *The Man God Uses.* Nashville: LifeWay, 1998.
Blackaby, Henry T., and Claude V. King. *Experiencing God: Knowing and Doing the Will of God.* Nashville: LifeWay, 1990.
Blackaby, Henry, and Richard Blackaby. *When God Speaks.* Nashville: LifeWay, 1995.
Bounds. E. M. *Power Through Prayer.* Grand Rapids: Baker, 1992.
Dalbey, Gordon. *Healing the Masculine Soul.* Nashville: Word, 1991.
Farrar, Steve. *Standing Tall: How a Man Can Protect His Family.* Portland: Multnomah, 1994.
Hunt, T. W., and Claude V. King. *In God's Presence.* Nashville: LifeWay, 1994.
Hunt, T. W., and Catherine Walker. *Disciple's Prayer Life: Walking in Fellowship with God.* Nashville: LifeWay, 1997.
Hybels, Bill. *Honest to God? Becoming an Authentic Christian.* Grand Rapids: Zondervan, 1990.
McGee, Robert S. *Search for Significance,* LIFE Support Edition. Nashville: LifeWay, 1992.
Morley, Patrick. *The Seven Seasons of a Man's Life.* Nashville: LifeWay, 1996.
Smalley, Gary, and John Trent. *The Hidden Value of a Man.* Colorado Springs: Focus on the Family, 1994.
Weber, Stu. *Tender Warrior.* Portland: Multnomah, 1993.

Notes
1. Adapted from *National Coalition of Men's Ministries Overview,* n.d., n.p., n.pag.
2. *Foundations for Effective Men's Ministry, Seminar Workbook* (Denver: Promise Keepers, 1993), 4.
3. George Barna, "The Battle for the Hearts of Men," *New Man,* January–February 1997, 42.
4. Ibid.
5. Ken Canfield, telephone interview, April 1998.
6. Barna, "The Battle for the Hearts of Men," 40.
7. Steve Sonderman, *How to Build a Life-Changing Men's Ministry: Bringing the Fire Home to Your Church* (Minneapolis: Bethany House, 1996), 221–22.
8. Phil Downer with Chip MacGregor, *Eternal Impact: Investing in the Lives of Men* (Eugene: Harvest House, 1997), 45.
9. Robert and Debra Bruce, *Becoming Spiritual Soulmates with Your Child* (Nashville: Broadman & Holman, 1996), 52.
10. Adapted from Henry T. Blackaby and Claude V. King, *Experiencing God: Knowing and Doing the Will of God* (Nashville: LifeWay, 1990), 20.
11. T. W. Hunt and Claude V. King, *The Mind of Christ* (Nashville: LifeWay, 1994), 17.
12. Blackaby and King, *Experiencing God,* 69–70.
13. Ibid., 71.
14. E. M. Bounds, as quoted by William Carr Peel, *What God Does When Men Pray* (Colorado Springs: NavPress, 1993), 11.

Answers to Activity
Page 16: 1. d, 2. b, 3. f, 4. a, 5. e, 6. c

POINT 2

◆

Propose a Purpose Statement

1. Partner and pray   2. Propose a purpose statement

Many men's ministries do a lot of good activities, but they have no focus and direction. These ministries are uncertain about what they are to be and do. Proverbs 29:18 says, "Where there is no vision, the people perish" (KJV). Men's ministry in a church must have a clear focus, or the men will be confused about what they are working toward. Therefore, the next step in building a strategy for men's ministry is to formulate a purpose statement. A purpose statement is like the goal line on a football field. Every player on a football team knows his assignment and works together with his teammates to cross the goal line. With your purpose statement serving as the goal line, you have a clear, common, intentional goal toward which all of the men and all of your ministries are directed. A purpose statement also gives you a way to determine whether the men's ministry is succeeding at what God has called it to accomplish.

BENEFITS OF A PURPOSE STATEMENT

A purpose statement benefits your men's ministry in at least five specific ways.

A purpose statement helps the pastor and the entire church body identify how your men's ministry supports the

---

Where there

is no vision,

the people perish.

Proverbs 29:18, KJV

---

total ministry of the church. In addition to addressing men's needs in a male context, men's ministry should be seen as an integral part of the church. Your purpose statement should therefore relate to and support the church's mission.

A purpose statement ensures that your ministry is purpose-driven rather than event-driven. A purpose statement provides focus and direction by helping you screen out distractions and major on priority activities. In men's ministry it is easy to begin without knowing where you want to end. You may schedule event after event, but often men stop attending if they do not see a larger purpose to the events. Every event should serve your ministry's purpose. Explain to the men how each event fits into the larger context of your men's ministry and the purpose of the church.

A purpose statement keeps you from taking on more than you can handle. At every leadership planning meeting, ask the same question: How does this fit our purpose? For every idea that comes along, ask: What is our purpose for men's ministry? Who is going to lead it? And what is your part in the ministry? The discussion that follows will keep you on track.

A purpose statement helps you make decisions. Without

a purpose statement, deciding for or against a ministry can be difficult. A purpose statement provides a fair way to determine which ideas serve your purpose and which don't.

A purpose statement allows you to work at your strengths. Many ministries try to do too many things too fast. It's better to start slowly and simply. Reach one group of men and minister to them effectively before you move on to another group.

✳ **State in your own words what you consider to be the two greatest benefits of developing a purpose statement.**

1. _____

_____

_____

2. _____

_____

_____

In 1996 the Southern Baptist Convention assigned men's ministry to LifeWay Christian Resources (then known as the Sunday School Board). In seeking to create a new model for men's ministry, one that seamlessly integrates and implements evangelism, discipleship, ministry, and missions, LifeWay invited men's ministry leaders from several Baptist state conventions and the North American Mission Board to work together to develop a purpose statement for the Convention's ministry to men. The desire of all those in attendance was to develop a purpose statement that reflects God's purpose for the local church, assists the local church in giving visionary leadership to men's ministry, and combines and utilizes the strengths of all agencies of the Southern Baptist Convention. Together they concluded that although many passages describe what men's ministry should be and do, two statements by Jesus summarize them all: the Great Commandment—" 'Love the Lord your God with all your heart and with all your soul and with all your mind. ... Love your neighbor as yourself.' " (Mark 12:30-31, NIV)—and the Great Commission—" 'Go and make disciples of all nations, baptizing them in the name of the Father and of the Son and of the Holy Spirit, and teaching them to obey everything I have commanded you' " (Matt. 28:19-20, NIV). From these foundational Scriptures the leaders developed this purpose statement for LifeWay's ministry to men:

To help men discover how they have been uniquely called and shaped by God to live the Great Commandment and to fulfill the Great Commission in every aspect of their lives—personal, home, church, workplace, community, and world

This statement shapes everything LifeWay does to provide resources, training, and events for men and to equip churches to minister to men. In the same way, your purpose statement will keep your ministry on track as you develop programs and activities for men.

DETERMINE TO KEEP FIRST THINGS FIRST

As you establish the purpose of your men's ministry and begin planning men's activities, keep your focus on obedience to God. Through your relationship with Him, He will reveal His plans and purposes for your men's ministry. Henry Blackaby wrote: "God didn't call us to be successful. God called us to be obedient. The success is His doing, not ours. Our role is to be His servant and let Him accomplish what He will through us."[1]

Many Christians are obsessed with planning, just as the apostle Paul zealously worked to destroy the early church before his conversion. After Paul met Jesus Christ, his agenda changed. He considered his old plans "rubbish" and adopted a new purpose: to "gain Christ and be found in him, ... to know Christ and the power of his resurrection and the fellowship of sharing in his sufferings, becoming like him in his death, and so, somehow, to attain to the resurrection from the dead" (Phil. 3:8-10, NIV). Similarly, men may set and reach admirable goals, but they may not be obedient to God. If we are not careful, our goal setting can become man-centered. When that happens, we celebrate reaching goals rather than obeying God. Only God can grow His kingdom. Our role is to be obedient to His purposes.

What if your men's ministry adopted goals like the following?
• Men will know Christ and be found in Him.
• Men will experience and demonstrate the power of Christ's resurrection in their lives.
• Men will fellowship through sharing in Jesus' sufferings.
• Men will become like Christ in His death and so attain the resurrection from the dead when He returns.

Your ministry would burst at the seams! Men would be attracted to a ministry in which men earnestly seek to be found in Christ, demonstrate the power of Christ in their lives, and aren't afraid to suffer as Christ did in order to be raised again to eternal joy.

Goals aren't bad as long as we let God set them. How do we do that? Blackaby writes that "God will reveal to us only what is important for the moment."[2] God revealed to Moses His vision for Moses' leading the Israelites to the promised land, but because the immediate future can shift abruptly, Moses had to rely on God for every detail along the way. In the same way, men's ministry leaders must build on God's purposes and then seek His direction at every turn.[3]

✳ Evaluate whether your planning for men's ministry so far has been God-centered or man-centered. List evidence in the columns.

God-Centered	Man-Centered

✳ Establishing your men's ministry on God's purposes is imperative. Before writing your purpose statement, set aside a day your leadership team can spend in prayer and fasting. Use this time to examine your lives before the Lord, for He cannot use unclean vessels. Confess any sin and ask for His forgiveness and for strength and wisdom to change. Ask God to show you where He is at work in men's lives. Seek His will for your men's ministry and commit it to His purposes. Let God speak to you through His Word about the direction your men's ministry will take. Start with these passages: Proverbs 27:17; Matthew 28:19-20; Mark 12:30-31; John 13:34-35; Acts 1:8; Romans 12:1-2; Galatians 6:1-2; Ephesians 4:11-16; Colossians 1:28-29; 2:6-7; 3:19,21; 2 Timothy 2:2.

DISCOVER THE PURPOSE OF YOUR CHURCH

God wants the church to reach men with the gospel of Christ and to help them grow to maturity. In the Great Commission (see Matt. 28:19-20) Jesus calls us to make disciples by sharing His message. In Ephesians 4:11-13 Paul teaches that God gives some people special abilities to equip others for works of service. Leaders, then, are called to disciple and equip people to serve and to mature in Christ. The purpose of your men's ministry needs to be in line with this overarching purpose and with the particular purpose of your church. This way

your men's ministry's purpose statement will reflect the fact that men's ministry is not separate from the church but is an integral part of the church and, as such, is responsible for helping communicate and carry out the church's mission.

✳ **Does your church have a purpose statement? If so, write it here.**

_____

_____

_____

DEVELOP YOUR PURPOSE STATEMENT

Remember these two foundational principles as you think about the purpose of your men's ministry.
1. It takes a long time to make a disciple. Even Jesus invested 3½ years of His life in the 12 disciples. Have a long-term perspective. Don't look for a quick fix in a few months. Instead, pray and plan for what God wants to do over the next several years.
2. Most meaningful changes take place in the context of relationships. Men change as they interact with other men. Your men's ministry should help men develop meaningful relationships with other men.[4]

While it would be easy for your men's group to adopt someone else's purpose statement, God is interested in developing a relationship with you and your men. He wants you to place your trust in Him rather than in someone or something else. Consider taking your leadership team through a study of Gene Mims's book *Kingdom Principles for Church Growth* (see "Resources," p. 22). From a biblical perspective Mims describes the church's purposes in terms of a 1-5-4 Principle, which states that the New Testament identifies one driving force of church growth, five essential church functions for church growth, and four accompanying results.[5] This study will better acquaint your men with the process God has chosen for building His kingdom.

As you study Scripture, pray, and discuss with other men God's purposes for the church, God will begin to give your men's leadership team a passion for the things about which He is passionate. You and your men will have the assurance that the purpose statement you adopted grew from what God placed in your hearts.

Here are steps for writing your men's ministry's purpose statement.
1. Have the leadership team read as many passages of Scripture as possible that are relevant to your ministry's mission.
2. Identify scriptural themes that highlight what you believe God could be calling your ministry to be and do (examples: equip men, evangelize men, mobilize

men for service, build disciples, engage the community, reconcile men, instruct men, encourage men).

✳ **Beside the references, note key themes you might want to include in your purpose statement. Add other verses on a separate sheet of paper.**

Proverbs 27:17: _____

Matthew 28:19-20: _____

Mark 12:30-31: _____

John 13:34-35: _____

Acts 1:8: _____

Romans 12:1-2: _____

Galatians 6:1-2: _____

Ephesians 4:11-16: _____

Colossians 1:28-29: _____

Colossians 2:6-7: _____

Colossians 3:19,21: _____

2 Timothy 2:2: _____

3. Take time to talk and pray through these ideas. Narrow your list of words and phrases to those you believe give direction to your ministry.

4. Examine surveys or other data that identify the needs of men in your church and community.

✳ **List the five greatest needs of men in your church and community.**

Church	Community

5. Examine your church's purpose statement if it has adopted one. You should have recorded this on page 20. Effective men's ministries mirror and support the church's mission.

6. Write a rough draft of your purpose statement. You might want to begin your statement with something like "Our ministry exists to glorify Jesus Christ by …" What you write will communicate the main business of your ministry. Your statement should be qualitative: "Our men's ministry is dedicated to building men into Christlike leaders for their families, friends, church, and community." It should also be quantitative: "Our men's ministry is committed to having 30 men in small groups so that they will become godly men who influence others for Jesus Christ."

✳ **If your men's ministry has a purpose statement, write it here. If not, write a sentence that captures the essence of what you believe God wants your church's men's ministry to accomplish. Remember, this is only a rough draft.**

_____

_____

_____

7. Refine your purpose statement. Here are some questions to ask yourselves: *Is it clear and concise—not more than two sentences? Does it state who we are and what we do as a ministry? Is it easy to communicate to the leaders and men of our church? Does it empower us as leaders? Is it consistent with who we are as a church?*

✳ **Write your revised purpose statement here.**

_____

_____

_____

8. When you have settled on a purpose statement, take time to evaluate it. Pray over it. Work on grammar and phrasing to make it clear. Share it with others and get their input. As a leadership team, review it after one month to determine whether it accurately reflects your ministry's identity and mission.

✳ **Write your final draft here.**

_____

_____

_____

Down the road it will be important to have a purpose statement for each ministry that develops within your men's ministry. If you start small groups, for example, those leaders should develop purpose statements of their own that flow from the overarching one. Here are some examples:

- "Our men's ministry is committed to having at least one man from each Sunday School class on its men's ministry prayer team."
- "We commit to involve every man in a small group so that he can grow through Bible study and mission action."

The process of identifying individual parts of the ministry can be exciting and gratifying. With purpose statements in hand, leaders of the various ministries have a greater sense of mission and ownership in the ministry.

DECLARE YOUR PURPOSE STATEMENT

Widely publicize your men's ministry purpose statement. Frequently state and repeat it so that all men in the church can recite it from memory.

Keep in mind that most of the men you are trying to reach through this ministry are busy and easily distracted. Even those who are actively involved can become consumed with only one aspect of the ministry and lose sight of the goal line. Therefore, you must find creative ways to keep your purpose statement before them. Rick Warren calls this need for restating your purpose the Nehemiah Principle. In *The Purpose-Driven Church* he cites the account of the people of Israel returning to rebuild the ruined walls of Jerusalem (see Neh. 4:6-15). Warren writes: "Although the wall took only fifty-two days to complete, the people became discouraged at the halfway point: just twenty-six days into the project! Nehemiah had to renew their vision."[6] From this incident Warren says that God taught him a valuable lesson on leadership: "Vision and purpose must be restated every twenty-six days to keep the church moving in the right direction."[7]

Since all people can quickly become distracted and discouraged, your men's ministry's purpose statement must be stated on a monthly basis. With the help of your pastor, church staff, media library, Sunday School classes, women's ministry leadership team, missions committee, and men's ministry leadership team, develop a variety of creative ways to promote your vision. Rick Warren offers several suggestions:

1. Use Scriptures that explain the biblical basis for your purpose statement.
2. Create an identifiable symbol that can be displayed on golf shirts, on hats, on bulletin boards, and in the church newsletter.
3. Invent slogans that can be easily remembered.
4. Share success stories of lives that have been changed through involvement in recreation, support groups,

Bible studies, conferences, and mission trips.
5. Personalize the purpose statement so that it attracts others and helps them see their part in the ministry.
6. "Always give practical, clear, concrete action steps" that explain how the men's ministry will "fulfill its purposes."[8]

✳ **Check the ways you will commit to declare your purpose statement.**
❑ **Use Scriptures.**
❑ **Create a symbol.**
❑ **Invent slogans.**
❑ **Share success stories.**
❑ **Personalize the purpose statement.**
❑ **Give practical action steps.**

Constantly be on the lookout for men who have stories to tell. Watch to see if God brings men with video- or audio-production skills into your church to help tell His story. Look for men in the community with similar skills, like a printer, a newspaper reporter, or an editor, who may not know Jesus Christ or may not have a church home but could become involved by helping you communicate your vision for men's ministry.

The best way to get a message across to a man is to develop a personal relationship with him. Therefore, when communicating your vision for men's ministry, don't rely solely on public announcements. Men respond best to other men who have demonstrated a genuine concern for them.

Resources
Barna, George. *The Power of Vision*. Ventura: Regal, 1997.
Biehl, Bobb. *Masterplanning: A Complete Guide for Building a Strategic Plan for Your Business, Church, or Organization*. Nashville: Broadman & Holman, 1997.
Blackaby, Henry, and Tom Blackaby. *The Man God Uses*. Nashville: LifeWay, 1998.
Bright, Bill, et al. *Seven Promises of a Promise Keeper*. Nashville: Word, 1994.
Dale, Robert. *To Dream Again*. Nashville: Broadman & Holman, 1981.
Hemphill, Ken. *The Antioch Effect: Eight Characteristics of Highly Effective Churches*. Nashville: Broadman & Holman, 1994.
Mims, Gene. *Kingdom Principles for Church Growth*. Nashville: Convention, 1994.
Roesel, Charles, and Donald Atkinson. *Meeting Needs, Sharing Christ*. Nashville: LifeWay, 1995.
Warren, Rick. *The Purpose-Driven Church*. Grand Rapids: Zondervan, 1995.

Notes
[1] Henry and Tom Blackaby, *The Man God Uses* (Nashville: LifeWay, 1998), 70.
[2] Ibid., 71.
[3] This section adapted from Blackaby, *The Man God Uses*, 70–71.
[4] *Men's Ministry Action Plan* (Casselberry: Man in the Mirror, Inc., n.d.), 8–9.
[5] Gene Mims, *Kingdom Principles for Church Growth* (Nashville: Convention, 1994), 6.
[6] Rick Warren, *The Purpose-Driven Church* (Grand Rapids: Zondervan, 1995), 111.
[7] Ibid.
[8] Ibid., 112–14.

POINT 3

◆

Prepare Leaders

1. Partner and pray   2. Propose a purpose statement

3. Prepare leaders

OUR GOAL

Great teams almost always have great coaches. Most championship teams in the past had one thing in common: a man at the head of the team superbly able to motivate and manage players. Players could come and go, but the coaches remained the same. The Cowboys had Landry, the Dolphins had Shula, UCLA had Wooden, the Reds had Anderson, the Steelers had Knoll, the 49ers had Walsh, North Carolina had Dean Smith, and the Packers had Lombardi. All of these men molded other men into winners. They shaped an environment in which players worked and won together.

If you are going to develop a lasting men's ministry in your church, it starts with leadership. Nothing in ministry—and, for that matter, in life—happens without leadership. Point 3 will examine a team structure for your men's ministry; the importance of leadership; some characteristics to look for in a leader; and how to recruit, train, and develop leaders. But let's begin by looking at the leadership model of our Lord Jesus Christ.

> *It was he who gave some to be apostles, some to be prophets, some to be evangelists, and some to be pastors and teachers, to prepare God's people for works of service.*
>
> Ephesians 4:11-12, NIV

FOLLOW JESUS' LEADERSHIP MODEL

A men's ministry leader has a leader—Jesus Christ. Jesus is a constant guide, empowering His servant to do His work. Remember that making disciples of men has a double purpose: ministry to men and ministry with men. Jesus called and equipped 12 common, everyday men. He did His greatest work in them. He also worked with them. As they developed personal love relationships with Christ, He was training and teaching them, perfecting them in their life assignments. They changed the whole known world as they became His men, experienced His love, and were filled with the power of the Holy Spirit. Jesus is still the best example of and the best source for spiritual leadership. He declares, "You must follow Me."

Jesus spent time with the multitudes, but most of His time went toward preparing 12 men for ministry. He took 12 men and poured His life into them so that when He was finished, they would be prepared to continue His ministry.

God knows that nothing changes people like relationships. That's why He sent a Son, not a tract. Jesus called certain men to join Him. Luke 6:12-13 says that "He went off to the mountain to pray, and He spent the whole night in prayer to God. And when the day came, He called His disciples to Him; and chose twelve of them, whom He also named as apostles" (NASB). Jesus didn't put up a notice on the office wall. After praying all night, He selected the men He thought were right for Him. Then the Lord made sure He didn't just have class once in a while; He spent all His time with them. He taught the twelve not only in formal situations but also in everyday conversations. He constantly looked for teachable moments.

Sometimes Christ had a sermon He wanted the disciples to hear. Other times He answered their questions. He made sure they saw Him spend time alone praying, and He used Scripture often, making it a normal part of His life. Christ would occasionally ask questions to initiate a discussion, and He spent much of His time ministering to others' needs. Once, when the disciples were arguing about who was the greatest, He took a towel, wrapped it around His waist, and began washing their feet, performing the most menial of services. The Lord demonstrated putting others first by placing the disciples ahead of Himself. Those 12 men got to experience the direct ministry of God in their lives. Imagine if someone could spend that sort of time with you.[1]

✳ **Based on Jesus' model, why do you think relationships are important in men's ministry?**

_____

_____

You might have written that developing relationships is the most effective way to guide men in their Christian walk. Let Jesus Christ be your model for servant leadership.

DEVELOP A TEAM STRUCTURE

God reveals His activity to His people from their love relationships with Him. When you formulated a purpose statement for your men's ministry in point 2, you probably identified how your ministry will respond to God's work among men in your church and community. Your ministry's organizational structure needs to grow from that spiritual base.

A team structure is recommended for men's ministry because men like determining their course of action and having hands-on experiences. The more you develop men spiritually, the more ministries God will call them to participate in. Having a team structure in place will allow you to plug in these men as God calls them to serve and grow.

Look at the diagram on page 25. It suggests a sample team structure for men's ministry leaders.

As you begin to think about a leadership structure, remember that it must be based on your purpose statement, that is, your response to God's activity among men in your church and community. The teams shown on the diagram are only examples. Your ministry may organize different teams, but the key is to build teams that support your ministry's purpose.

Also remember that it takes time to develop a structure like the one depicted in the diagram. Begin by enlisting a leadership team. At the center of your organizational structure is the men's ministry leadership team. The men's ministry leadership team works together to maintain a balanced men's ministry. As servant leaders, these team members are responsible for—

- maintaining an exemplary Christian lifestyle;
- supporting the pastor and church staff with prayer and encouragement;
- seeking God's direction for men's ministry through intense prayer;
- casting the vision for men's ministry;
- communicating the vision to the congregation;
- recruiting, training, and empowering other men to carry out the ministry.

A fully developed men's ministry leadership team includes the following six members.

1. The *pastor or church-staff representative* focuses on motivating believers (see John 13:5,12-16; Eph. 4:11-12). This man—
   - models servant leadership (see Matt. 20:25-28);
   - regularly prays for and with men's ministry team leaders;
   - helps the leadership team see how men's ministry can support the church's total ministry;
   - empowers the men's ministry team leader to lead the men's ministry;
   - attends and speaks at men's ministry events/activities, as his schedule permits;
   - gives support in developing the men's ministry budget;
   - provides a means for handling check requests related to the men's ministry budget.

2. The *men's ministry team leader* focuses on mobilizing believers (see Matt. 28:19-20). This man—
   - models servant leadership (see Matt. 20:25-28);
   - demonstrates a passion for reaching men, seeing the potential for a great ingathering;
   - understands the church's total ministry and how men's ministry helps the church fulfill its mission;
   - serves as the administrator who leads enthusiastically and by example in devotion to Christ and ministry;
   - convenes and presides over monthly men's ministry leadership-team meetings;

SAMPLE TEAM STRUCTURE

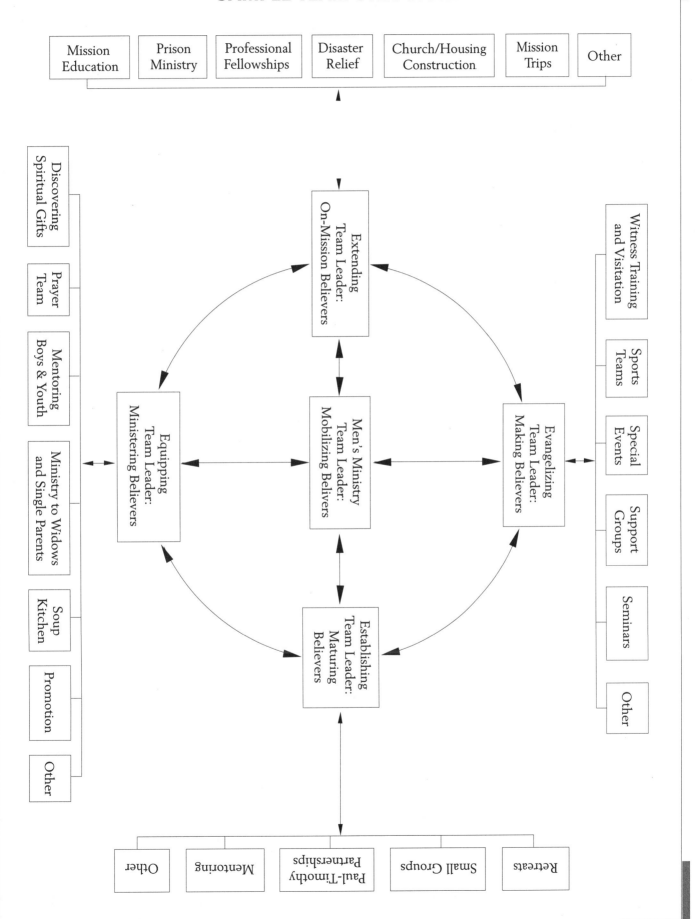

- maintains the annual calendar for men's ministry;
- communicates prayer requests and praises to the prayer team;
- identifies, evaluates, and secures resources for men's ministry and empowers others to lead;
- works with the leadership team to develop a balanced ministry and an annual budget;
- presides at all churchwide men's ministry events;
- serves on the Church Council or pastor's advisory council;
- guides the men's ministry leadership team in planning and evaluating churchwide men's ministry celebrative events.

3. The *evangelizing team leader* focuses on making believers (see Rom. 1:14-16). This man—
   - models servant leadership (see Matt. 20:25-28);
   - has a passion for lost men and is active in sharing his faith;
   - is an active participant in the church's outreach program;
   - identifies resources for evangelism training and support;
   - plans and conducts evangelism training to equip men to share their faith;
   - helps develop strategies for reaching lost men and recruits others for ministry to the lost;
   - presents an annual budget to the leadership team for the evangelism ministry;
   - attends the monthly men's ministry leadership team meeting;
   - communicates prayer requests and praises to the prayer team;
   - serves on the church evangelism committee and works with revival preparation.

4. The *establishing team leader* focuses on developing maturing believers (see Col. 2:6-7). This man—
   - models servant leadership (see Matt. 20:25-28);
   - is driven to see men discipled from spiritual infancy to spiritual maturity;
   - has participated in a discipleship group and has led a small group;
   - understands the Paul-Timothy process and is actively discipling another man;
   - conducts ongoing leadership training for small-group leaders at least once a quarter;
   - communicates prayer requests and praises to the prayer team;
   - develops a process for helping men get involved in small groups;
   - identifies, evaluates, and suggests potential resources for discipling men;
   - presents an annual budget to the men's ministry leadership team for the establishing ministry;
   - attends the monthly men's ministry leadership team meeting.

5. The *equipping team leader* focuses on developing ministering believers (see 1 Cor. 12:7,12-25). This man—
   - models servant leadership (see Matt. 20:25-28);
   - is active in ministering to others in the church and community;
   - develops a process for helping men discover and match their spiritual gifts and abilities with local ministry;
   - enlists and empowers leaders to develop a variety of ministry teams and projects;
   - communicates prayer requests and praises to the prayer team;
   - identifies, evaluates, and utilizes resources for equipping men for ministry;
   - presents an annual budget to the men's ministry leadership team for the equipping ministry;
   - attends the monthly men's ministry leadership team meeting.

6. The *extending team leader* focuses on developing on-mission believers (see Acts 1:8). This man—
   - models servant leadership (see Matt. 20:25-28);
   - is a Great Commission Christian who takes an active part in mission education and action;
   - supports the church's mission organizations;
   - enlists and empowers leaders to develop a variety of mission-action projects;
   - communicates prayer requests and praises to the prayer team;
   - identifies, evaluates, and utilizes resources for educating and involving men in missions;
   - presents an annual budget to the men's ministry leadership team for the extending ministry;
   - attends the monthly men's ministry leadership team meeting.

✳ Beside each key position on the men's ministry leadership team, write the name of a man in your church you think would be right for the job.

Men's ministry team leader: _____

Evangelizing team leader: _____

Establishing team leader: _____

Equipping team leader: _____

Extending team leader: _____

✳ Begin praying specifically about their involvement on the men's ministry leadership team.

IDENTIFY LEADERS

Until you have a man willing to be the primary leader for your men's ministry, it will be difficult for your ministry to go forward. Can you identify the leader of your team? He may already be in place. The men of your church may be waiting for someone to take the lead. There's a good chance your leader is the man holding this manual—a man passionate about men's ministry. This man needs a clear vision of where God is going and the incredible harvest that is before us. He also needs to possess leadership skills or at least a willingness to learn.

It isn't enough to find one man who can see where God is going and can motivate and manage a group of men to get there. You need men serving alongside that man. Building a men's ministry leadership team is a very important step in starting your men's ministry. A leadership team sets you up for quality ministry now and positions you for future growth. The key to effective ministry is found in the quality of the leadership team. Ministries that move forward and make a difference are those that have solid leadership teams.

Look for the following five qualities in the men you want to join your men's ministry leadership team.

Servant Spirit

In Mark 10:42-45 Jesus shared with His disciples the key element in spiritual leadership. He told them that the way up is down, that the person who will lead is the one who will serve. Our society is obsessed with climbing the ladder, upscaling, promotions, and upward mobility. Jesus declared that those who will lead in the kingdom of God will be obsessed with descending the ladder, downscaling, spiritual demotions, and downward mobility. Those who lead will be servants to all.

It is easy to find men who want to be involved in ministry if they can start at the top and don't have to do ordinary, dirty jobs. They want to be up front teaching or around the table making decisions, not in the back making coffee or setting up chairs. Some men feel that they are above certain tasks. They import their marketplace position, power, and philosophy, believing that it will work in the church. It doesn't, and it shouldn't.

Getting a ministry going requires an enormous amount of work. Some tasks—making calls, compiling surveys, sending out mailings—are repetitious and menial. But they need to be done. One man on your leadership team who thinks he is above that kind of work breeds instant division.

Character

It isn't how you look, where you work, what you have, whom you know, or what you know that counts. It is who you are when no one is looking. It is a man's character that counts.

Men of character drive real ministry. A great passage on leadership is 1 Samuel 16:7. God told Samuel not to look at a man's outward appearance. God looks at the heart. This is a key principle for selecting a leadership team. Some additional helpful guidelines are the lists Paul gave to Timothy for selecting elders and deacons (see 1 Tim. 3:1-13). And 1 Timothy 4:12 offers one of the best measuring tools for choosing leaders. It provides five standards to measure a man's character:

Speech. Does he use his tongue to tear down or build up? Does he lie or speak the truth? Is he sarcastic and cutting or loving and kind?

Life. Is there consistency between his behavior on Sunday and Monday? Does he visualize what he verbalizes, behaving in accordance with what he believes? There is no room on a leadership team for someone who doesn't live his faith in the marketplace.

Love. Is he interested in others' well-being? Does he show compassion and tenderness toward others?

Faith. Is he willing to take wise risks and live on the edge? Is he willing to trust God, or does he live purely by human strength?

Purity. Is this man seeking to be morally, ethically, and spiritually pure before God?

Godliness

The greatest gift your leadership team can give the men of your church is their personal holiness. Nothing is more important in leading other men to Christ than a vital, authentic relationship with Jesus. Men today want the real thing, not secondhand religion. They want reality, not ritual. In selecting men to be on your leadership team, start with men you know who are in love with Jesus. Here are some things to look for.

Strong private life. Do they regularly spend time with Jesus? When you get together with men, ask them what they are learning in their daily devotions. A long stare after that question is a good clue that not much is happening in that area of their lives. Unless they regularly spend time with Jesus, they will have nothing to give to others. What they are in private with Jesus will directly influence what they do in public with other men.

Obedience. Are they seeking to obey God in all areas of life, or is there an area in which they knowingly continue to sin? Are they open to accountability to others for their life and actions?

Worship. Godly men love to worship. They make sure they regularly meet with God's people to worship. If a man's hobby, golf game, or favorite spectator sport regularly causes him to miss Sunday worship, he's making a loud statement about his priorities.

Passion

To have passion is to be enthusiastic about what you are doing, to eagerly anticipate the next time you get together with your men. You love what you are doing and are thankful that God has given you gifts and the incredible privilege of serving Him. When you interview men for your leadership team, ask these questions to gauge their passion for ministry: What is your vision for men's ministry? What gets you the most excited about serving? Where do you see yourself fitting in? From these questions and others you will get a sense of whether they really want to do ministry or are motivated by guilt or a feeling that they should do something for the sake of doing something.

Giftedness

The final quality to seek in a man for your leadership team is giftedness. Every man is gifted, but you must make sure that he is gifted for his area of responsibility.

Our natural tendency is to surround ourselves with men just like us—those we want as friends. Men with different gifts think differently. They might laugh at opposite things. They process experiences and emotions in a variety of ways. It can be death to a ministry if everyone on the team is the same. Although Green Bay Packers head coach Mike Holmgren was a great offensive coordinator, he was relatively weak in defense. Holmgren led two Packers teams to the Super Bowl because he surrounded himself with strong defensive minds that complemented his offensive schemes. In the same way, a leader of men needs to surround himself with other men who complement his giftedness.

✳ Name men in your church who exemplify the qualities you have studied.

Servant spirit: _____

Character: _____

Godliness: _____

Passion: _____

Giftedness: _____

✳ Now compare your list with the men you listed on page 26. Do you need to revise your considerations for your men's ministry leadership team, based on the qualities you have studied?

As you pull together a men's ministry leadership team, think through the following areas to ensure a well-rounded team.

Is there a man with the gift of leadership? Many leaders—even pastors—do not have the gift of leadership. A leader has the abilities to develop a vision and to get others involved to make that vision a reality. Every team needs someone with the gift of leadership.

Is there a man with the gift of administration? A ministry launch generates endless numbers of administrative tasks. Find someone who likes administration—keeping ministry details organized and workers on task and on time. Any man with the adventurous spirit of a leader needs a man like this on the leadership team.

Is there a man with the gift of helps? With so much to get done, you need to have someone on your leadership team who relishes doing little things, behind-the-scenes things that make a ministry work.

Is there a man with the gift of mercy? Sometimes a leadership team full of men who like to get things done leaves a bunch of battered people in their wake. You need someone who can care for the men, be a kinder and gentler example to overeager leaders, and shepherd the other leaders as the team develops.

These four gifts keep a leadership team working well. They bring balance to one another. It's possible, though, to have the proper gift mix but still get nowhere. Each man must bring with him not only a gift but also a deep willingness to be a team player.

✳ **What gifts are needed on your men's ministry leadership team to balance the team leader's gifts?**

_____

_____

✳ **Beside the gifts you listed, write the names of men in your church who demonstrate these gifts.**

✳ **Do any of these men appear on the two previous lists you have made? Examine your lists and, prayerfully considering qualities and gifts, make a final list of prospects for your leadership team.**

Men's ministry team leader: _____

Evangelizing team leader: _____

Establishing team leader: _____

Equipping team leader: _____

Extending team leader: _____

RECRUIT YOUR LEADERSHIP TEAM

It's one thing to know what kind of men you want on your leadership team—even to set your sights on which ones you want. It's another thing to get them involved. If your church is like most, 20 percent of the people do 80 percent of the work. All of the church's key people are pulled in many different directions. So it's a good policy not to steal leaders from another ministry. Instead, develop your own leaders from the many men who are on the outside looking in. Here are steps you can take to recruit men for your leadership team.

Pray them out. In Matthew 9:37-38 Jesus told the disciples that the harvest is plentiful. That's true in our day as well. But what was the first thing He told them to do? Hire a headhunter? No! The first step is to pray to the Lord of the harvest to send workers for the harvest.

When you see a man at church who isn't involved but should be, put his name on a list. Regularly pray through this list, asking God to thrust these men into the harvest, in men's ministry or in another area. Pray that God will bring just the right position for each man, based on his giftedness, passion, and availability.

Develop relationships with them. Ministry happens best through friendships. Do things with potential leaders to get to know them. Take them out for breakfast or lunch. In this informal setting you can learn more about their walk with the Lord.

Meet them one-to-one. The best way to ask a man to be involved is in a one-to-one setting. Meet him for a meal or in his office or your office. Try hard to connect face-to-face before you settle for a phone conversation. Then share your vision for the ministry and where it is going—the big picture—in order to recruit to a vision, not a program. After he grasps the big picture, share more specifically about the area in which you see him getting involved. Tell him why you think he is the right man for the job and explain how he would fit on the leadership team.

Share a job description. At this one-to-one meeting give a straightforward job description for the specific area in which you would like the man to help. Put it in writing to ensure that everything is as clear as possible, even though you might also cover this verbally. The job description tells him specifically what you would expect of him. It includes—

• what he would do—the ministry responsibilities;
• how much time it would take to do it;
• to whom he would report;
• the term of service;
• what the men's ministry leadership team and the church would do to support him in his ministry;
• the qualifications for the job.

After reviewing the job description with the man, ask him whether he has any questions about the ministry opportunity.

Ask for a commitment. Finish the conversation by asking the prospective leader to pray about the opportunity and, if he's married, to talk with his wife about it before making a commitment. Give him a copy of "A Covenant of Expectations for Men's Ministry Leaders" on page 30. State a specific time when you need a response, usually a maximum of one or two weeks. At that time meet with him again to discuss any questions and to sign the covenant together.

You could use the same steps to recruit any leader for men's ministry. Remember, as you begin your ministry, all you are looking for are five men to form your men's ministry leadership team. If you have two or three already, then you need to decide how many men you want on your team and who should contact potential leaders.

✳ **Use the steps in this section, "Recruit Your Leadership Team," to recruit each man God is leading to join your men's ministry leadership team.**

TRAIN YOUR LEADERS

For many men a huge roadblock to serving in the church is their fear that they won't do the job right. Men fear failure. One key to working with your leadership team is to provide the training they need to do what you have asked them to do. It is not enough to recruit them and then let them go. You squelch fears when you give men skills, instruction, and resources to do the job properly. Never ask a man to do anything you aren't willing to train him to do.

The most effective training takes place in short, informal settings. Here are ways you can train your leaders.

Small groups. If you are just starting your ministry, it may be hard to wait to begin small groups or a monthly meeting, but you can't go wrong taking your first year to develop your leaders. This will set a solid foundation for whatever course you take in the future. And the best way to do that is to meet with a small group of men. Plenty of great leadership books are available that can help you prepare your men (see "Resources,", p. 31).

In the small-group experience, model leading discussions, handling tough questions, dealing with problems, and so on. Give leaders training in the basics:

• The purpose of small groups
• Small-group dynamics
• Listening skills and feedback
• Inductive Bible study
• How to start and finish a group
• How to choose group members
• How to handle difficult questions and participants
• How to lead an effective prayer time

Committee meetings. The normal give-and-take of a planning meeting often opens opportunities to interject good leadership principles. Briefly coach the men on church procedures like how to reserve rooms, place bulletin announcements, and work in cooperation with the custodial staff.

Books and courses. Another good thing to do with your leadership team is to read a leadership book or complete a discipleship study together and discuss it when you meet monthly. Studying books together gives all of the leaders a common understanding of service and ministry, and it encourages them to read, which most men do not like to do. If you like to read, pass on a good book when you finish it.

A COVENANT OF EXPECTATIONS FOR MEN'S MINISTRY LEADERS

I understand that my leadership role in this ministry is important for the growth of God's kingdom.

I understand that God has called me to assume this leadership role, and I am totally dependent on Him for guidance, direction, sensitivity, and spiritual discernment. Therefore, a committed prayer life is a necessity.

I understand that God has raised up a generation of men He wants to use in creative and mighty ways to reach others for Christ.

Recognizing my total dependence on God, I will seek to do the following.

- I will be a man of integrity by maintaining a close walk with Jesus Christ and by demonstrating Christlike character in my words and actions.
- I will be a partner with our pastor and the other members of our men's ministry leadership team in developing and implementing activities and meetings for our men's ministry.
- I will support and regularly pray for our pastor, our church, and our men's ministry. I will also lead men to do the same.
- Acknowledging that men's ministry is a valuable outreach and discipling tool of the local church, I will do whatever it takes to reach men wherever they are through a balanced focus on evangelizing men to salvation and church membership, establishing men to spiritual maturity, equipping men for ministry, and extending men on mission.

- I will seek God's direction in identifying men in our church who need to lead specific men's ministry activities.
- I will ensure that each men's activity has a written spiritual goal that will be evaluated later. This goal will be shared frequently with all men.
- I will participate in regular gatherings of men to celebrate and share what God has done in and through our men's ministry.
- I will cooperate with denominational men's ministry leaders in joint efforts to reach and minister to men in the name of Christ.
- I will promote biblical unity in the body of Christ.

_____   _____
Signed   Date

_____   _____
Signed   Date

Other resources. One way to train your men informally is to provide them resources. Besides books, you can use discipleship and leadership periodicals from your denomination's publishing house. Ask your pastor or minister of education to pass on good articles he discovers. Some video series make great take-home helps that men can view at their convenience.

Consulting. It's often helpful to enlist an outside consultant to meet with your leadership team, hear what you're doing, and provide objective feedback.

On-the-job training. When possible, work alongside another man before asking him to do a job alone. Have your men do the same. On your special-events team, for example, each member would groom a man to take his place. These men would attend all of the meetings and take some responsibilities. These men would then be more prepared to lead a small group if they chose.

Outside seminars and conferences. Your pastor probably knows the training available in your area. LifeWay Christian Resources offers men's ministry training across the country. For information contact Sid Woodruff, MSN 151; LifeWay Christian Resources; 127 Ninth Avenue, North; Nashville, TN 37234-0151; (615) 251-2028. Also contact the men's ministry director at your state denominational office or a representative for mission education and mobilization at the North American Mission Board; 4200 North Point Parkway; Alpharetta, GA 30022-4176; (770) 410-6000.

✳ **Think about your men's ministry leadership team or your prospective team members. What competencies do they need to develop most?**

_____

_____

✳ **Check the methods you can use to meet these training needs.**
  ❏ Small groups   ❏ Committee meetings
  ❏ Books and courses   ❏ Other resources
  ❏ Consulting   ❏ On-the-job training
  ❏ Outside seminars and conferences

✳ **Describe the first step you will take toward providing this training.**

_____

_____

GIVE AWAY THE MINISTRY

In the movie *Miracle on Ice*, the story of the 1980 U.S. Olympic hockey team, an interesting scene occurs after Herb Brooks's American squad defeats the Russian team in the semifinals of the medal round. Players on the ice hug one another, others cry in ecstasy, flags wave everywhere, and the Lake Placid crowd chants, "USA! USA!" Then there's a shot of Brooks. An assistant coach tells Brooks to go out on the ice with the guys to celebrate one of the greatest upsets of all time. Herb looks at his assistant. "This is their time of glory," he says. "They earned it. Let's let them enjoy it." Brooks turns his back and walks to the locker room.

Real leadership gets excited seeing others minister. It pulls together a group of men, equips them, trains them, and releases them to do ministry. Your ministry will grow only as you develop leaders and allow them freedom. If you try to do everything yourself, the scope of your men's ministry will be small and its impact limited. Use these basic principles to give away the ministry—to delegate ministry to the men you lead.

Point men in the right direction. Your first task as a leader or a leadership team is to decide what you want to do. Vision is deciding where you are going with the ministry and discerning what must happen for you to get there. You should have identified the direction of your men's ministry when you developed your purpose statement in point 2 of this manual.

Transfer ownership. You may be sure where your group should go. But you can't get your men anywhere without help. Give your men the authority, freedom, and resources they need to perform as God has gifted them. Biblical delegation starts a man with small tasks, then moves him to bigger assignments when he proves himself faithful. Start by putting men in charge of things, then move them to projects, and finally move them to people. Since people are our most precious commodity, make sure the men you choose to lead them possess character and ability.

You have to consciously work to give away ministry. Your first step in letting go is to make known what you need and expect. To get a man to plan a fall kickoff, for example, sit down with him and go over the following:

• What has to be done
• How it will be done
• When it will be done
• Who will help

Release your leaders. A good phrase to keep in mind is "Catch and release." Leadership means helping men catch a vision for using their gifts and then releasing them to do it. Releasing men is difficult. When you give a job away, your men won't do it as you would. They won't avoid the mistakes you would have seen a mile away. And they may never do their job as well as you could. But that's OK. Ministry isn't about perfection.

It's about men—developing them to be who God wants them to be.

Stay in touch with your leaders. Be available to meet with the men to discuss how they are doing. One problem with delegation is the dump-and-run phenomenon, when a leader gives away an aspect of the ministry but never checks on progress or offers follow-up help. As you give away your ministry, be available to support and encourage your hard-working men. What each man needs will be different. Some like a lot of room. They run with a job and forget all about you. Others need more of your time and attention.

Even if you are just beginning a men's ministry, decide now to give away the ministry as men are called and equipped.

✳ **Match the principles you studied with practical ways to give away the ministry.**

___ 1. Point men in the right direction.
___ 2. Transfer ownership.
___ 3. Release your leaders.
___ 4. Stay in touch with your leaders.

a. Help leaders discover their spiritual gifts.
b. Follow up with leaders.
c. Regularly communicate the men's ministry vision.
d. Give men authority, freedom, and resources.

Check your answers below.

Resources

Blackaby, Henry, and Tom Blackaby. *The Man God Uses*. Nashville: LifeWay, 1998.

Blackaby, Henry, and Henry Brandt. *The Power of the Call*. Nashville: Broadman & Holman, 1995.

Chambers, Oswald. *My Utmost for His Highest*. Edited by James Reimann. Grand Rapids: Discovery House, 1992.

Coleman, Robert. *The Master Plan of Evangelism*. 2nd ed. Westwood: Fleming H. Revell, 1994.

Downer, Phil, with Chip MacGregor. *Eternal Impact: Investing in the Lives of Men*. Eugene: Harvest House, 1997.

Hanks, Louis B. *Vision, Variety, and Vitality*. Nashville: Convention, 1996.

Hemphill, Ken. *The Antioch Effect: Eight Characteristics of Highly Effective Churches*. Nashville: Broadman & Holman, 1994.

Hybels, Bill. *Too Busy Not to Pray: Slowing Down to Be with God*. Downers Grove: InterVarsity, 1998.

Maxwell, John. *21 Irrefutable Laws of Leadership*. Nashville: Thomas Nelson, 1998.

McCasland, David. *Abandoned to God*. Nashville: Thomas Nelson, 1993. Out of print.

Swindoll, Charles R. *Hand Me Another Brick*. New York: Bantam, 1983.

Wallis, Arthur. *God's Chosen Fast*. Fort Washington: Christian Literature Crusade, 1993.

Wilkes, Gene. *Jesus on Leadership: Developing Servant Leaders*. Nashville: LifeWay, 1996.

Note

[1]This section adapted from Phil Downer with Chip MacGregor, *Eternal Impact: Investing in the Lives of Men* (Eugene: Harvest House, 1997), 38–39.

Answers to Activity

Page 31: 1. c, 2. d, 3. a, 4. b

POINT 4

◆

Plan a Balanced Ministry

1. Partner and pray   2. Propose a purpose statement

Establish   Equip

Evangelize   Extend

3. Prepare leaders

4. Plan a balanced ministry

It's easy to grow a ministry that gets so caught up in one biblical mandate that it ignores the others. It's possible, for example, to pour a great deal of energy, money, and time into bringing lost men to Christ but then to spend little time grounding them in the basics (see Col. 2:7) and helping them mature in Christ (see Eph. 4:13). It's also possible to spend so much time perfecting your care for the men in your church (see Gal. 6:2) that you never reach out to those outside the faith (see Acts 1:8). That's why planning a balanced ministry is so important. You can do this by keeping these four biblical mandates in mind.

Evangelize. The gospel of Jesus Christ has the power to save those who believe (see Rom. 1:16). Evangelism is presenting the gospel of Jesus Christ in the Holy Spirit's power and leaving the results to God. Approximately four billion people don't know Jesus Christ. Most men in your men's ministry are surrounded daily by people in this category. Part of your ministry needs to be designed to reach those who are without Christ.

Establish. Many men aren't well grounded in the basics of Christianity even after years of church involvement. They can say and do the right things, but they

> *We proclaim him, admonishing and teaching everyone with all wisdom, so that we may present everyone perfect in Christ.*
>
> Colossians 1:28, NIV

lack vitality in their relationships with Christ. In Colossians 2:6-7 Paul wrote, "Just as you received Christ Jesus as Lord, continue to live in him, rooted and built up in him, strengthened in the faith as you were taught" (NIV). In the establishment area of your ministry, you can help men develop the basic spiritual disciplines of prayer, Bible study, and Scripture memorization, as well as help them develop relationships with other men who will challenge and support them in their walk with Jesus.

Equip. The third part of a balanced ministry is getting men off the bench and into the game. Your ministry should seek to help men become contributing members of the body of Christ by discovering and using their spiritual gifts (see Eph. 4:11-13).

Extend. Nothing is more exciting than seeing men become on-mission Christians, catching a vision for influencing their own Jerusalem, Judea, and Samaria and for carrying the gospel to all the world (see Acts 1:8).

Points 4A, 4B, 4C, and 4D will help you plan a balanced ministry to men that includes all four areas. Don't expect to be able to address each area equally well at first. Rather, try to give balanced attention to each area as you plan and move forward.

POINT 4A

◆

Plan a Balanced Ministry: Evangelize Men to Salvation and Church Membership

Evangelize

1. Partner and pray 2. Propose a purpose statement

3. Prepare leaders

4. Plan a balanced ministry

OUR GOAL

obby was active in his church teaching Sunday School, working on committees, and serving as a deacon. On the job he mingled with employees and customers who were not Christians, making friends with each person God brought into his life. Bobby also had hunting and fishing buddies who were not saved. When Bobby enrolled in a witness-training group at church, he learned how to share Christ with others. His faith grew dramatically as he began to lead some of his friends to a saving knowledge of Jesus Christ. Later, by studying *Experiencing God*, Bobby realized that God had already been at work in the lives of those with whom he shared a witness. When he witnessed to his friends, he was simply joining God in His saving activity. It was God who was causing his friends to be receptive to the gospel even before Bobby opened his mouth.

The predominant message of this manual is for men to live the Great Commandment (see Mark 12:30-31) and to fulfill the Great Commission (see Matt. 28:19-20). A man obeys these commandments by loving God with all his mind,

> *I am not ashamed of the gospel, because it is the power of God for the salvation of everyone who believes.*
>
> Romans 1:16, NIV

heart, soul, and strength and by loving his neighbors enough to share Christ with them. The concept of relationship is key in these Scriptures. To help men come to God, we must be willing to intentionally build loving, caring relationships with them.

ACCEPT RESPONSIBILITY FOR WITNESSING

In Romans 1:14-16 the apostle Paul expressed his feelings about being a witness for Christ. Although Paul had not personally met the people of Rome, he felt that he owed them a debt: to tell them about Jesus. Do we also feel obligated to tell others about Jesus?

Following are four reasons men need to witness.

Your neighbor. The people of the United States probably have greater access to the gospel than any other people in history. In spite of that, many have not heard it at all. Many more have not understood it. Here are some of the most common misunderstandings.

• You get salvation by earning it. Do more good than bad, and you will go to heaven.

- All religions are the same. The important thing is to believe in a higher power.
- God loves us so much that He could never let anyone go to hell.

Men with ideas such as these do not know the message of Jesus. From Romans 10:17 we learn, "Faith comes from hearing the message, and the message is heard through the word of Christ" (NIV). Men need to hear the gospel in order to believe.

This need is especially important in light of the consequences of unbelief.

✷ **Read John 3:18,36. What is the result of a lack of faith in Christ?**

_____

_____

A man without a saving faith in Jesus is missing abundant and eternal life in the present and will face God's wrath and judgment in the future. The needs of our neighbors obligate believers to be personal witnesses.

✷ **List the names of three lost men you know.**

_____

✷ **If these men became Christians today, how would their lives be affected?**

_____

_____

✷ **Are the potential changes worth the effort it would take to share the gospel with them?** ❑ Yes ❑ No

Yourself. Talking about Jesus is also something Christian men need to do for themselves. Personal witnessing is necessary for a believer's spiritual health. Dialogue about your faith makes your spiritual life stimulating and meaningful. The more you talk to others about Jesus, the more excited you will become about your own faith and relationship with God. Talking to others about Jesus is a natural part of a Christian man's life. If you spend time with God each day, you will naturally witness of your relationship with Him. Furthermore, as you grow in that relationship, others will come to you with questions or for help because your life resembles that of Jesus. Because you are growing in Christlikeness, you genuinely care about people. Therefore, you do not mind taking risks to witness to those you meet, even if you are initially uncomfortable doing so.

Personal witnessing is also a trigger that releases power in our lives. In 1 Corinthians 2:1-5 Paul admitted feeling weak and inadequate as he considered the task of bearing witness to Christ in the city of Corinth. As he spoke about Jesus, however, God demonstrated the presence and power of the Holy Spirit. Believers who witness about Christ experience the Holy Spirit working in and through their lives. God always gives power and strength to those who do His work.

Many Christians feel intimidated when they consider telling someone about Jesus. Yet those moments of weakness can be times when God provides His greatest strength. When Paul complained about the weakness he felt from a thorn in the flesh, the Lord taught him an important lesson: " 'My power is made perfect in weakness' " (2 Cor. 12:9, NIV).

Your church. Personal witnessing is also a necessity for the life and ministry of a man's church. The number of new, baptized believers in most evangelical mainline denominations has declined over the past several decades. If churches multiply the number of people doing the work of evangelism, they can grow by adding new believers to the membership. Personal witnessing is a necessity for churches to grow through evangelism.

Your Lord. Although God does not need us to accomplish the salvation of lost people, He chose to involve us in the process. In His wisdom the Lord chose to use human agents to spread the news about new life in Jesus. God's plan for evangelism obligates Christian men to be witnesses.

Among the last words of Jesus in each of the Gospels was a command for His followers to be witnesses of what they had seen and experienced. In Matthew He told the disciples to " 'make disciples of all nations' " (Matt. 28:19, NIV). In Mark they were commanded to " 'preach the good news to all creation' " (Mark 16:15, NIV). Luke records Jesus' reminding the disciples that " 'repentance and forgiveness of sins will be preached in his name to all nations, beginning at Jerusalem' " (Luke 24:47, NIV). After the resurrection narrative in John, Jesus said: " 'Peace be with you! As the Father has sent me, I am sending you' " (John 20:21, NIV). Clearly, Jesus expected His followers to be witnesses for Him.

Throughout the New Testament Christ's followers are admonished to speak about Jesus in the world. In 2 Corinthians 5:20 the apostle Paul noted: "We are therefore Christ's ambassadors, as though God were making his appeal through us. We implore you on Christ's behalf: Be reconciled to God" (NIV). *Ambassador* may be defined as *an official messenger with a special mission.* Christians are official representatives of Jesus. Our special mission is to urge others to be reconciled with God through faith in Jesus.

Jesus referred to His disciples as fishers. In Matthew 4:19 He said, " 'Come, follow me, ... and I will make you fishers of men' " (NIV). Jesus expected those who followed Him to become personal witnesses. Neither personality nor Bible knowledge makes us fishers of men. We become witnesses as a result of what Jesus has done for us. Since He chooses us to share, He will do what is necessary to enable us to witness. We must be involved in evangelism, for that is the work Jesus intends for us to do.[1]

✳ Summarize each reason to witness.

Your neighbor: _____

_____

Yourself: _____

_____

Your church: _____

_____

Your Lord: _____

_____

PRAY

In Matthew 9:36-38 when Jesus saw multitudes of people suffering distress and despair, He was moved with compassion. He realized that the number of workers did not match the size of the ready harvest. Instead of immediately sending the few workers available into the field to reap as much of the harvest as possible, Jesus told His disciples to " 'beseech the Lord of the harvest to send out workers into His harvest' " (Matt. 9:38, NASB). Witnessing involves prayer. The disciples looked at the multitude and saw a large group of people. Jesus looked at the crowd and saw broken lives (see Matt. 9:36). His vision of their needs stirred His compassion. When our compassion is stirred, we want to witness.

As we pray, God opens our eyes to see the harvest as He sees it. He gives us His vision, and that vision will compel us to share Jesus. Men who pray for the harvest will want to work in the field, just as the disciples who prayed for laborers in Matthew 9 went out to share in Matthew 10.

Prayer also reminds us of the One to whom the harvest belongs. We are to ask the Lord to "send forth labourers into his harvest" (Matt. 9:38, KJV). The harvest is from the Lord, not from the laborer. As laborers we are instrumental in bringing men to Christ, but God is responsible for their salvation (see 1 Cor. 3:6).

Although we cannot produce evangelistic fruit, we can participate in the evangelistic process. God saves, but He saves the lost through our involvement in evan-

gelism. We pray and work for His harvest. Realizing who produces the harvest reduces the pressure to win converts. We are successful when we tell someone about Jesus, regardless of the results. The witness is accountable for participation, not for production.[2]

✳ Recall the three lost men you listed on page 34. Begin praying every day for their salvation.

SEEK THE SPIRIT

To be ready to share their faith, men must seek the filling of the Holy Spirit. In Acts 1:8 Jesus told His disciples to be witnesses after the Holy Spirit came upon them. In Acts 4:18-21 Jesus' followers were told that persecution would follow if they continued speaking about Jesus. After being filled with the Holy Spirit, however, they began to witness boldly in spite of the threats (see Acts 4:31). The Holy Spirit will help us overcome our fears and find a way to share the gospel.

A common misunderstanding about the filling of the Holy Spirit is that it refers to the coming of the Holy Spirit into our lives. In John 7:38-39 Jesus said that the Holy Spirit would be sent to those who believe in Him. The Holy Spirit comes into your life when you become a Christian. As you place your faith in Jesus, the Holy Spirit comes to dwell in you. According to Jesus, the indwelling is permanent (see John 14:16).

The filling of the Holy Spirit refers not to the Spirit's coming into our lives but to the Spirit's empowering us for witness and ministry. As we are filled with the Holy Spirit, we receive the courage and strength necessary to tell others about Jesus. Our lives and our lips become channels for the Spirit to use in spreading the gospel.

In Ephesians 5:18 Christians are commanded to "be filled with the Spirit." The Greek language reveals some important truths about this commandment. The verb is plural in form, indicating that the commandment is for all Christians. It is also an imperative verb, meaning that the action is required. Because it is a passive verb, the filling of the Spirit must be something God does for us. We cannot fill ourselves. The command is also in the present tense, indicating continuous action: "Keep on being filled." Unlike salvation, the filling of the Spirit is not a one-time experience. Each time we go out to witness, we should seek to be filled with the Holy Spirit.

How can you be filled with the Spirit? Filling begins with *seeking*. In Matthew 7:7 Jesus said, " 'Ask and it will be given to you; seek and you will find; knock and the door will be opened to you' " (NIV). The Lord delights in giving to those who want to receive.

The next step is *cleansing* our hearts of all known sin. The Holy Spirit will not honor or bless a sinful life. The Bible tells us what to do about sin in 1 John 1:9: "If we confess our sins, he is faithful and just and will forgive us our sins and purify us from all unrighteousness"

(NIV). When our sin is forgiven and cleansed, we are ready to be filled.

The final step is *yielding* control of our lives to the Holy Spirit. When we accept His control, we will do His work. That work is to bear witness to Jesus (see John 15:26-27).

As men tell others about Jesus, they will experience the power and help of the Holy Spirit in three ways.
1. The Holy Spirit prepares the lost person to receive their witness (see John 16:8).
2. The Holy Spirit guides them in what to say and do as they witness (see Matt. 10:19-20).
3. The Holy Spirit keeps their witness alive in the minds and souls of those who hear it (see John 15:26).[3]

✳ **Match the way each step helps a witness experience the filling of the Holy Spirit.**

___ 1. Seeking   a. **When we accept the Spirit's control, we can bear witness to Jesus.**

___ 2. Cleansing   b. **When our sin is forgiven and cleansed, we are ready to be filled.**

___ 3. Yielding   c. **The Lord will give to those who want to receive.**

    Check your answers on page 42.

God not only works in your life as a yielded Christian witness, but He also works in the life of a man who does not know Him. The Holy Spirit empowers our witness by convicting the man of sin, righteousness, and judgment (see John 16:8-9). The Holy Spirit also converts the lost man from death to life. This takes a great responsibility off our shoulders. It is ultimately God's job to get men to heaven. All God desires and expects from us is that we are obedient in telling other men about His Son and in giving them an opportunity to respond.

BUILD WITNESSING RELATIONSHIPS

The apostle Paul is an excellent example of a Christian who wanted to lead others to Christ. Many have called him the greatest personal soul-winner of all time, other than Jesus. First Corinthians 9:19-23 reveals Paul's strategy for winning the lost.

> Though I am free and belong to no man, I make myself a slave to everyone, to win as many as possible. To the Jews I became like a Jew, to win the Jews. To those under the law I became like one under the law (though I myself am not under the law), so as to win those under the law. To those not having the law I became like one not having the law (though I am not free

from God's law but am under Christ's law), so as to win those not having the law. To the weak I became weak, to win the weak. I have become all things to all men so that by all possible means I might save some. I do all this for the sake of the gospel, that I may share in its blessings (1 Cor. 9:19-23, NIV).

✳ **In the previous Scripture underline every time Paul said "to win."**

✳ **What was Paul's priority in life?**

_____

Paul's priority was to win the lost for Jesus. To reach his goal, Paul developed the following strategy for soul-winning.

Be Inclusive, Not Exclusive

Paul did not write off groups of people because they were different from him. In 1 Corinthians 9:19-23 Paul listed several groups he might have written off but did not. He disregarded potential barriers between him and these groups.

Paul exemplified the heart and mind of Jesus, who included all persons in His redemptive plan. Peter said that Jesus did not want "anyone to perish, but everyone to come to repentance" (2 Pet. 3:9, NIV). The angel who announced Jesus' birth proclaimed " 'good news of great joy that will be for all the people' " (Luke 2:10, NIV). In Jesus' earthly ministry He continually included those who had previously been excluded. He broke down centuries-old barriers to embrace outcasts.

Many of us exclude certain groups from those with whom we should share the gospel. Some of us tend to witness only to those of our same background. Some of us will not witness to our peers but will witness to persons with whom we have only minimal exposure. Either way we miss the blessing of winning men for Jesus, and they miss the blessing of eternal life.

✳ **Look again at 1 Corinthians 9:19-23. Circle every group Paul included in his witnessing strategy. Then check your answers on page 42.**

Be Willing to Become

Paul was willing to become something in order to win someone. Becoming something to someone means finding common ground on which to establish credibility or trust. It means finding a point of connection, a way to identify.

A relationship is made up of what two persons have become to each other. A relationship is defined by what goes through two persons' minds when they think of each other. Until you become something to someone, there is no relationship. When you have found common ground and have established credibility and trust, you have the basis for a relationship. Something you have in common with another man might be fishing, hunting, playing basketball, eating lunch together, or having children who are in the same class at school.

✳ From 1 Corinthians 9:19-23, list what Paul said he would become in order to win the lost for Jesus. Then check your answers on page 42.

Verse 19: _____

Verse 20: _____

Verse 21: _____

Verse 22: _____

Paul's statement in verse 22 holds the key to cultivating a witnessing relationship: "I have become all things to all men so that by all possible means I might save some." Becoming something or someone positive to a lost person is the way you cultivate a witnessing relationship. When a Christian becomes Christlike to a lost man, the Holy Spirit uses the resulting relationship to prepare the man for the gospel. Witnessing relationships are cultivated by witnesses who are empowered by the Holy Spirit.[4]

✳ Recall the three lost men you listed on page 34. Name interests you have that might become or that have already become common ground for establishing a relationship with each of them.

1. _____

2. _____

3. _____

✳ If you have already established relationships with these three lost men, what have you already become to them? In other words, what comes to their minds when they think of you?

1. _____

2. _____

3. _____

✳ Do you need to change their perception of you? Should you become something different or some-thing more? What do you think you should become for these men to allow you to present the gospel?

1. _____

2. _____

3. _____

✳ If you have not already established relationships with these three men, get to know each over a meal with or without his spouse.

BE PREPARED

A foundational aspect of any men's ministry should be that every man is active in building caring relationships with other men and in leading them to Christ. Men must be equipped to test other men for receptivity to the gospel, to present the gospel, and to give a testimony when they have opportunities.

Test for Receptivity

Receptivity may be thought of as a continuum. On one end is a man who is very interested in and open to discussing spiritual issues with you. On the other end is a man who absolutely will not discuss anything religious with you. In the parable of the sower (see Matt. 13:1-9,18-23) Jesus described four different types of soil, which represent the hearts of men.

That same day Jesus went out of the house and sat by the lake. Such large crowds gathered around him that he got into a boat and sat in it, while all the people stood on the shore. Then he told them many things in parables, saying: "A farmer went out to sow his seed. As he was scattering the seed, some fell along the path, and the birds came and ate it up. Some fell on rocky places, where it did not have much soil. It sprang up quickly, because the soil was shallow. But when the sun came up, the plants were scorched, and they withered because they had no root. Other seed fell among thorns, which grew up and choked the plants. Still other seed fell on good soil, where it produced a crop—a hundred, sixty or thirty times what was sown. He who has ears, let him hear.

"Listen then to what the parable of the sower means: When anyone hears the message about the kingdom and does not understand it, the evil one comes and snatches away what was sown in his heart. This is the seed sown along the path. The one who received the seed that fell on rocky places is the man who hears the word and at once receives it with joy. But since he has no root, he lasts only a short time. When trouble or persecution comes because of the word, he quickly falls away. The one who received the seed that fell among the thorns is the man who hears the word, but the worries of this life and the deceitfulness of wealth choke it, making it unfruitful. But the one who received the seed that fell on good soil is the man who hears the word and understands it. He produces a crop, yielding a hundred, sixty or thirty times what was sown."

Jesus said that when the seed of the gospel falls on men's hearts, men respond in different ways. Your men can learn how to determine which category a lost man fits and ways to enhance the receptivity of a lost man in each category. The receptivity categories give men a biblical way to evaluate attitudes that create barriers to the gospel so that they can plan an effective witnessing strategy tailored to each lost man's specific, individual need. The purpose of receptivity categories is never to label or pigeonhole men. We rate attitudes, not men.

✳ In Jesus' teaching in Matthew 13:1-9,18-23, what might the sower represent?
❑ Jesus   ❑ The world   ❑ The witness

✳ What might the seed represent?
❑ The word of God   ❑ The witness   ❑ The world

✳ What might the soil represent?
❑ Jesus   ❑ The witness   ❑ The hearts of lost men

✳ Now read the passage again and circle each type of soil on which the seed fell. Underline the descriptions of the different results when the seed fell on each type of soil.

The sower in the parable represents the man who witnesses, the seed represents the word of God, and the soil represents the hearts of lost men. This is not the only way to interpret this parable. The parable of the soils is used here not to interpret the Scriptures but to show men what to expect when they approach lost men with the gospel. When the gospel seed is sown in the hearts of lost men, they respond in different ways.

The receptivity categories that can be identified are:
Good soil. Very receptive.
Rocky soil. Gives the gospel only a shallow hearing and has accepted only a part. Depends on good works to attempt to earn salvation.
Thorny soil. Either does not understand or does not accept Jesus' lordship. Rates his spiritual need by health, wealth, success, and peer acceptance.

Hard soil. Agnostic. Thinks that it is not possible to know for certain that God exists. Feels no need for God or religion.

Notice that the sower in Jesus' parable is not nearly as choosy as most witnesses are today. He does not say to himself: *This looks like good soil. I will sow here.* He sows everywhere and allows the soil to make its response to the seed. In other words, he tests the soil by sowing the seed. We should not sow our witness only where the soil looks good. We may not know what the Holy Spirit and another sower have been doing to prepare this soil.[5]

✳ Match each response to the gospel with its corresponding receptivity category.

Receptivity Category	Response
___ 1. Good soil	a. "I must be living right. God is blessing me. I have health, wealth, success, and peer acceptance."
___ 2. Rocky soil	b. "I'm sure I will go to heaven when I die. Look at all the good things I do!"
___ 3. Thorny soil	c. "I would love for you to tell me how I can be saved."
___ 4. Hard soil	d. "God is for weak people. I don't need religion."

Check your answers on page 42.

As a men's ministry leader, you can help men become confident in their ability to test another man's receptivity to the gospel. This competence will help them cross the transitional bridge and actually share the gospel message. The acrostic FIRE is one way to test receptivity.

Family: Would you mind telling me about your family?
Interests: Do you have any special interests or hobbies?
Religious background: When you attend church, where do you attend?
Exploratory questions:
• Do you ever think much about spiritual things?
• Do you know for certain that when you die, you will go to heaven?
• Suppose you were standing before God right now and He asked you, "Why should I let you into My heaven?" What do you think you would say?[6]

A lost man's answers to these questions reveal his attitude toward spiritual need, church and religion, the witness, and testing the soil. An analysis of these four attitudes indicates his receptivity to the gospel.

Attitude toward spiritual need. This refers to the man's realization of his need for God and his openness to spiritual counsel. Reflecting the degree of realization and admission of need for God, this attitude indicates whether the man is being drawn toward or convicted by the Holy Spirit. Attitude toward spiritual need determines the depth of communication to which the lost man is open. Is the lost man convicted that he is a sinner? Does the man understand that he will be held accountable and judged by God sometime in the future? Lost men who understand and admit their lostness and need for the Lord are more receptive than those who refuse to admit spiritual need. Attitude toward spiritual need is indicated by the lost man's response to *E* in the FIRE acrostic.

Attitude toward church and religion. This reflects the man's degree of willingness to attend church and the perceived credibility of church leaders. It demonstrates the degree of probability that the lost man will hear God's Word by going to church or by associating with Christians. This attitude affects how the lost man will listen to God's Word. Were past church-related experiences good or bad? What are his contacts at church? Does he know a pastor or a church leader in whom to confide? Which kinds of church events are likely to evoke the best response? Lost men who have confidence in a church or a church leader are more receptive than those who do not. Attitude toward church and religion is indicated by the lost man's response to *R* in the FIRE acrostic.

Attitude toward the witness. How well does the man relate to you as a witness for Christ? This attitude is based on trust in the messenger and determines in whom the lost man will confide. Ask yourself these questions: *What has affected my credibility? What have I already become to this lost man? How likely would the lost man be to respond favorably if approached with the gospel today? What are the indications for the future of the relationship? What do I need to become to gain this man's trust and bridge the gap to a successful witnessing encounter?* Lost men are more receptive when approached by a witness in whom they have confidence. Attitude toward the witness is indicated by the lost man's responses to *F* and *I* in the FIRE acrostic.

Attitude toward testing the soil. This describes the man's response to the witnessing approach. How far were you allowed to progress? The answer to this question determines the probability that the lost man will listen to the gospel and make a positive response. The attitude toward testing the soil is one of the clearest receptivity indicators. In most cases, it indicates whether the witness can present the gospel at that time or, if not, which receptivity category should be assigned to the lost man. Attitude toward spiritual need is indicated by the lost man's responses to *R* and *E* in the FIRE acrostic.[7]

✳ **Draw lines connecting each component of the FIRE acrostic with the attitude it is most likely to reveal.**

Family	Attitude toward spiritual need
Interests	Attitude toward church and religion
Religious background	Attitude toward the witness
Exploratory questions	Attitude toward testing the soil

Check your answers on page 42.

✳ Use the information in this section to test the receptivity of the three lost men you listed on page 34. Record what you discover on the chart "My Circles of Witnessing Influence" on page 40. Plan to use this tool with the men you train to witness.

✳ As the three men indicate that they are receptive, ask them for prayer requests. Check with them to learn how they are doing. Later, invite them to men's outreach events, Bible studies, or church. Continue praying for them and exposing them to evangelistic opportunities.

Give a Testimony

A basic tool for a Christian man's witness is his story of what Jesus did for him. That story is called a personal testimony. Some people think that a testimony is effective only if dramatic or unusual. Fortunately, that is not the case. God can use any testimony as an evangelistic tool. A testimony is effective because it is a personal story. Unlike something heard or read, the personal testimony has been experienced. Since it is firsthand information, a testimony has unique authority. Lost people may not accept the authority of the Bible, but most will not deny the reality of a personal experience. Every testimony carries with it the authority of experience.

A personal testimony also arouses interest by allowing you to present the gospel in terms of what God did in your life. When you express the story of what Jesus did for you in a brief and interesting way, men usually listen to the gospel.

You may choose from two types of testimonies.
1. A salvation testimony is the story of how you became a Christian.
2. A recovery testimony is the story of how Jesus helped you with a problem or a need in your life.

The principles involved in preparing your testimony for witnessing are simple.

MY CIRCLES OF WITNESSING INFLUENCE[8]

Family	Test Soil (Date)	Receptivity Category	Friends	Test Soil (Date)	Receptivity Category
Neighbors	Test Soil (Date)	Receptivity Category	**Work/School Associates**	Test Soil (Date)	Receptivity Category
Relatives	Test Soil (Date)	Receptivity Category	**Other Contacts**	Test Soil (Date)	Receptivity Category

Follow an outline. Using an outline keeps you on course. Many people find that it also makes their testimonies easier to remember. Your experience can be outlined in many ways. A helpful one is:
1. My life before Christ
2. How I realized my need for Christ
3. How I received Christ
4. My life after receiving Christ

Write it. Writing your testimony helps you clarify what you want to say. It also enables you to control the length of time you take to tell your story.

Begin by saying, "I have not always been a Christian." This gives you a common bond with each lost person you encounter. Your background and lifestyle may be different, but that statement means that you have shared the experience of being an unbeliever.

Close your testimony by asking, "Has anything like this ever happened to you?" If the person says no, ask permission to share the way to experience new life in Jesus. If the person says yes, ask him or her to share a testimony. If the testimony sounds unclear, you may still be able to share the gospel.

Keep it short. It is best to hold your testimony to two minutes or less.

Emphasize Jesus more than yourself. Keep your focus clear. Sharing your testimony is not sharing your life story. It is giving an account of what Jesus did for you. Your purposes are to introduce Jesus and to explain briefly what He has done in your life.

Avoid Christianese. The most common problem for believers who use their testimonies to witness is Christianese. *Christianese* is a word coined to describe the language we use in church. Terms like *coming down the aisle* or *getting saved* have little meaning to persons who do not go to church. Avoid using words and phrases unbelievers might not understand. When you use religious expressions, clarify them.[9]

✳ **Using the suggested outline, write your testimony on another sheet of paper. Practice presenting it to a family member or your witnessing partner. Request suggestions for improvement. When opportunities arise, share your testimony with the three lost men you have been cultivating.**

Share the Gospel
Men can choose from a number of ways to share the gospel. They can use a personal testimony, a witnessing booklet, a memorized presentation of the gospel, selected Scriptures such as the Roman Road, a single-Scripture-verse method, or a combination of these methods with a personal testimony. A simple Roman Road presentation is provided here.
1. Romans 1:16: "I am not ashamed of the gospel, because it is the power of God for the salvation of everyone who believes: first for the Jew, then for the Gentile" (NIV).
2. Romans 2:4: "God's kindness leads you toward repentance" (NIV).
3. Romans 3:23: "All have sinned and fall short of the glory of God" (NIV).
4. Romans 5:8: "God demonstrates his own love for us in this: While we were still sinners, Christ died for us" (NIV).
5. Romans 6:23: "The wages of sin is death, but the gift of God is eternal life in Christ Jesus our Lord" (NIV).
6. Romans 10:9-10,13: "If you confess with your mouth, 'Jesus is Lord,' and believe in your heart that God raised him from the dead, you will be saved. For it is with your heart that you believe and are justified, and it is with your mouth that you confess and are saved. ... For, 'Everyone who calls on the name of the Lord will be saved' " (NIV).
7. Romans 8:16-17,38-39: "The Spirit himself testifies with our spirit that we are God's children. Now if we are children, then we are heirs—heirs of God and co-heirs with Christ, if indeed we share in his sufferings in order that we may also share in his glory. ... For I am convinced that neither death nor life, neither angels nor demons, neither the present nor the future, nor any powers, neither height nor depth, nor anything else in all creation, will be able to separate us from the love of God that is in Christ Jesus our Lord" (NIV).
8. Romans 12:1-2: "I urge you, brothers, in view of God's mercy, to offer your bodies as living sacrifices, holy and pleasing to God—this is your spiritual act of worship. Do not conform any longer to the pattern of this world, but be transformed by the renewing of your mind. Then you will be able to test and approve what God's will is—his good, pleasing and perfect will" (NIV).

✳ **When you sense that the time is right, present the gospel to the three men you have been cultivating.**

Lead a Prayer for Salvation
Many times men who are lost and want to be saved do not know how to pray for salvation. The language the man uses in prayer is not nearly as important as his attitude. For many lost men, however, even a simple prayer is difficult to express. If the lost man needs help praying, lead him through a prayer similar to this one.

Dear God, I know that Jesus is Your Son and that He died and was raised from the dead. Because I have sinned and need forgiveness, I ask Jesus to save me. I am willing to change the direction of my life by acknowledging Jesus as my Savior and Lord and by turning away from my sins. Thank You for giving me forgiveness, eternal life, and hope. In Jesus' name. Amen.

Always clarify your role in praying for salvation. Be sure the man understands that your words are not more holy or effective than his. You are only helping him express what he wants Jesus to do in his life.[10]

✳ **Every Christian should know how to lead a prayer for salvation. Write one in your own words.**

_____

_____

_____

_____

_____

_____

✳ **Compare your prayer to the previously suggested one. The language used is not the primary issue. A man's genuine commitment of his life to Christ matters most.**

Witness with a Partner

When Jesus sent the disciples to minister, He sent them in pairs (see Luke 10:1). His model is still effective today. Witnessing with a partner has several benefits.

- A partner provides support when you witness. If you have a sense of inadequacy about witnessing, a partner makes it easier to be confident.
- A partner can help handle distractions that arise in a witnessing situation. For example, a partner can play with children so that the parent can listen to the message the witness is sharing.
- A partner can strengthen your commitment to pray about personal evangelism. Men who witness together pray together.
- Witnessing with another man promotes accountability and responsibility. Accountability usually results in productivity.[11]

✳ **Many of the activities in point 4A have guided you to identify and develop witnessing relationships with three lost men you know. Using the steps in the following box, communicate the same process to train men in your ministry to reach out to men in their circles of influence.**

---

1. Identify three lost men you know.
2. Pray every day for their salvation.
3. Invite each man to a one-to-one meal.
4. Test each man's receptivity to the gospel.
5. As appropriate, ask the lost men for prayer requests.
6. Invite the lost men to men's outreach events, Bible studies, or church.
7. Continue praying for the lost men and exposing them to evangelistic opportunities.
8. When the time is right, present a personal testimony and the gospel.

After men accept Christ, they need to be discipled. Point 4B in this manual will focus on establishing men to spiritual maturity.

Resources

Fay, Bill, and Ralph Hodge. *Share Jesus Without Fear*. Nashville: LifeWay, 1997.
How to Have a Full and Meaningful Life (tract). Nashville: The Sunday School Board, 1971.
Kelley, Chuck. *Learning to Share My Faith*. Nashville: LifeWay, 1994.
Robinson, Darrell. *People Sharing Jesus*. Nashville: Thomas Nelson, 1995.
Sanderson, Leonard, and Arthur H. Criscoe. *DecisionTime: Commitment Counseling*. Nashville: LifeWay, 1999.
Smith, Jack R., and Jennifer Kennedy Dean. *Witnessing Through Your Relationships*. Nashville: LifeWay, 1994.
Welch, Bobby H., and Doug Williams with David Apple. *A Journey in FAITH*. Nashville: LifeWay, 1998.
Welch, Bobby H., and Doug Williams with David Apple. *FAITH Advanced: The Journey Continues*. Nashville: LifeWay, 1999.

Notes

[1]Adapted from Chuck Kelley, *Learning to Share My Faith* (Nashville: LifeWay, 1994), 5–8.
[2]Ibid., 9–10.
[3]Ibid., 13–15.
[4]Adapted from Jack R. Smith and Jennifer Kennedy Dean, *Witnessing Through Your Relationships* (Nashville: LifeWay, 1994), 23–25.
[5]Ibid., 61–63.
[6]Ibid., 55–56.
[7]Ibid., 58–59.
[8]Ibid.
[9]Kelley, *Learning to Share*, 10–12.
[10]Ibid., 25.
[11]Ibid., 13.

Answers to Activities

Page 36, column 1: 1. c, 2. b, 3. a
Page 36, column 2: everyone, Jews, those under the law, those not having the law, the weak, all men
Page 37: Verse 19: slave. Verse 20: Jew, one under the law. Verse 21: one not having the law. Verse 22: weak, all things.
Page 38: 1. c, 2. b, 3. a, 4. d
Page 39: Family: attitude toward the witness. Interests: attitude toward the witness. Religious background: attitude toward church and religion, attitude toward testing the soil. Exploratory questions: attitude toward spiritual need, attitude toward testing the soil.

POINT 4B

◆

Plan a Balanced Ministry: Establish Men to Spiritual Maturity

To establish men to spiritual maturity means to develop faithful, maturing Christians. You and other church leaders must be intentional in planning events, activities, and studies that will develop men into mature believers. You must catch the vision of involving men in Christian discipleship that literally transforms their lives. This process requires commitment, planning, and hard work. Accept the responsibility for providing a balanced ministry that establishes all men in their Christian faith.

Your challenge of establishing men involves providing all types of opportunities to help them grow in—

- Christlikeness;
- their ability to apply biblical truth to every area of life;
- their responsibility to share their Christian faith with others;
- becoming multiplying leaders in the church.

Your target audience includes all men in one or more of the following categories.

- Are new Christians and/or older Christians who need to become well grounded in the basics of the Christian life

- Want to become true disciples of Jesus Christ
- Want to grow spiritually and know Christ better
- Are members of your church
  - Hurt and need caring relationships and encouragement
  - Need accountability and support
  - Have been Christians for a long time but have never been systematically discipled
  - Are leaders or potential leaders

Learning to live as a Christian disciple in our culture can be overwhelming and challenging. Many men feel uncertain; others feel intimidated. Men need other men who can guide them and show them the way as they walk in this new, transformed life in Christ.

As you take the challenge of developing a ministry to men, resolve in your heart to meet men where they are spiritually and lead them to become fanatical in their love for Jesus Christ, positively influencing their personal lives, families, churches, workplaces, communities, and world for Christ.

Jesus said, " 'Go and make disciples of all nations, baptizing them in the name of the Father and of the

> *Continue to live in him [Jesus Christ], rooted and built up in him, strengthened in the faith as you were taught, and overflowing with thankfulness.*
>
> Colossians 2:6-7, NIV

Son and of the Holy Spirit, and teaching them to obey everything I have commanded you' " (Matt. 28:19-20, NIV). Our command is to make disciples, which suggests a process rather than an instant occurrence. Christian discipleship may be defined as the process of developing a personal, lifelong, obedient relationship with Jesus Christ in which He—

- transforms our character into Christlikeness;
- changes our values into Kingdom values;
- involves us in His mission in the home, the church, and the world.[1]

If we do not make disciples who are able to disciple others, then our going, baptizing, and teaching may end with the next generation. How do we establish men to spiritual maturity? We will consider the following questions to help us understand this important process.

- What is spiritual transformation?
  —How does God transform a man into Jesus' likeness?
  —What are characteristics of spiritual transformation?
  —What are hindrances to spiritual transformation?
- What is the biblical model for establishing men in the Christian faith?
- How can you determine where your men are in the discipleship process?
- What are the 12 steps for establishing men to spiritual maturity?

WHAT IS SPIRITUAL TRANSFORMATION?

The goal of discipleship is spiritual transformation. Spiritual transformation is God's work of changing men into Jesus' likeness by creating a new identity in Christ and by empowering a lifelong relationship of love, trust, and obedience to glorify God. Paul wrote in Romans 12:2: "Do not conform any longer to the pattern of this world, but be transformed by the renewing of your mind. Then you will be able to test and approve what God's will is—his good, pleasing and perfect will" (NIV). Paul's use of the word *transformed* means *to be remodeled or changed into another form*. Not just the outward appearance but the essential person—character, nature, and perspective—is being changed. Spiritual transformation is a change of inward essence rather than a mere transition from one way of living to a different way. Christ is being formed in all who belong to Him (see Gal. 4:19). Spiritual transformation is the process of becoming like Christ.

Spiritual transformation begins with a new identity in Christ. When men receive Jesus as Savior and Lord, they receive a new identity established by a new relationship with Jesus (see Eph. 2:4-6,19-20). Salvation is a defining experience in which we become new persons. We take on His identity. We are sanctified or set apart for God's purposes at the moment of spiritual new birth in Christ (see John 3:5-6).

At the moment of conversion—when a man surrenders to a relationship with Jesus as Savior and Lord—God provides—

- justification (see Acts 13:39; Col. 2:13-15);
- regeneration (see John 3:1-16; 17:3);
- redemption (see Eph. 1:7);
- deliverance (see Col. 1:13);
- sanctification (see John 17:15-19).

Spiritual transformation continues in a growing relationship of love, trust, and obedience. Spiritual transformation is a process—a progressive change of worldview, values, attitudes, and behavior. Beginning with the heart and reaching out to touch the life and witness of God's people at every level, God's Word and God's Spirit bring transformation. Spiritual transformation at its foundation is a change of the heart that expresses itself in the outward life. The "good tree" (inner person) bears "good fruit" (outward actions; see Matt. 12:33). This growing relationship with Jesus affects all other relationships, such as marriage, parenting, work, and friendships.

Love and trust result in obedience. Obedience in our relationship with Jesus produces greater love and stronger faith.

Spiritual transformation glorifies God. The goal of the new identity in Christ and the lifelong relationship of love, trust, and obedience is to glorify God. God is glorified through a relationship of love. God is glorified as men fulfill Christ's mission. God is glorified as He is made known to others through His relationship with His people.

A man's intimate relationship with Jesus produces a new heart that is being transformed into the likeness of Christ: "We, who with unveiled faces all reflect the Lord's glory, are being transformed into his likeness with ever-increasing glory, which comes from the Lord, who is the Spirit" (2 Cor. 3:18, NIV).

✳ **Complete the three statements about spiritual transformation. Then check your answers on page 52.**

Spiritual transformation begins with _____

_____

Spiritual transformation continues in a growing relationship of _____

_____

Spiritual transformation _____

_____

How Does God Transform a Man into Jesus' Likeness?

Spiritual transformation begins and continues by the Holy Spirit's work (see John 16:7-15) in the heart of a man who is saved by grace through faith (see Eph. 2: 8-10). The transforming work of the Spirit begins at the moment of salvation as God provides the new believer a new identity.

The Holy Spirit continues this transforming process through the believer's relationship of love, trust, and obedience with Jesus. There is no spiritual transformation apart from a relationship with God. It is a process of moral and spiritual transformation.

Major agents of transformation are:

Scripture. God's Word imparts His being to believers. We are established by His Word in a unique relationship with God in which obedience is expected of us (see John 14:23).

Family/home. God uses family members and homes as His instruments of spiritual growth.

The people of God. Jesus provides gifts to His church so "that the body of Christ may be built up until we all reach unity in the faith and in the knowledge of the Son of God and become mature, attaining to the whole measure of the fullness of Christ" (Eph. 4:12-13, NIV). Every man being transformed by the Holy Spirit's work should help other men grow in Christlikeness (see Prov. 27:17; Eph. 4:15-16).

Life circumstances. "We know that in all things God works for the good of those who love him, who have been called according to his purpose" (Rom. 8:28, NIV).

Spiritual disciplines. To open ourselves to God's work in us, we must train ourselves to be godly (see 1 Tim. 4:7). Spiritual disciplines are the means by which we place ourselves before God for Him to work in us. Examples include prayer, Bible study, fasting, worship, evangelism, serving, stewardship, and learning. However, we know that the most iron-willed discipline will not make us more holy, because growth in holiness is a gift from God (see John 17:17; 1 Thess. 5:23; Heb. 2:11).

God's discipline. God disciplines His children to make us holy and to transform us into the likeness of Christ (see Heb. 12:10-11).

✳ **Rank the following agents of transformation according to the degree to which the men in your church need growth in these areas. Let 1 = most important and 6 = least important.**

___ Scripture
___ Family/home
___ **The people of God**
___ Life circumstances
___ **Spiritual disciplines**
___ **God's discipline**

It is not the time but the intensity of the relationship with Jesus that determines spiritual growth. Such growth develops from obedience with the appropriate motive—love of God and trust in Him.

What Are Characteristics of Spiritual Transformation?

The measure of discipleship is the degree to which a man is like Jesus. Consider these qualities.

Men who are transformed are characterized by love, trust, and obedience.

Men who are transformed live in harmony with God's Word. The outward evidence of the inner spiritual transformation into Christlikeness is—

- living by Jesus' teachings, His Word (see John 8:31-32; 14:21,23-24);
- loving God and loving others (see Matt. 22:37-39; John 13:34-35);
- bearing fruit (see John 15:8; Gal. 5:22-23).

Men who are transformed see the world through the lens of Scripture. Men are made different from the world by God's Word (see John 17:14). Their minds and hearts are being transformed through a continual learning process led by the Spirit of God (see Rom. 12:1-2). As the Spirit transforms their minds, men do not want to be conformed to this world (see Rom. 12:2). The desires of the mind will be satisfied by the things of God: "Set your minds on things above, not on earthly things" (Col. 3:2, NIV). This will transform men's perspective on work in a secular society and on God-given opportunities to make a difference in society.

Men who are transformed have relationships with other believers. The Spirit brings fellow believers together into a dedicated and distinct relationship with the Father, united as one spiritual family (the church), a people for His own possession and use. The Spirit of God dispenses spiritual gifts to believers to fulfill their purposes of doing the work of ministry and building up the church (see Rom. 12:4-8; 1 Cor. 12:12-31; Eph. 4:11-16).

Men who are transformed make God's love known to others. A man's love for God is reflected in loving people so much that he is compelled to make God's love known. His heart focuses on fulfilling God's purpose, corporately and individually, to proclaim the good news of salvation by grace through faith in Christ so that all people become believers. We are to go into our world to make disciples, who make disciples, who make disciples.

What Are Hindrances to Spiritual Transformation?

Becoming a believer in Christ ensures lifelong conflict. Some hindrances to spiritual transformation are:

Satan. Satan is powerless against the Father. This powerlessness to defeat Christ assures us that we have the same power when we are in Christ. Even though the ultimate victory has been determined by Christ, we live in a battle against evil (see Eph. 6:10-18).

The world. Men face temptation to conform to the world's perspective and its way of doing things. The world represents everything that is totally opposed to God's love and purposes. God's love cannot dwell in the same heart that loves the world.

Personal desires of the flesh. The old nature of self-centeredness engages a believer in a spiritual war against God-centeredness.

Lack of faith. " 'Do not let your hearts be troubled. Trust in God; trust also in me' " (John 14:1).

Lack of knowledge. Men can be unaware of the new identity they possesses in Christ. The Bible is the source for understanding the way of salvation, the gospel, and guidance for daily living.

Unintentional drifting. Sometimes men begin an unplanned drift and thus no longer "grow in the grace and knowledge of our Lord and Savior Jesus Christ" (2 Pet. 3:18, NIV).

Deliberate rebellion. Rebellion is saying no to God.

Distraction. Perhaps one of the most effective hindrances Satan uses against men is distraction. He can distract men—

- from the centrality of Christ;
- from spiritual priorities to activities that may or may not be good;
- from the victory we have in Christ to occupying our minds with our fears and failures;
- from Christ's grace and mercy to pursuing legalistic self-righteousness;
- from God's purposes to personal ambitions that consume our energy;
- from a balanced relationship with Christ to preoccupation with one doctrine or aspect of the Christian life.

✳ **Name the three greatest distractions you see to men's spiritual growth.**

1. _____

2. _____

3. _____

A believer lives by faith in Jesus and grows in a relationship of love, trust, and obedience, while yielding to the transforming power of the Holy Spirit.[2]

WHAT IS THE BIBLICAL MODEL FOR ESTABLISHING MEN IN THE CHRISTIAN FAITH?

Biblical discipleship is a process that identifies five stages of spiritual development in a disciple's life, describes what happens in each stage, and outlines ways a discipler enables disciples to become what Christ wants them to be.

As a disciple of Jesus Christ, each one of us is on a journey traveling down a path of spiritual growth. The path shown in the diagram on page 47 represents our lifelong spiritual growth. Notice that the path goes up and down because spiritual growth is not a consistently upward process. In some periods we grow fast, and in others we seem to plateau. However, a disciple should have a distinctively upward growth trend. The words at the bottom of the diagram name the tasks of a discipler. The words at the top name the tasks of a disciple in response to a discipler's actions.

Five stages of spiritual growth may be identified in a disciple's life.

Spiritually dead. Men are spiritually dead in their sins and do not know Christ. Spiritually dead men cannot respond to Christ except as the Holy Spirit draws them.

Spiritual child. When the Spirit of God convicts men and they repent of their sin, call on Jesus, and are saved, they become spiritual children. Spiritual children have many of the same traits as physical children.

Spiritual disciple. As spiritual children grow, they become spiritual disciples.

Disciple maker. As spiritual disciples mature, they become disciple makers, helping other men in the same growth process.

Colaborer in ministry. As disciple makers continue to develop, they become colaborers in ministry with other spiritual disciples, who continue to reach the lost and make disciples. The mission, then, is to develop disciples as Jesus did, who will make disciples of all nations.

As you consider this process of discipleship, determine your stage of spiritual development and identify ways you can help other men develop at each stage of spiritual growth.

✳ **Match the five stages of a man's spiritual growth with the correct summary statements.**

___ 1. Spiritually dead   a. **A man who has repented of his sin, has called on Jesus, and is now saved**

___ 2. Spiritual child   b. **A man who is in the process of spiritual growth**

___ 3. Spiritual disciple   c. **A man who has joined other disciples to reach the lost and make disciples**

___ 4. Disciple maker   d. **A man who does not know Christ**

___ 5. Colaborer in ministry   e. **A man who helps others grow spiritually**

Check your answers on page 52.

How Jesus Made Disciples

Jesus helped His disciples grow at each stage of development.

Spiritually dead. When Jesus first called His disciples, they were spiritually dead, so His task was to witness to them. Jesus witnessed to what the Father was saying and doing. He continually bore witness to the Father in everything He taught and did (see John 14:10).

Spiritual child. After the disciples started following Jesus, He began to establish them in the faith and in relationship to the Father and to one another. However, as spiritual children, the disciples often showed childlike characteristics. They argued about who would be first in the kingdom of God. They showed their anger at a Samaritan village that did not receive Jesus, threatening to call down fire from heaven. They acted impulsively and made many mistakes. However, Jesus continued to nurture them so that He could present them to the Father (see John 17:6).

Spiritual disciple. Jesus helped these spiritual children grow. Jesus continually had to teach the disciples and to correct them until they finally understood.

Disciple maker. Jesus expected His disciples to bear fruit in the form of other disciples. He equipped His disciples to make disciples. Jesus helped His disciples understand concepts and skills so that they could adjust to any situation and complete the task. After Jesus ascended to heaven, the Holy Spirit worked in the disciples' lives to help them remember His teachings, with which they could train others.

Colaborer in ministry. Jesus spent three years with the twelve not only for their benefit but also so that they would make disciples of all nations. When Jesus called the disciples to follow Him, He said that He wanted them to be with Him. When He had finished discipling them, He told them to go make disciples of all nations and that He would be with them. The disciples then became colaborers in ministry with Him. God intended for all nations to be blessed through the disciples. As colaborers in ministry, they became a team, continuing to multiply disciples, as recorded in the Book of Acts.

How the Disciples Made Other Disciples

Spiritually dead. First, the disciples bore witness to spiritually dead persons who had killed the Lord Jesus (see Acts 2:23). They said they must witness in Jesus' name even if it meant going to prison. They testified that they had seen Him, had known Him, and had experienced Him. In response more than three thousand people came to Christ at Pentecost.

THE PATH OF SPIRITUAL GROWTH[3]

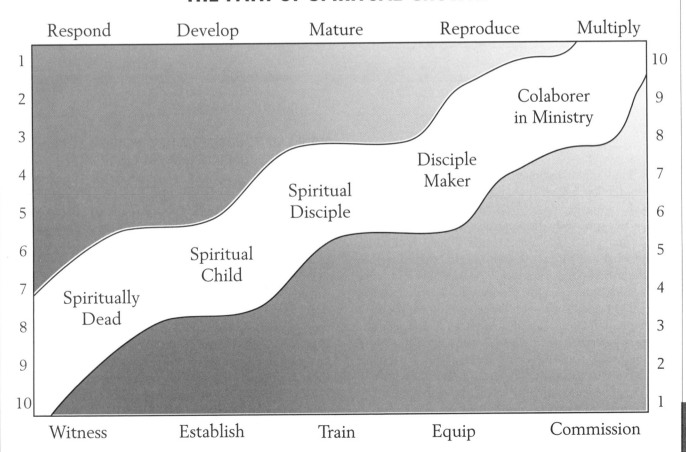

Spiritual child. The disciples immediately began to establish spiritual children. They did the same things Jesus had done with them (see Acts 2:42-46).

Spiritual disciple. The thousands of people who responded began to develop into spiritual disciples as the disciples continued to train them. In Acts 6:3 seven believers who were "known to be full of the Spirit and wisdom" (NIV) were selected for ministry.

Disciple maker. The disciples continued to equip the believers until they became disciple makers. In Acts 8 Philip, one of the seven, went to Samaria and proclaimed the gospel to the Samaritans. Then the Holy Spirit led him to the desert to witness to the Ethiopian eunuch.

Colaborer in ministry. When persecution came, Acts 8:4 says that "those who had been scattered preached the word wherever they went" (NIV). The disciples who were scattered abroad felt commissioned as colaborers in ministry and began to multiply throughout the known world.

✳ **Check your current stage of spiritual maturity.**
  ❑ **Spiritually dead**
  ❑ **Spiritual child**
  ❑ **Spiritual disciple**
  ❑ **Disciple maker**
  ❑ **Colaborer in ministry**

✳ **Why did you answer as you did?**

_____

_____

_____

_____

How Paul Made Disciples
Spiritually dead. Paul persecuted the church until his life-changing experience on the road to Damascus, when this spiritually dead person responded to Christ.

Spiritual child. God sent Ananias to help Paul understand what had happened and to begin establishing him as a spiritual child. Paul developed quickly and began witnessing and preaching. He went to Jerusalem, where Barnabas began to establish him more fully in the faith.

Spiritual disciple. Then Paul went to Arabia for three years, where the Lord trained and equipped him. After he matured in the faith and became a spiritual disciple, he went back to Tarsus and began to make disciples.

Disciple maker. About 10 years later, Barnabas was called to go to Antioch to help many Gentile Christians who had come to faith in Christ. Remembering Paul, Barnabas traveled the 120 miles to Tarsus to find him.

He brought Paul back to Antioch, and he and Paul taught the new Christians there for one year. Barnabas was training and equipping Paul to be a disciple maker.

Colaborer in ministry. As Paul and Barnabas reproduced disciples, God blessed their ministry and called them to take the gospel to the nations. The church at Antioch commissioned them to take the gospel to those who had not heard. They went as colaborers in ministry to multiply disciples.

Paul continued to follow this same process of developing spiritual disciple makers and colaborers in ministry. Timothy, as a young man, came to Christ and began to develop, mature, and reproduce as Paul established, trained, and equipped him. Later, Paul wrote to Timothy, "The things you have heard me say in the presence of many witnesses entrust to reliable men who will also be qualified to teach others" (2 Tim. 2:2, NIV).

Five generations of disciples are represented: Barnabas discipled Paul, who discipled Timothy, who discipled faithful men, who were to teach others also. Paul not only lived this process but also taught it and commanded Timothy to follow it.[4]

✳ **Name at least two men you know in each stage of spiritual maturity.**

Spiritually dead: _____

Spiritual child: _____

Spiritual disciple: _____

Disciple maker: _____

Colaborer in ministry: _____

HOW CAN YOU DETERMINE WHERE YOUR MEN ARE IN THE DISCIPLESHIP PROCESS?
The stage of a man's spiritual maturity is indicated by the way he partakes of spiritual food. Paul wrote, "I gave you milk, not solid food, for you were not yet ready for it. Indeed, you are still not ready" (1 Cor. 3.2, NIV).

Spiritually dead men do not eat and assimilate God's Word.

Spiritual children cannot feed themselves. Others, such as a Sunday School teacher, the pastor, and books, must feed them the Word by making it simpler so that they can understand it.

Spiritual disciples can feed themselves. Although they continue to benefit from others, they learn to study the Bible for themselves so that they can grow and mature.

Disciple makers desire to feed others. They want to help others grow as they have grown.

Colaborers in ministry concentrate on multiplying the food so that multitudes can feed on the gospel.[5]

✳ Read the names of the men you listed in the previous activity. Pray about discipling one of the men who is at a stage you have already experienced. Record his name and his stage of development.

Name: _____

Stage of development: _____

✳ Examine the chart "Stages of Spiritual Development" on this page. As you identify your role and task as the discipler and the man's commitment and development as the disciple, summarize what you can do to begin discipling him.

_____

_____

_____

_____

WHAT ARE THE 12 STEPS FOR ESTABLISHING MEN TO SPIRITUAL MATURITY?

1. *Pray.* Ask God to give you a clear vision for discipling men and to direct you to the men He has chosen for you to disciple.
2. *Evangelize.* Share a witness of what God has done and is doing in your life daily.
3. *Establish.* God wants you to establish spiritual children in the disciplines of the Christian life until they become spiritual disciples.
4. *Equip.* Equip spiritual disciples to become disciple makers. Help disciple makers understand concepts and skills so well that they can adjust to any situation and can complete a task.
5. *Extend.* Equip disciple makers to reproduce themselves as colaborers in ministry with you so that the number of disciples continues to multiply.
6. *Develop.* As you develop, help men through the stages you have already experienced. As you train another man in the stage you have passed through, you learn more about it and make it more a part of your life. Examples:
   • A spiritual child can witness to spiritually dead persons.
   • A spiritual disciple can establish spiritual children.
   • A disciple maker can train spiritual disciples.
   • A colaborer in ministry can equip disciple makers.
7. *Model.* Although your ministry to men may focus on discipling men at a particular stage, it is helpful to simultaneously disciple men at different stages. You are the model for the men you train. You have the responsibility to model all stages of spiritual discipling to encourage your disciples to reproduce at each stage they have completed. As a disciple maker, you may spend most of your time training spiritual disciples, but you should never stop witnessing to the spiritually dead or establishing spiritual children. If you do not continue to witness regularly, those you train will tend not to witness.
8. *Remember.* Remember that you are only one component of the discipling process. God is the One who makes disciples. He also uses the church, small discipleship groups, and other colaborers to help a man grow. You are not completely responsible for failures or successes (see 1 Cor. 3.5-8).

STAGES OF SPIRITUAL DEVELOPMENT

	Discipler		Disciple	
Stage	Role	Task	Commitment	Development
Spiritually Dead	Witness (1 Cor. 1:18; 2:15)	Evangelism	Friendship, which leads to claiming Christ's lordship	From unbeliever to spiritual child
Spiritual Child	Parent (1 Cor. 3:1-3)	Follow-up	Claiming Christ's lordship, which leads to discipleship	From spiritual child to spiritual disciple
Spiritual Disciple	Servant (1 Cor. 3:5-6)	Training	Discipleship, which leads to leadership	From spiritual disciple to disciple maker
Disciple Maker	Steward (1 Cor. 4:1; 3:10-16)	Equipping	Leadership, which leads to partnership	From disciple maker to colaborer in ministry
Colaborer in Ministry	Encourager (1 Cor. 3:7-9; 4:16-17)	Supporting	Partnership, which leads to churchmanship	From colaborer in ministry to discipler

9. *Vision.* Maintain a vision of what God wants to accomplish through you and through those you train. Keep looking for the needs of men at every stage and keep looking beyond those needs to God's purposes. At each stage ask a different question:
   - What would make this spiritually dead man open to the gospel?
   - What food would best feed the hunger of this spiritual child?
   - What would help this spiritual disciple grow to maturity?
   - How can I equip this disciple maker to be concerned with the spiritual growth of others?
   - What would keep this colaborer in ministry focused on Kingdom growth and on a world vision of God's mission as he disciples others? What equipping does he need to move into that ministry?

10. *Focus.* As men show more interest, give them more time and help. The natural tendencies are to spend more time with the weak and needy and allow the growing man to continue on his own. You need to focus on those who are growing in order to produce multipliers and colaborers who can help with the spiritually dead or spiritually immature.

11. *Share.* Shift the responsibility from yourself to the man you disciple as you see that man develop. Notice the numbers 1 through 10 on the sides of the diagram "The Path of Spiritual Growth" (p. 47). The numbers on the left reflect the disciple maker's responsibility, while those on the right represent the disciple's responsibility. The discipler and disciple's responsibilities gradually shift as the disciple grows. For example:
   - When sharing the gospel with a nonbeliever, the responsibility lies very heavily (9 or 10) with the discipler.
   - As the new disciple grows and learns to feed himself, the discipler's responsibility gradually lessens until he shares only a small level of responsibility (1 or 2) for the colaborer in ministry.

12. *Pray.* Ask God to give you patience and discernment to take men through each stage in this discipleship process. Continue to evaluate as men's lives are truly being transformed.[6]

✳ **As you examine the chart "A Strategic Game Plan for Establishing Men," page 51, think about the men you listed on page 48. Answer these questions about their spiritual needs in relation to your men's ministry.**

What can your men's ministry do to make these spiritually dead men open to the gospel?

_____

_____

_____

_____

What can your men's ministry do to make these spiritual children spiritually hungry?

_____

_____

_____

_____

What can your men's ministry do to make these spiritual disciples want to grow to maturity?

_____

_____

_____

_____

What can your men's ministry do to make these disciple makers concerned about other disciples' spiritual growth and multiplication?

_____

_____

_____

_____

What can your men's ministry do to keep these colaborers in ministry focused on Kingdom growth and on a world vision of God's mission?

_____

_____

_____

_____

A STRATEGIC GAME PLAN FOR ESTABLISHING MEN

Stage	Spiritual Child: Being Fed	Spiritual Disciple: Feeding Self	Disciple Maker: Feeding Others	Colaborer in Ministry: Multiplying Others
Phase	*Beginning.* This phase primarily addresses needs of new Christians but also needs pertinent to older Christians.	*Growing.* This phase lasts for the rest of a man's life as he continually expands knowledge and applications.	*Ministering.* Although a sequence can be observed throughout the four phases, this phase actually begins earlier, even in the beginning phase, not only after the growing phase.	*Reproducing.* This phase moves one step farther in that the believer not only ministers to others but also equips them to reproduce in the lives of others, who will do the same.
Focus	• Following up with new Christians • Reviewing the basics	• Deepening • Broadening	• Witnessing • Serving • Disciple making	• Building disciple makers • Building spiritual leaders
Biblical Basis	• 1 Peter 2:2 • Hebrews 5:12-13	• Hebrews 5:14	• Hebrews 6:1 • John 21:17	• 2 Timothy 2:2
Objectives	• To ground new Christians in the basics of the Christian life • To review and establish the basics in the lives of older Christians	• To lead men to go deeper than the surface, living the gospel in daily life • To expand concepts of what it means to be a Christian, applying Christ's lordship to all of life	• To involve men in others' lives through personal witness, ministering to needs, mission projects, and discipling other Christians.	• To equip men to build disciple makers, leading others to do the same • To equip men to become spiritual leaders in all aspects of church and Christian life
Topics	Salvation, assurance, essentials of growth, basic Bible study, church	Advanced Bible study, lordship, personhood, life purpose, spiritual gifts, decision making, career, God's will, priorities and values, ownership and stewardship, relationships, dealing with problems, conflict management, sexuality, singleness, marriage, parenting, character development, spiritual warfare, worldview, ethics, worship, theology, Baptist life, other denominations, world religions, cults, churchmanship	Helping, counseling, teaching, ministering, witnessing, apologetics, follow-up, missions, serving	Leadership, discipling, multiplying, mentoring, apprenticing, imparting vision
Resources	Survival Kit, Beginning Steps, Taking the Next Step, How to Study Your Bible, Basics for Baptists, MasterLife, Living God's Word, In God's Presence, Destination: Principles for Making Life's Journey Count	Experiencing God; The Mind of Christ; Life in the Spirit; MasterLife; Disciple's Prayer Life; The Man God Uses; Living Your Christian Values; Meeting Needs, Sharing Christ; The Kingdom Agenda; The Seven Seasons of a Man's Life, LifeAnswers; Serving God; Stand Firm; When God Speaks, Legacy Builders; Growing Disciples Weekend manuals	MasterLife; Meeting Needs, Sharing Christ; FAITH evangelism courses; Share Jesus Without Fear; Witnessing Through Your Relationships; DecisionTime; WiseCounsel; Jesus on Leadership; Leading Discipleship in a Church; Drawing Men to God: Men's Ministry Manual	MasterLife, Jesus on Leadership, Drawing Men to God: Men's Ministry Manual, Start a Revolution: Nine World-Changing Strategies for Single Adults

The disciples Jesus made were bold witnesses who were able to teach others and establish the church. You may not feel qualified or ready to make disciples. However, as you begin to disciple others, you will become a better disciple yourself. As you prepare, explain, model, teach, and encourage others, your own faith will be strengthened.

Remember, Christian discipleship is developing a personal, lifelong, obedient relationship with Jesus Christ in which He transforms your character into Christlikeness; changes your values into Kingdom values; and involves you in His mission in the home, the church, and the world. As you develop in your relationship, character, and values and as you increase your involvement in Christ's mission, you have the blessed opportunity of bringing others along with you. The window into your life is for many people a glimpse into Jesus.[7]

Resources

Arnold, Jeffrey. *The Big Book on Small Groups.* Downers Grove: InterVarsity, 1992.

Atkinson, Donald, and Charles Roesel. *Meeting Needs, Sharing Christ.* Nashville: LifeWay, 1995.

Beginning Steps: A Growth Guide for New Believers. Alpharetta: North American Mission Board, 1993.

Biehl, Bobb. *Mentoring: Confidence in Finding a Mentor and Becoming One.* Nashville: Broadman & Holman, 1996.

Blackaby, Henry, and Richard Blackaby. *When God Speaks.* Nashville: LifeWay, 1995.

Blackaby, Henry, and Tom Blackaby. *The Man God Uses.* Nashville: LifeWay, 1998.

Blackaby, Henry T., and Claude V. King. *Experiencing God: Knowing and Doing the Will of God.* Nashville: LifeWay, 1990.

Burton, Jim. *Legacy Builders.* Memphis: The Brotherhood Commission of the Southern Baptist Convention, 1996.

Burton, Jim. *Legacy Builders Retreat Preparation Manual.* Memphis: The Brotherhood Commission of the Southern Baptist Convention, 1995.

Burton, Jim. *Legacy Builders Retreat Participant Workbook.* Memphis: The Brotherhood Commission of the Southern Baptist Convention, 1995.

Criscoe, Arthur H., and Leonard Sanderson. *DecisionTime: Commitment Counseling.* Nashville: LifeWay, 1987.

Drakeford, John W., and Claude V. King. *WiseCounsel: Skills for Lay Counseling.* Nashville: LifeWay, 1988.

Edgemon, Roy T., and Steve Williams. *Leading Discipleship in a Church.* Nashville: Convention, 1998.

Edwards, David. *Destination: Principles for Making Life's Journey Count.* Nashville: LifeWay, 1997.

Experiencing God Weekend Manual. Nashville: LifeWay, 1997.

Fay, Bill, and Ralph Hodge. *Share Jesus Without Fear.* Nashville: LifeWay, 1997.

Gorsuch, Geoff, and Dan Schaffer. *Brothers: Calling Men into Vital Relationships.* Colorado Springs: NavPress, 1994.

Growing Disciples Weekend Administrative Guide. Nashville: LifeWay, 1997.

Hemphill, Ken. *LifeAnswers: Making Sense of Your World.* Nashville: LifeWay, 1993.

_____. *Serving God: Discovering and Using Your Spiritual Gifts.* Nashville: LifeWay Christian Resources, 1995.

Hendricks, Howard and William. *As Iron Sharpens Iron: Building Character in a Mentoring Relationship.* Chicago: Moody, 1995.

Hodge, Ralph, and Jerri Herring. *Taking the Next Step: A Guide for New Church Members.* Nashville: Convention, 1996.

Hunt, T. W., and Claude V. King. *In God's Presence.* Nashville: LifeWay, 1994.

Hunt, T. W., and Claude V. King. *The Mind of Christ.* Nashville: LifeWay, 1994.

Hunt, T. W., and Catherine Walker. *Disciple's Prayer Life: Walking in Fellowship with God.* Nashville: LifeWay, 1997.

The Kingdom Agenda Weekend Manual. Nashville: LifeWay, 1997.

Lea, Thomas D. *How to Study Your Bible.* Nashville: LifeWay, 1986, 1989.

Life in the Spirit Weekend Manual. Nashville: LifeWay, 1997.

MasterLife Weekend Manual. Nashville: LifeWay, 1997.

McQuilkin, Robertson. *Life in the Spirit.* Nashville: LifeWay, 1997.

Morley, Patrick. *The Seven Seasons of a Man's Life.* Nashville: LifeWay, 1996.

Moore, Waylon B. *Living God's Word: Practical Lessons for Applying Scripture to Life.* Nashville: LifeWay, 1997.

Mosley, Ernest, and Betty Hassler. *Basics for Baptists.* Nashville: Convention, 1996.

Neighbour, Ralph, and Bill Latham. *Survival Kit: Five Keys to Effective Spiritual Growth.* Nashville: LifeWay, 1996.

Rogers, Mike, and Debi Rogers. *The Kingdom Agenda: Experiencing God in Your Workplace.* Nashville: LifeWay, 1997.

Smith, Jack R., and Jennifer Kennedy Dean. *Witnessing Through Your Relationships.* Nashville: LifeWay, 1994.

Stand Firm (magazine). Nashville: LifeWay Christian Resources.

Welch, Bobby H., and Doug Williams with David Apple. *A Journey in FAITH.* Nashville: LifeWay, 1998.

Wilkes, Gene. *Jesus on Leadership: Becoming a Servant Leader.* Nashville: LifeWay, 1996.

Wilkinson, Bruce. *The Seven Laws of the Learner.* Nashville: LifeWay, 1994.

Willis, Avery T., Jr. *MasterLife.* Nashville: LifeWay, 1996–97.

Notes

1. Avery T. Willis, Jr., *MasterLife 1: The Disciple's Cross* (Nashville: LifeWay, 1996), 5.
2. This section adapted from Ralph Hodge, "Spiritual Transformation" (Discipleship and Family Division, LifeWay Christian Resources, Nashville, June 1998), 1–7.
3. Avery T. Willis, Jr., *MasterLife 4: The Disciple's Mission* (Nashville: LifeWay, 1997), 123.
4. Ibid., 123–26.
5. Ibid., 126.
6. Adapted from Willis, *MasterLife 4,* 126–27.
7. Avery T. Willis, Jr., *MasterLife: Developing a Rich Personal Relationship with the Master* (Nashville: Broadman & Holman, 1998), 259.

Answers to Activities

Page 44: a new identity in Christ; love, trust, and obedience; glorifies God
Page 46: 1. d, 2. a, 3. b, 4. e, 5. c

POINT 4C

◆

Plan a Balanced Ministry: Equip Men for Ministry

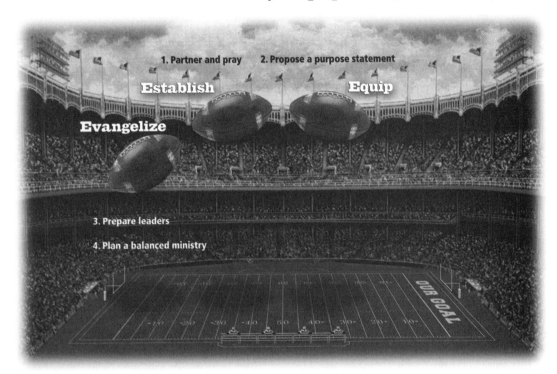

Nothing is more exciting than helping men come to God and enter a personal relationship with Jesus Christ. Nothing is more encouraging than helping men grow in Christ as fully devoted disciples. And nothing is more empowering than helping men serve through their church in ways that match their God-given gifts, abilities, personalities, and life experiences.

It's common to find men in the church whose growth has been stunted because no one has helped them discover the unique way God has made them and how that corresponds with what God wants to do in and through the church. Instead of helping men find their unique fit in effective service and ministry, churches often limit themselves to merely filling vacancies in the existing church structure. In doing so, they may miss additional ministry opportunities for the church, and they may frustrate and minimize the effectiveness of those who have something new to offer.

Ask yourself, for example:

- Are there men in our men's ministry who have come to Christ and are growing as disciples but

We are God's workmanship, created in Christ Jesus to do good works, which God prepared in advance for us to do.

Ephesians 2:10, NIV

have found no meaningful place of service in the church? Or are there men who have merely been given something to do that hardly utilizes the abilities and gifts God has given them for service?

- Do we know enough about each man in our men's ministry to help him find an effective and fulfilling place of service in our church?
  - Might God show us something of His will for our church as we discover more about the human resources He has given us through our church's men?
  - Does our men's ministry have an intentional strategy for matching men with the ministries He intends for our church to carry out?
  - Do the men actively serving in the church have the training and support they need to keep going and growing in their service?

These questions show the value of having an ongoing placement process that helps men find meaningful, fulfilling places of service in the church. Well-matched places of service can give a man practical applications of his spiritual growth in discipleship and valuable training for understanding and developing his unique life mission to the world.

Steps in developing a placement process include—
1. analyzing each man's ministry readiness;
2. discovering each man's unique makeup for ministry;
3. identifying the needs and opportunities of church and community;
4. matching men with ministry;
5. equipping and encouraging men as they serve.

ANALYZE EACH MAN'S MINISTRY READINESS

As a leader in men's ministry, you have the responsibility for guiding men in their Christian journeys from lostness into salvation, from salvation into discipleship, from discipleship into ministry in and through the church, and from ministry into joining God in His redemptive mission to the world. Because each man's Christian journey is different, it is important to identify the primary stage of Christian growth and ministry for each man in your ministry and the next stage toward which you can encourage and empower him. You can better guide each man in his journey of faith if you can identify what has taken place, what is taking place, and what he has not yet experienced in his Christian life.

Ask the Right Questions

As simple as it sounds, developing relationships in which the right questions can be asked at the right time can produce breakthroughs both in your men's ministry and in the spiritual lives of the men you serve. Because men's ministry can be characterized by friendships and activity-based programs, it is possible to operate on a superficial level at which spiritual matters are assumed or ignored. There may be men who have attended your church longer than you but have never received Christ as their personal Savior. Men whose faithful participation implies spiritual maturity may have little scriptural foundation in their lives. A man who has served in the same church role for years may be woefully mismatched or underemployed. And tragically, a man who has been growing, training, and developing in your local church may be ready to take his gifts to the world to reach others but has never been challenged to do so.

An effective men's ministry leader knows where most of the men he serves are in their Christian journeys, and in the cases when he doesn't know, he works hard to find out. He intentionally asks questions and listens to the answers that reveal spiritual needs and help assess each man's spiritual growth and ministry readiness. He follows up sensitively and respectfully with the information he discovers, using it in the context of a trusting relationship to help each man discover and move toward the next arena of Christian growth and service.

✳ **After examining the chart on this page, begin working the questions into conversations with men in your men's ministry to discover their stages of spiritual growth and ministry involvement.**

Questions That Reveal the Need for Salvation	Questions That Reveal the Need for Discipleship	Questions That Reveal the Need for Placement in Ministry	Questions That Reveal the Need for Awakening to Mission
• How would you describe your relationship with God? • Have you ever explained to someone what it means to be a Christian? What did you say? • What first led you to this church? What was your church background before attending here? Is this church's teaching different in any way? • When do you feel closest to God? Do you ever feel that He's far away? • Have you ever had a Mormon missionary or a Jehovah's Witness come to your door? How did you handle the situation?	• Did you grow up going to Sunday School? Was it a good experience? Did you have good teachers or feel that you learned much? • What is your favorite part of the Bible? • Do you have a certain Bible you use all the time, or do you use the one that is available? • What is the most practical Bible study you've ever been involved in? • Who is the best Bible teacher you've ever heard? What made him or her so effective?	• If you could do any job in the church besides what you're already doing, what would it be? • Do you feel that you've really found your fit in the church? • You're really good at _____. Have you ever considered using that gift at church? • Have you ever thought about what you were made for—what God intends to do through your life? • Have you ever studied spiritual gifts in the Bible? Do you think you have a good understanding of what your spiritual gift is?	• Have you ever helped someone come to Christ? How did God use you? • Do you seek ways to use your God-given skills outside the church? • Do you think our church is effective in reaching our community with the gospel? What could we do to be more effective? • If our men's group planned a mission project, what are we best equipped to do? • What parts of our community aren't being touched by our church? Do you think our church can reach those people?

Encourage Further Growth

As you analyze each man's Christian journey, don't make anyone feel scrutinized or judged. Your purpose is not to grade his spiritual maturity, and you don't want to create feelings of inadequacy or inferiority. Instead, you want to discover each man's ministry readiness and to equip each one for further growth and ministry.

Use the information and insight you discover to—

Identify. Relate your Christian journey and experiences to those you discover in other men. If you sense that a man does not yet have a personal relationship with Christ, talk with him about your life before Christ and what led you to desire salvation. If the answers to your questions demonstrate little biblical knowledge or spiritual discipline, explain how much you still have to learn or how valuable your small group or Sunday School class has been. Identifying with a man's growth and ministry experiences will build trust. It will also empower him to speak more openly as he senses that his experiences are not uncommon and that you are willing to reflect his honesty and vulnerability with your own.

Encourage. Encourage the progress you find. If a man hasn't yet made a commitment to Christ, encourage the openness, attendance, or friendliness you find in his seeking efforts. If he has rarely or never helped someone else come to Christ, encourage the discipleship or service you find in his life. Create the feeling that a man can build on his current forward momentum rather than feel inadequate about his lack of past progress.

Connect. Think about who would be a good match with the man, both in spiritual development and personal compatibility. Try to connect him with another man who has recently or closely walked where he is walking—a friend and mentor who can encourage him toward his next steps in Christian growth and service.

✳ Identify your men's stages of Christian growth and ministry by listing their names on the chart on this page. You may want to begin by identifying a small sample of men for now, like a men's Sunday School class, and expanding this exercise later to include all men in your ministry.

Provide Opportunities for Self-Analysis

Just as important as your efforts to analyze men's ministry readiness are the opportunities you create to help them do their own self-analysis. While most analysis may come in the context of informal conversations and growing relationships, take occasional (at least annual) opportunities in a group context to teach biblical principles of Christian growth and ministry and to let men reflect individually and confidentially on their lives.

Elements of a study or a meeting designed for this purpose might include—

- Bible passages or examples of men coming to God through Jesus (salvation), growing in Christ (discipleship), serving through the church (ministry), and going to the world (missions)
- Clear explanations of salvation, discipleship, ministry, and missions in modern contexts
- Examples of ways Christian growth and ministry are nurtured and encouraged
- Exercises men can use privately to analyze their own ministry readiness
- Direction on what the next steps might be for men to become involved in ministry (see the following material in this point of the manual)

You could present these opportunities in other ways besides a Bible study.

- Hold a planning meeting at which the stages of Christian growth and ministry can be presented as the purpose or goals of your men's ministry.

OUR MEN'S STAGES OF CHRISTIAN GROWTH AND MINISTRY

Salvation: Come to God	Discipleship: Grow in Christ	Ministry: Serve Through the Church	Missions: Go to the World

- Ask the pastor to preach a sermon on Christian growth and ministry as part of a special Men's Day.
- Invite a well-known or respected speaker to speak on Christian growth and ministry at a father-son outing or another outreach event.
- Develop a series of short studies for your men's small groups or Sunday School classes.
- Develop a placement questionnaire encompassing all of the elements discussed in this section.

✳ Reread the previous five ways your men's ministry can present men opportunities to analyze their ministry readiness. In the margin draw a star beside one method you would like to use soon.

It is important to have an intentional strategy and method for analyzing the ministry readiness of each man in your ministry. After you have done this, you can help each man discover the unique way God has hand-crafted him for ministry.

DISCOVER EACH MAN'S UNIQUE MAKEUP FOR MINISTRY

Many men's ministries have intentional strategies and processes in place for bringing men to God and discipling them. Unfortunately, the important ministries of helping men find their unique places of service in the church and their unique missions to the world often go unattended.

✳ Examine the chart on page 55 on which you identified the stages of Christian growth and ministry for selected men in your men's ministry. What is the next step for most men on your list?
❑ Come to God ❑ Grow in Christ
❑ Serve through the church ❑ Go to the world

You most likely discovered what many churches find. The longest list of men consists of those who have come to Christ and are growing but who have not found highly effective places of service. And of those who have found places of service, too few are serving with the passion and effectiveness that indicate they are fulfilling God's plan for them and the church.

✳ Focus on the men you identified whose next step in their Christian journeys is finding a meaningful place of ministry. How well do you know each of those men? Do you know them deeply enough to steer them to places of service that maximize who God made them? As you think about each man, mentally answer the following questions.
- Does this man understand what the Bible teaches about spiritual gifts? Has he discovered his gift?

- What are this man's hobbies and interests? What does he love to do?
- What natural abilities does this man have? Does he recognize how strong they are?
- What kind of personality does this man have? Is he outgoing or shy? Is he a thinker or a doer? Is he organized or impulsive?
- What is this man's background? What do I know about his education, his family, his past and present employment, his victories, and his heartaches that could give me clues to how God might have prepared him for service?

If you cannot answer these kinds of questions about your men, many of them may be mismatched in their places of service. Others may not be matched at all. That's why an effective placement process that begins by analyzing each man's ministry readiness must be followed by discovering each man's unique makeup.

Use a Discovery Instrument

God has uniquely shaped each man for ministry in the church. Every life experience, behavioral trait, ability, and passion helps prepare him for ministry. Your men's ministry will greatly benefit from developing a formal system to plug men into the church's ministry. One such model is found in *Jesus on Leadership* by C. Gene Wilkes. In this model the acrostic SERVE is used as an outline to help men discover how God has uniquely shaped each Christian for ministry in the church. The five factors forming the acrostic SERVE are:

Personal Factor	Key Personal-Application Question
Spiritual gifts	What am I gifted to do?
Experiences	What experiences have I had?
Relational style	Where does my personality best suit me to serve?
Vocational skills	What natural talents and skills do I have?
Enthusiasm	What do I love to do?

Participants in the *Jesus on Leadership* study are led through the five areas and corresponding diagnostic tools. The following paragraphs summarize what is included in each section of the study.

Spiritual gifts—gifts God gives through His Holy Spirit to empower men for service. This section provides an overview of spiritual gifts and help in identifying which ones God has given to men. Elements you might find valuable in your placement process include—
- a simple, practical definition of *spiritual gifts;*
- cautions about spiritual gifts and an explanation of the purpose of spiritual gifts;
- advice on how to discover spiritual gifts;

- a list of spiritual gifts and brief definitions as presented in Scripture (see Rom. 12:3-8; 1 Cor. 12:1-11,27-31; Eph. 4:11-12; 1 Pet. 4:9-11);
- biblical teaching on how the church at Antioch acknowledged God's call, their giftedness, and their obedience in setting members apart for service;
- a spiritual-gifts survey to help your men start identifying gifts they have or may have.

Experiences—events God allows to mold men into servant leaders. This section helps men review their histories to discover how God has prepared them for unique ministries only they can fulfill. Elements you might find valuable in your placement process include—

- encouragement that God uses all past experiences—positive and negative—to prepare men for ministry to others;
- exercises in which men record their past experiences (spiritual markers) and how God has used those experiences;
- scriptural examples of how God used the experiences of His people to accomplish His purposes.

Relational style—behavioral traits God uses to give men a leadership style. This section helps men recognize how their God-given temperaments can best be used in ministry. Elements you might find valuable in your placement process include—

- encouragement that everybody is different and that there are no wrong or right personality types;
- a relational survey that ranks instinctive behaviors to reveal strengths and help men consider how these strengths can be used in servant leadership;
- accounts of biblical leaders' leadership styles and ways God accomplished His purposes through them.

Vocational skills—abilities men have gained through training and experience that they can use in service to God. This section helps men appreciate their natural talents and vocational skills. Elements you might find valuable in your placement process include—

- explanations of *vocation* as what men do to provide for their needs in society and of *vocational skills* as abilities learned to enhance their careers;
- clarification that God's call is to follow Him, which takes priority over career choice;
- biblical and present-day examples of persons whose vocations God used to make a difference;
- a practical exercise in which men list skills, how those skills are used in their vocations, and how God can use those skills for His mission.

Enthusiasm—passion God has placed in a man's heart for a particular ministry to others. This section helps men clarify what they really love to do. Elements you might find valuable in your placement process include—

- a study of the word *enthusiasm* as it relates to a person's innermost being and how it affects his role as a servant leader;
- exercises that call men to name what they have a passion for and how they can use it in God's service;
- biblical examples of servant leaders who were enthusiastic about their service to God.

In *Jesus on Leadership* each man's responses to these studies and diagnostic tools are woven into a SERVE Profile. When men complete the course and work through each diagnostic tool as homework, they have the information needed to match their profiles with existing or new church ministries.[1]

✳ **Examine the list of men you developed earlier. Complete the chart on this page about them. This is the type of information needed about all men who become involved in your ministry.**

✳ **How can understanding your spiritual gifts, experiences, relational style, vocational skills, and enthusiasm help you as a men's ministry leader?**

_____

_____

You probably responded that your ministry profile will tell you how you are best equipped to serve and equip other men.

MINISTRY PROFILE

Name	Spiritual Gifts	Experiences	Relational Style	Vocational Skills	Enthusiasm

Personalize the Discovery Process

Jesus on Leadership is only one valuable source of help. You could add many other study elements or diagnostic tools to the previous outline (see "Resources," p. 64). The important thing is that your men's ministry have an intentional process for helping each man discover his unique makeup in a way that is specific and personal both to him and to your church. The SERVE model is helpful in that it doesn't limit the discovery process to one factor, such as spiritual gifts. Instead, it employs a discovery process that gives multiple perspectives on each man's God-given uniqueness. Your process of helping men discover their unique makeup for ministry should be multifaceted.

✳ **If your men's ministry does not have in place a process for discovering men's makeup for ministry, use the following checklist to get started.**

DISCOVERY-PROCESS CHECKLIST

❑ Decide who will be responsible for evaluating potential resources for helping men discover and match their gifts with ministries.

❑ Develop a timeline for obtaining and reviewing these resources and for reporting options to the men's ministry leadership team.

❑ Allow the men's ministry leadership team to make the final decision about the process to be used for helping men discover and match their gifts with ministries.

❑ Have your leadership team be the first to work through the training process. In a smaller church the pilot group may consist of the pastor and a few deacons.

❑ Prayerfully identify a lead trainer who will serve as the administrator of the process to match men with ministry.

❑ Watch to see where God is at work around you and maintain an ongoing list of ministry needs.

❑ Involve your men's ministry prayer team by communicating ministry needs, trusting God to call men to meet these needs.

❑ Frequently communicate ministry needs to the men of the church by posting needs on a bulletin board, printing them in the church newsletter, or mentioning them from the pulpit.

❑ Resist the temptation to do too much too fast. Wait for and trust the Holy Spirit to call men to particular places of service.

❑ Constantly remind your men's leaders that the goal of men's ministry encompasses more than huddling in small-group Bible studies. Men need to be involved in ministry.

In addition to developing a formal process that includes course work and diagnostic tools, provide opportunities like the following to help men discover their unique makeup.

Mentorships. Consider matching each man with a mentor who can help that man discover his unique makeup for ministry.

Partnerships. A mentor may or may not have a similar ministry makeup as the man he is guiding. As you identify men's unique skills and interests, look for opportunities to introduce them to other men who seem to share those skills or interests. Invite them to lunch together. Take them golfing, bowling, or fishing. If they find kinship and mutual support in their similar gifts, backgrounds, or personalities, step back and watch them reinforce one another's ministry potential.

Ministry and mission projects. Use short-term ministry and mission projects as laboratories for helping men discover their makeup for ministry. You can learn someone's ministry shape simply by giving him a job to do. Make sure these assignments are short-term.

Intentional observation and affirmation. You can help men discover their unique makeup for ministry by intentionally looking for their strengths and quickly affirming what you see. Tremendous empowerment and encouragement can come from positive affirmation.

Bible studies and small groups. Numerous small-group studies are available on discovering your spiritual gifts, understanding your personality type, and applying your skills to ministry.

Self-directed resources. In some cases men may be unwilling to join a formal group or use a discovery process that requires time commitment and accountability. For these men, talking about the process in a large group and then using the resource on their own might be more effective. Self-directed resources, such as spiritual-gifts inventories, personality profiles, and skills-assessment tools, could be made available for men to use in privacy and at their own pace.

Exercises with spouses. Often the best mirror a man has into his strengths, weaknesses, untapped potential, personality, and heart passions is his wife. Consider facilitating an exercise for public or at-home use that empowers a man's wife to tell him what she sees in him. Include the following questions or directions.

• Name three things you love most about your spouse.
• What is one thing you think your spouse would enjoy immensely if he tried it? Why?
• What is something your spouse is very good at that few people know about?
• What kind of work is your spouse doing when he seems happiest?
• When have you seen your spouse bring out the best in others?

✳ Reinforce your grasp of each method of self-discovery by matching it with the correct benefit.

___ 1. Mentorships
___ 2. Partnerships
___ 3. Ministry and mission projects
___ 4. Intentional observation and affirmation
___ 5. Bible studies and small groups
___ 6. Self-directed resources
___ 7. Exercises with spouses

a. Offer self-assessment tools that can be used in privacy and at a man's own pace
b. Match a man with another who can help him discover his unique makeup for ministry
c. Provide laboratories for trying abilities and gifts
d. Match men of similar ministry makeup
e. Provide formal learning opportunities
f. Empower a wife to identify her husband's strengths
g. Empower and encourage men

Check your answers on page 64.

Record Ministry Profiles

No matter what processes you use for helping men discover their unique makeup for ministry, the intentionality of your placement process will be greatly strengthened by recording in writing or in a computer database each man's spiritual gifts, experiences, relational style, vocational skills, and enthusiasm. And if you can get him involved in recording what he is discovering through some of the processes previously discussed, the result will be even more powerful.

One of the most beneficial exercises in which you could lead your men would be to develop a life-ministry statement that incorporates the spiritual discoveries they are making about the way God has uniquely created them for service. Another possibility would be to lead them to develop a life-ministry statement that would more specifically describe how they sense God has shaped them to serve in the church.

Recording your discoveries about each man's unique ministry makeup will help you formalize and summarize the diverse blend of men God has placed in your church. Next comes the other half of the equation: identifying the needs and opportunities for service God has placed in your church and community.

IDENTIFY THE NEEDS AND OPPORTUNITIES OF CHURCH AND COMMUNITY

In *Experiencing God* Henry Blackaby identifies four ways God speaks to us and invites us to join Him in His work: the Bible, prayer, circumstances, and the church. While churches (and men's ministries) often emphasize

Bible study and prayer, they frequently overlook circumstances and the church as sources of God's direction. Blackaby writes: "In the church, the need does not constitute the call. The need, however, is not to be ignored. Don't ever be afraid to let the body of believers assist you in knowing God's will. … What you will find is that a number of things begin to line up. What you are hearing from the Bible and prayer and circumstances and the church will begin to say the same thing. Then you can proceed with confidence."[2]

In the context of men's ministry, listening to the church means getting to know the men God brings your way and understanding how he has uniquely shaped them for His purposes in your midst. That's why analyzing each man's ministry readiness and discovering each man's unique makeup for ministry are so important. You can view each man God brings your way as a living letter from Him and as a clue about what He intends to do in the life of your men's ministry.

✳ Think about a man who recently joined your church or participated in a men's ministry activity. What do you think he is telling you about what God wants to do through your men's ministry?

_____

Listening to circumstances also means being alert to the needs and opportunities of both your church and your community. God is preparing your church and your men's ministry for " 'such a time as this' " (Esth. 4:14, NIV), and the needs and opportunities you sense are other valuable clues for discerning God's direction. A large part of visionary leadership is looking for ministry opportunities your men are uniquely shaped to fit.

Determine Needs

Almost every church has more jobs than volunteers, more places of service than servants. So a logical place to start in sensing where the men in your men's ministry could serve is the list of vacant positions in your church's existing structure. Your church probably has a nominating committee or another group that places people in ministry positions in the church. The chairperson of that group would likely be delighted to develop a relationship with men's ministry so that the placement process could be linked to the church's ongoing needs. If that process is not centralized, contact the pastor, Sunday School director, or others in the church who could help connect men with places of service in the regular church structure.

As you become acquainted with your church's ministry needs, develop a list of those needs and an understanding of specific gifts and qualifications required for each place of service. If job or task descriptions have been written, collecting copies of those will help you better picture the shape of the hole that needs to be filled. However, you may find a shorthand list or chart to be most versatile in helping you keep track of the church's specific needs.

✳ Use the chart on this page to identify the best makeup for meeting some of your church's needs in the upcoming year.

Discern Opportunities

One of the most exciting ways you can help men serve through the church is by discerning new opportunities for ministry. In Acts 6:1-7, for example, an emerging and previously unmet need confronted the young church in Jerusalem. Because the Greek-speaking Jews felt that their widows were being neglected, the church created deacon ministry. They looked to maturing, spiritual men in the church to bring a ministry solution to an increasingly obvious need. As a result, the need was met, the church was unified, the men grew in their service to Christ's body, and the church's evangelism and discipleship expanded. Wouldn't it be exciting to re-create that dynamic in your church by discerning emerging ministry opportunities and enthusiastically meeting them with your spiritually maturing men?

✳ Answer the following questions to discern new ministry opportunities your men could address.

Which groups in the church seem neglected or discouraged?

_____

What new people are noticeably emerging either in your church or in your community? ❏ Senior adults ❏ Young families ❏ Ethnic groups ❏ Single adults ❏ Poor ❏ Affluent ❏ Other: _____

What skills and shapes of men are being drawn together? For what might they be well suited that has not been a ministry of your church in the past?

_____

_____

What is happening in your community that will have an effect on your church members and other local residents, such as an economic depression, problems with crime or gambling, or a big event coming to town that will draw lots of people?

_____

_____

How could a new ministry by your men help meet needs created by these situations and build bridges for evangelism or discipleship?

_____

_____

MINISTRY NEEDS

Need or Position	Spiritual Gifts	Experience	Relational Style	Vocational Skills	Enthusiasm

What is consuming your church staff's time and energy and distracting them from their primary responsibilities?

_____

_____

Could any of these responsibilities be undertaken by maturing men in your men's ministry?
❑ Yes ❑ No

Balance Needs and Opportunities

Of course, there is likely to be ongoing tension between current needs based on the existing church-ministry structure and emerging needs the church has not yet addressed. Consider the following ways to bring balanced sensitivity to your church's ministry needs.

- Work with your church leaders to establish clear ministry plans and priorities for the church. Prioritize the needs that are most critical to the church's overall purpose.
- Guide your men toward multifaceted service that is directed toward God (see Acts 13:2), believers (see Heb. 6:10), and unbelievers (see Matt. 5:13).
- Encourage your men to balance their service among people's physical (see Matt. 10:42), emotional (see Rom. 12:15; 2 Cor. 1:3-4), and spiritual (see 2 Cor. 5:18) needs.
- Seek to maintain a balance between ministry in the church to its members and ministry through the church to the community.
- Make the process of helping men discover their unique makeup for ministry as multidimensional as possible. Steering men into service based only on their past experiences or only on their natural abilities may tend to place them repeatedly in the same kinds of service.

Dream Big

As a group, do some Spirit-led dreaming about—
- ministry positions your church staff or nominating committee hasn't had time to creatively construct;
- emerging and unmet needs only one or two men in your group have noticed;
- relationships and heartbeats forming among your men that are ready to synergize into innovative and unprecedented ministry ideas and strategies. Ask, "What do you think God might want to do _through_ us, given what He's been doing _in_ us?"

Identifying the needs and opportunities confronting your church and understanding the shape of each of those voids will prepare you for the next step in helping men serve through the church: matching men with the ministries for which God has been preparing them.

MATCH MEN WITH MINISTRY

With analysis-and-discovery processes in place and a list of church and community needs, you can begin the process of strategically matching men with ministry. To make good matches, you'll want to involve your church leaders and the men themselves.

Seek the Support of Church Leaders

Church leaders and the pastor in particular play an important role in establishing the value and importance of active church service. They can continually reinforce the fact that every member is a minister, not just the church staff or elected offices, and they can lead the church to understand that matching gifts to meaningful church service is a natural outgrowth and evidence of Christian maturity. For this to happen, your church leaders need to provide the following forms of support.

Strong biblical teaching on serving and church ministry. Your men and your church will benefit from compelling preaching and teaching that reveal what the Bible says about the purpose of ministry, the believer's call to ministry, the rewards of ministry, and how to discover personal ministry. Work with church leaders to follow up these teaching times with clear presentations of the ministry opportunities and placement processes available through men's ministry and the church. Possible Scripture passages include Matthew 25:14-30; Romans 12; Ephesians 4—6; 1 Corinthians 12; and many others.

Clear direction on the church's ministry priorities. Your church leaders can help match men with ministry by clearly articulating the church's mission and vision for your community and for the world. From that can come more specific priorities and goals that help clarify where the church is going and what kinds of ministries are most needed to accomplish the church's vision. You may even want to create a formal philosophy-of-ministry statement for your church, which describes the roles of members and pastors and outlines the standards of training and performance to which your church wishes its ministries to be accountable. As you learn more about the makeup of your men, you can also help church leaders see the kinds of human resources God is sending you. Together you may discover something new about God's direction for the church.

Endorsement of your role and process in helping men serve. If you work with your church leaders to create a credible placement process that serves your men and the church, you can rely on the leaders to be your advocates and to endorse your efforts to match men with ministry. That process might include some or all of the elements discussed in this point of the manual, including attendance at training events, completion of a personal profile, and meeting with men's ministry leaders. Consider developing a ministry covenant or an at-your-service certificate that formalizes each man's completion of that process and his commitment to serve in the church.

✳ **Evaluate the extent to which your church leaders provide the support your men's ministry needs to match men with ministry. Rate each means of support on a scale of 1 to 5, with 1 indicating the greatest support.**
  - **Strong biblical teaching on**   1 2 3 4 5
    serving and church ministry
  - **Clear direction on the church's**   1 2 3 4 5
    ministry priorities
  - **Endorsement of your role and**   1 2 3 4 5
    process in helping men serve

✳ **Discuss your evaluation with your men's ministry leadership team, as well as strategies for increasing the church's support.**

Expect the Cooperation of Your Men

Effectively matching men with ministries that fit their unique makeup also requires the patient participation of the men themselves. Ask your men for the following commitments.

Prayerful consideration of a full list of ministry opportunities. Boyish enthusiasm can sometimes lead to quick decisions, perhaps to do the first thing that comes along that looks like a good match. Make sure you have a list of ministry options that is as comprehensive as possible and that each ministry option is updated and clear in its expectations. You might even rank that list according to your church's strategic priorities or according to where the most help is needed. Then ask each man to spend time prayerfully considering the entire range of options before hastily choosing the first thing that sounds good or the place of service a friend is considering. Ask him to narrow his list to three or four things, then to rank them according to his giftedness and passion for each.

Consideration of ministry needs as well as giftedness. The better the match between the man's shape and the ministry need, the better. And you should always urge a man to find a primary place of service for which he is obviously gifted and in which he will be effective and fulfilled. Many times, however, the body of Christ may have urgent or important needs that must be met regardless of giftedness. The irony is that the need may have been created because the person well suited to meet that need is mismatched in another place of service. Help your men understand that although giftedness is the most important factor in a primary place of service, willingness is the most important factor in a secondary place of service.

Willingness to consider trial periods as learning laboratories. Urge your men to match with a ministry as soon as they've completed the analysis-and-discovery processes. Make clear the next step to take and point them to the next training or involvement, even if there doesn't seem to be a perfect fit. One of the best ways to discover and affirm a well-matched place of service in the church is simply to try it. And if you as a leader establish the expectations that serving is also learning, that no one is perfect, and that no job is permanent, you will free your men to move smoothly and confidently from one place of service to the next until they find a match that may be confirmed by gradual comparison as much as others are confirmed by immediate compatibility.

✳ **Evaluate the extent to which your men provide the cooperation your men's ministry needs to match them with ministry. Rate each means of involvement on a scale of 1 to 5, with 1 indicating the greatest involvement.**
  - **Prayerful consideration of a full**   1 2 3 4 5
    list of ministry opportunities
  - **Consideration of ministry**   1 2 3 4 5
    needs as well as giftedness
  - **Willingness to consider trial**   1 2 3 4 5
    periods as learning laboratories

✳ **Discuss your evaluation with your men's ministry leadership team, as well as strategies for increasing men's participation.**

Seek Matches Made in Heaven

Ultimately, what you are seeking are matches made in heaven—matches that bring together uniquely crafted men with the specially prepared work God has planned for them to do in your church (see Gal. 1:15; Eph. 2:10; 2 Tim. 1:9). Prayerfully ask God to show you matches between the human resources He has placed in your church and the human needs you have discovered. Look for logical matches. But more importantly, look for "Aha!" matches that require spiritual discernment and Spirit-led direction.

- As you consider a man's spiritual gifts, picture voids that keep your church from being a fully functioning, healthy church. Where is encouragement needed, or wisdom, or service, or mercy? Where is potential or talent abundant but leadership or administration lacking? Where is the desire to grow and learn present but teaching or knowledge absent?
- As you consider a man's life experiences and background, ask yourself who else has a similar past journey that could be brought together with this man for great synergy in serving together or great healing in crying together. Whom could this man help because of what he's done, what he knows, or what he's been through? Does someone in crisis

need this man's experience? Could this man be a life-changing mentor for a younger man or a boy?

- As you consider a man's unique personality, think about the neediest persons in your church, not just the obviously needy. Who are strong leaders who are burning out and need someone to listen and laugh with? Who are shy persons who need someone to help them find bonds of true fellowship? Which persons need a complementary personality to help them be all God made them to be?

- As you consider a man's natural abilities, make a long list of practical tasks that need to be done. Is the need for manual labor? musical accompaniment? careful research? written expression? What are the needs for which you would have to hire a specialist or trained professional if God hadn't given you someone with that natural ability?

- As you consider a man's heart passion, look around for signs of neglect. Where have people been overlooked or projects stalled because no one cared deeply enough to bring them the persevering energy they require? Where are the broken-down walls of your church, and who are the Nehemiahs and Ezras?

When a man is well matched in a place of service, he will not only be effective and fulfilled personally, but he will also be in a position to draw others to Christ. Though we are all shaped differently, we are all shaped to share Christ. And a man who finds his perfect fit in the body of Christ is a man who finds ways to make that body grow (see 2 Cor. 5:16-20).

✳ As a practice exercise, try matching the sample list of men you developed earlier with the ministry needs you identified on page 60. Use the criteria you have studied in this section.

Man	Ministry

EQUIP AND ENCOURAGE MEN AS THEY SERVE

No matter how well you match men with ministries, your men are certain to face times of frustration and discouragement. Ministry in the church is often difficult work with imperfect people in the face of spiritual

opposition (see Eph. 6:12). Actively follow up with men to promote their perseverance and success.

The key lies in the same ongoing relationship in which you discern a man's ministry readiness, discover his unique makeup, and determine his match with ministry needs. That relationship should be sprinkled with "How's it going?" questions and an open atmosphere in which a man can share his frustrations in serving, as well as his victories. Also find ways to infuse into that relationship a continuing diet of practical training and scriptural instruction that will both sharpen his effectiveness and help him maintain a more eternal perspective on the challenges and benefits of ministry.

Offer Equipping and Encouraging Words

The Bible reminds us at points such as James 3 that words are one of the most powerful tools we possess, especially in our relationships in the church body. We can't overestimate the impact our words can have—for good or for evil—in the lives of the men we are seeking to lead. Paul frequently wrote encouraging words to believers (see Eph. 4:1-2; 1 Thess. 5:14). As you relate to the men who are actively serving, look for opportunities to do the following.

Listen. Take time to really hear what's going on in a man's spiritual life as he serves. You're bound to hear evidence of growth, effectiveness, and victory. You're also bound to hear struggle, failure, and frustration. Many times all a man needs to confirm his call to service and press on with new energy is the opportunity to vent or share with a trusted friend.

Empathize. Before offering advice or solving a problem, take time to understand and relate to what the man is experiencing and to demonstrate that you know how it feels to be rejected, to make a mistake, or to revel in being used by God. We enjoy spiritual fellowship with Christ and with one another in the sufferings and sacrifices of ministry (see Phil. 3:10).

Suggest. Many times listening and empathizing are all a man needs to be encouraged and to renew his strength for serving. Sometimes, though, a man needs help navigating his way through difficult situations that arise in his place of service. If you feel you can help, offer suggestions and see how they are received. Men don't always feel comfortable asking for help. You may need to meet them more than halfway.

Equip. If a man who is serving seems to continually trip into the same problems or frustrations, he may need additional training or understanding. Just because a man is gifted or has a heart for a particular place of service doesn't mean he has all of the relational, organizational, or knowledge skills he needs to be effective. Look for areas in which a man might need to be equipped "for works of service" (Eph. 4:12, NIV).

Encourage. Encouraging—helping the men in your

men's ministry "not [to] become weary in doing good" (Gal. 6:9, NIV)—is one of the most important leadership roles you can play in helping men serve through the church. With your powerful words, affirm each man's giftedness, rekindle his passion, appreciate his uniqueness, and enlarge his perspective so that he doesn't give up before the harvest.

✳ Practice encouraging words with a man who is serving in your church. From your conversation what did you learn about his service?

_____

What did you learn about encouraging men?

_____

Recognize the Rewards of Service

Nothing is more encouraging to the men serving through the church than to know what God says about their service. Jesus' parable of the talents recorded in Matthew 25 shows the importance He placed on faithful stewardship of the gifts and resources God bestows. And of course, much of the New Testament consists of equipping and encouraging words from such believers as Paul or Peter or James to the Christians he had mentored and matched with service in the early church. In 1 Corinthians 3:10-15 Paul speaks of our work's being tested by fire and evaluated according to its quality on judgment day. Important and often underemphasized Scripture passages like Matthew 25:23; Acts 20:24; 1 Corinthians 12:7; Colossians 3:23-24; and 1 Peter 4:10 show not only our responsibility for serving Christ but also the rewards that accompany faithful service. Consider how such Bible passages could be encouraging, perspective-setting influences on men as you encourage them in their service.

The chart "Equipping Men for Ministry" on this page depicts the important process of mobilizing men for ministry. As you help men come to God, grow in Christ, and find their unique places of service in the church, you'll find that you are equipping them to go to the world with the gospel and love of Christ. As they stretch and exercise their gifts, your men will gain the confidence and boldness that come from being used by God in the way for which they were created. They will understand more and more deeply that the purpose of their service is to build up the body of Christ so that the body may draw others to Him. Then the whole cycle starts again, and more men (and women and children) come to God because your men have joined God in His mission to redeem the world through Christ.

So embrace the time, the relationships, the disciplined process, and the prayer it will take to help men serve through the church with effectiveness and love. You'll find that it's well worth the effort.

Resources
Hemphill, Ken. *Serving God: Discovering and Using Your Spiritual Gifts.* Nashville: LifeWay Christian Resources, 1995.
Lay-Mobilization System. Leadership Network; 2501 Cedar Springs Road LB-5, Suite 200; Dallas, TX 752011; call (800) 765-5323; fax (214) 969-9392; email 743233600@compuserve.com; or visit *www.leadnet.org.*
McQuilkin, Robertson. *Life in the Spirit.* Nashville: LifeWay, 1997.
Miller, Calvin. *The Empowered Leader: 10 Keys to Servant Leadership.* Broadman & Holman, 1997.
Roesel, Charles, and Donald Atkinson. *Meeting Needs, Sharing Christ.* Nashville: LifeWay, 1995.
Wilkes, Gene. *Jesus on Leadership: Developing Servant Leaders.* Nashville: LifeWay, 1996.
Willis, Avery T., Jr. *MasterLife.* Nashville: LifeWay, 1996–97.

Notes
[1] Adapted from C. Gene Wilkes, *Jesus on Leadership: Becoming a Servant Leader* (Nashville: LifeWay, 1996), 32–84.
[2] Henry T. Blackaby and Claude V. King, *Experiencing God: Knowing and Doing the Will of God* (Nashville: LifeWay, 1990), 107.

Answers to Activity
Page 59: 1. b, 2. d, 3. c, 4. g, 5. e, 6 a, 7. f

EQUIPPING MEN FOR MINISTRY

Analyze Ministry Readiness	Discover Makeup for Ministry	Identify Needs and Opportunities of Church and Community	Match Men with Ministry	Equip and Encourage
• Ask the right questions. • Encourage further growth. • Provide opportunities for self-analysis.	• Use a discovery instrument. • Personalize the discovery process. • Record ministry profiles.	• Determine needs. • Discern opportunities. • Balance needs and opportunities. • Dream big.	• Seek the support of church leaders. • Expect the cooperation of your men. • Seek matches made in heaven.	• Offer equipping and encouraging words. • Recognize the rewards of service.

POINT 4D

◆

Plan a Balanced Ministry: Extend Men on Mission

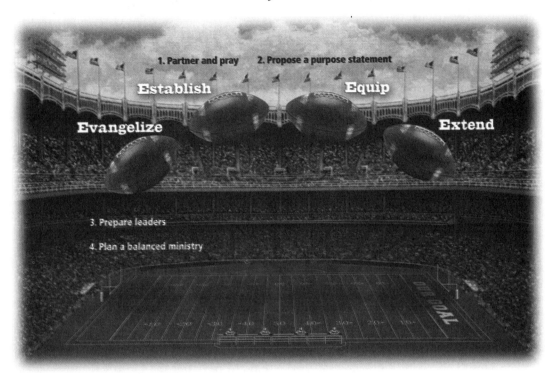

Two gunfighters were to duel it out in the old West. But the big fellow said to the small one: "It's not right. You've got a bigger target to shoot at than I do."

The little fellow replied: "Let's be fair. I'll take a paintbrush and make an outline my size on your body. Then, any place I hit outside the line doesn't count."

We laugh at that story, but anything your men's ministry hits outside the line drawn by the Lord Jesus Christ truly doesn't count.

Christianity was born with a map of the world in its hand. Jesus Christ presented the map in Matthew 28:19: " 'Go therefore and make disciples of all the nations' " (NASB). He drew the map even more clearly in Acts 1:8: " 'You shall be My witnesses both in Jerusalem, and in all Judea and Samaria, and even to the remotest part of the earth' " (NASB). When the church was born on the day of Pentecost, it instinctively turned toward this world and this mission.

Point 4 of this manual was written to show that healthy Christians are engaged in a spiritual process: *coming* to faith in Christ and church membership, *growing* in discipleship toward Christlike character and maturity, and *serving* in and through their local church as they discover their God-crafted gifts for ministry. But

> *"As the Father sent me, so I send you."*
>
> John 20:21, GNB

many Christian men stop there, never discovering or embracing the fact that a fully functioning Christian not only *comes* to God, *grows* in Christ, and *serves* through the church but also *goes* to the world with the gospel treasure he has discovered. As a men's ministry leader, you have the task of encouraging, enabling, and equipping all men to complete this spiritual-growth process by helping them become on-mission Christians.

HOW EFFECTIVE ARE YOU IN THE RED ZONE?

Many men's ministries do a good job of gathering men for special events and activities; grouping men together for Bible study, prayer, and accountability; and perhaps even matching men with ministry in the church. But they fall short of the goal line God identified in Matthew 28:19-20 and Acts 1:8. Your men's ministry must move beyond simply meeting the needs of the men already in the church. The goal of your men's ministry is to lead men into vibrant relationships with Jesus Christ, through which they become "fellow worker[s] in the gospel of Christ" (1 Thess. 3:2, NASB). They become fellow laborers in the gospel of Christ when they become completely aligned and identified with God's interests "by allowing God to take [them] directly into His purpose for the world."[1]

On a football field the area from the 20-yard line to the goal line is known as the red zone. It is the final 20 yards through which the offense must pass in order to score a touchdown or a field goal. Successful teams frequently score when inside their opponent's 20-yard line. In this men's ministry manual the red-zone area of the field corresponds to extending men on mission. It calls leaders to evaluate the effectiveness of their men's ministry on the basis of the number of men it equips to be on mission with God in their homes, workplaces, communities, and world. These on-mission men are passionate advocates of world-mission causes. They constantly make adjustments in their lives in order to share their faith with those within their spheres of influence who don't know Christ.

As a men's ministry leader, you have the responsibility of challenging men to complete the spiritual-growth process, of calling them to become on-mission Christians. You want to help men discover how they are uniquely called and shaped by God to live the Great Commandment (see Mark 12:30-31) and to fulfill the Great Commission (see Matt. 28:19-20) in every aspect of their lives—personal, home, church, workplace, community, and world.

WHAT MOTIVATES AN ON-MISSION CHRISTIAN?

God calls all Christians to take part in bringing the lost to faith in Christ. This includes witnessing to those in your immediate sphere of influence as well as those who dwell on the other side of the globe. Let's examine five biblical motivations for becoming an on-mission Christian.

Our Lord's Commission

There are approximately 4 billion non-Christians in the world, 1.7 billion of whom have never heard of Christ, do not have the Bible in their languages, and have never known a Christian.[2] We must always remember that Christ died for each one of these people, that He wants each one to be saved, and that He calls and empowers us to go and make disciples. Our marching orders come straight from our commander-in-chief, Jesus Christ, who said: " 'Go to the people of all nations and make them my disciples. Baptize them in the name of the Father, the Son, and the Holy Spirit, and teach them to do everything I have told you' " (Matt. 28:19-20, CEV). Believers in Christ are commanded to reach out to lost people everywhere, ministering and witnessing to them in His name. God has not designed a plan B. "As long as that text rings out its trumpet-toned commission, any man who opposes missions is implicitly saying he knows better than Christ."[3]

In John 20:21 Jesus said, " 'As the Father sent me, so I send you' " (GNB). In Latin the word for *send* is the same word that is used for *missions* or *missionary*. What Jesus was saying, then, is this: "As the Father has made Me a missionary, I'm making you missionaries." The resurrected Christ reinforced this commission with His words in Acts 1:8. Here Jesus promised to give His Holy Spirit to all Christians, in full measure and as a permanent possession, in order to empower them to carry out their missionary assignment locally, regionally, and internationally. The Great Commission provides all the motivation needed for placing a priority on enabling and equipping men to be on mission with God in the world. But what if the last lines of the Gospel of Matthew had been lost? Would there be any doubt that men are to take the good news of Jesus Christ to lost people everywhere? Certainly not! Our marching orders are not based on a single command. In every word Jesus spoke, sealed by His death and resurrection, is an injunction to go to a lost world with the message of salvation. As John said, "He [Christ] Himself is the propitiation for our sins; and not for ours only, but also for those of the whole world" (1 John 2:2, NASB).

Another aspect of our marching orders involves the gifts God has given us to glorify Him and to meet the needs of lost men: "Each one, as a good manager of God's different gifts, must use for the good of others the special gift he has received from God" (1 Pet. 4:10, GNB). Every Christian is uniquely called and shaped by God to carry out the Great Commission. He created us with certain talents and gifts to be used to touch the lives of other men. A major part of a men's ministry leader's responsibility is to help men identify and utilize their gifts. True missionary service takes place when our gifts intersect with the world's needs.

✳ **Think about the men in your men's ministry. What gifts do some of them possess that can be used to reach the lost?**

_____

_____

Compassion

Jesus ministered to both the physical and spiritual needs of people. Jesus performed two types of work: He reached out with both hands to do relief work and release work. Relief work provides for the immediate physical needs of a person in an emergency—food, clothing, and shelter. Release work provides deliverance from things that hold a person in bondage—release from sin and deliverance from the powers of evil. It is important that the body of Christ do both types of work. Programs that deal only with relief work can result in fatigue. Yet those concerned only with release can become callous to the immediate, basic cry of human need that surrounds us. Jesus is our example for providing both relief and release. In doing this, He showed people that He really loved them.

When Jesus was asked which commandment is the most important, He answered: " ' "Love the Lord your God with all your heart, with all your soul, with all your mind, and with all your strength." The second most important commandment is this: "Love your neighbor as you love yourself." There is no other commandment more important than these two' " (Mark 12:30-31, GNB). If we don't love people, we won't make much of an impact in their lives for Christ. " 'If you have love for one another, then everyone will know that you are my disciples' " (John 13:35, GNB). We show our love and compassion for lost men by sharing the truth about Jesus Christ and the relationship they can have with Him.

The eyes of on-mission Christians see wandering souls the way Jesus saw them. Matthew 9:36 says, "Seeing the multitudes, He [Jesus] felt compassion for them, because they were distressed and downcast like sheep without a shepherd" (NASB). Apart from a relationship with Jesus Christ, the lost will be eternally separated from God. On-mission Christians are controlled by Christ's love (see 2 Cor. 5:14). How thrilling to see men with a driving sense of urgency to bring men to Christ.

Community

Without a strong commitment to be on mission with God to bring all people together in Christ, our churches are nothing more than small social clubs with restrictive memberships. Being "baptized into one body, whether Jews or Greeks, whether slaves or free" and drinking of "one Spirit" (1 Cor. 12:13, NASB) are not just religious jargon; they are the only way for true community to be achieved. John the apostle calls us to look forward to the heavenly scene around His throne, where men "from every nation and all tribes and peoples and tongues" will be represented (Rev. 7:9, NASB).

With so many opportunities all around us to share the gospel with people from other countries, a men's ministry must encourage and empower Christians to seize opportunities. Consider these statistics.

- More than 22 million internationals pass through U.S. borders in a single year.
- These people represent more than 185 countries.
- More than 500,000 are students.
- Sixty percent of these current and future leaders come from countries in the Last Frontier, a term referring to more than two thousand people groups who have no access to the gospel.
- Twenty-five percent of all students come from countries where missionaries are prohibited.
- Eighty percent are never invited into an American home.[4]

Think what might have happened if someone had shared the gospel with Idi Amin, Saddam Hussein, and Muamar Kadaffi, who are only a few world leaders who have studied in the United States.[5]

Amid competing nationalism and outbursts of racism, Christ is the way for the people of our world to experience and share God's love with one another. Through the transforming power of Jesus, man can be reconciled to man and nation to nation.

Continuity

Christians are called to remember the rock from which we were hewn (see Isa. 51:1, NASB). The church is forever bound to continue the work Jesus and the apostles began. Jesus carried the mission of the Kingdom in His heart, and the early New Testament church followed His lead by being passionately missionary-minded. Speaking of those first-century believers, Acts 5:42 records that "day after day, in the temple courts and from house to house, they never stopped teaching and proclaiming the good news that Jesus is the Christ" (NIV). Other Bible passages state that they carried the gospel from town to town (see Acts 11:19-22). Thank God for the faithful saints who years later brought the gospel to America.

It has been said that Christianity is always only one generation away from extinction. The men in your church are responsible for leaving an on-mission legacy for future generations.

✳ Take a few minutes to review your life as a growing Christian. Who are some on-mission men who have influenced your relationship with God? Write their names here.

_____

_____

✳ Thank the Lord for these men and the influence they have had in your life. Consider the legacy you and the men in your men's ministry are leaving for those who come after you.

Christ

As important as commission, compassion, community, and continuity are to mission, not one of these—or even all of them added together—can compare to the ultimate reason for mission. The one true reason for mission is Christ. James Stewart captured what this statement means when he wrote, "To say 'I believe that God so loved the world that in Christ He gave everything He had, gave His very self,' to use such words not lightly ... but in spirit and in truth, means that the one who uses them binds himself irrevocably to make self-giving the controlling principle of life: and this is the very essence of mission."[6]

Mission can never be the responsibility of a few fanatics who happen to have a taste for it. It's not like walking along a cafeteria counter, selecting only the food items that suit your taste and passing over those that don't appeal to you. To have accepted Christ into your life is to have received His self-giving passion for reaching His world with the message of His love and grace.

As the apostle said in describing the way a person can know for certain that He belongs to God, "The one who does not love does not know God, for God is love. … Beloved, if God so loved us, we also ought to love one another. … By this we know that we abide in Him and He in us, because He has given us of His Spirit. And we have beheld and bear witness that the Father has sent the Son to be the Savior of the world" (1 John 4:8,11,13-14, NASB).

Did you catch that? The distinctive mark of being a Christian is that a person bears witness to the fact "that the Father has sent the Son to be the Savior of the world." A man who is on mission with God in the world has fully grasped the meaning of the life, death, and resurrection of Jesus Christ.[7]

WHAT DOES IT MEAN TO BE AN ON-MISSION CHRISTIAN?

Surveys indicate that many professing Christians are not on mission with God. In a given year fewer than one-third (29 percent) of churchgoing Christians talk about their faith with non-Christians. Fewer than one-fifth (17 percent) invite a non-Christian to church. And fewer than one-tenth (8 percent) lead someone to faith in Christ.[8] Such statistics are alarming, especially when we consider the number of witnessing opportunities Christian men have in their workplaces and communities every day. So how do you turn ordinary Christians into on-mission Christians?

Participation in God's redemptive mission can become personal, practical, and passionate if we follow four timeless, biblical principles. These key on-mission principles motivate men both to support distant missionaries and to be on mission in their own spheres of influence.

An on-mission man spiritually awakens to his personal responsibility for the Great Commission of Jesus. " 'I tell you, open your eyes and look at the fields! They are ripe for harvest. Even now the reaper draws his wages, even now he harvests the crop for eternal life' " (John 4: 35-36, NIV).

An on-mission Christian begins as someone who knows Christ, has a growing relationship with Him, and is serving in a local church. He understands mission causes, prays for non-Christians, and gives to reach

beyond his direct influence. The awakening that leads to on-mission service comes as his heart breaks and his motivation grows to reach lost people. This motivation is grounded in love, not guilt, and is profoundly real and personal. It is a realization that people need to know God and that He wants to use on-mission Christians to make that happen.

This realization is illustrated in one man's story:

I have to admit, missions studies never kept my attention. Witnessing courses sounded too intimidating and too demanding. Church visitation was a matter of duty, not desire. Most of those opportunities—and most of the people leading them—left me feeling guilty and uncomfortable. Though I knew it wasn't completely true, I felt they were trying to get me to do something that worked for them but not for me. And, to be honest, I wondered why they didn't seem to make more of a difference. My church was seeing very few people become Christians. I was personally seeing even fewer.

But because I was committed to my church, I continued to listen, and study, and pray, and give help to people I sensed were on mission reaching others for Christ. I wasn't awake yet, but I was stirring.

Increasingly, I couldn't miss the dissonance between what the Bible was describing as normal and healthy, and what I was experiencing personally. The Great Commission was emerging to me as the direct responsibility and mission of all believers, and I was beginning to realize that coming and growing and serving in the church weren't all God wanted for me. Somehow He wanted me to be involved in leading others to Christ. At first, I just couldn't figure out what that meant for me personally, and I couldn't find my style with others who seemed to be doing it.

About that time a handful of Christian friends, including my wife and me, started talking and praying about why our churches didn't seem to be impacting our community and why our lives weren't drawing others to Christ.

And for me, that's where it began. I believe the Holy Spirit was stirring in our hearts and creating an "awakening," a realization that was very real and very personal. I began to realize that people need to know God—no, it was more than that—people around me need to know God, and loving Him meant letting Him use me to make that happen.[9]

An on-mission man continually adjusts to remove barriers that keep people from hearing the gospel. "To the weak

I became weak, to win the weak. I have become all things to all men so that by all possible means I might save some" (1 Cor. 9:22, NIV).

On-mission Christians are "God-crafted pegs of all shapes and sizes who have adjusted—twisted, turned, rotated—until they discover how God has uniquely positioned them to 'go' and bring others to Christ rather than 'stay' an insider whose faith is only connected to God and other Christians."[10] Many Christian men are successful at coming, growing, and serving, but they do very little to go. On-mission men are committed to adjusting their lives as well as their view of other men's lives. They adjust by looking at how they are living their lives and leading in their churches. They adjust by finding out who the men around them are, what they are like, how they spend their time, and what interests them—all in order to know how to reach these men for Christ. "Perhaps the most painful adjustment an *on-mission* Christian makes is the commitment to change, and to embrace new patterns and create new strategies in order to reach new people. ... An adjusting, on-mission Christian is a lifelong learner who twists and turns and flips and rotates until his or her unique style as a Christian forms a creative bridge between Jesus Christ and people who don't know him."[11]

An on-mission man has an evangelistically active lifestyle in which his unique, God-given gifts are used naturally by the Holy Spirit to lead people to Christ. "How, then, can they call on the one they have not believed in? And how can they believe in the one of whom they have not heard? And how can they hear without someone preaching to them?" (Rom. 10:14, NIV).

On-mission Christians understand that spiritual awakening and spiritual adjustments inevitably lead to spiritual activity. They are liberated in the discovery that God made them personally to share Christ. "Activated Christians find increased opportunities to share Christ. They develop patterns of living and disciplined behaviors which somehow utilize their unique shape and situation to create occasions of divine appointment."[12] Active, on-mission Christians take initiative with men, sharing through every avenue that provides an opportunity. They help other men discover their gifts and utilize those gifts, believing that every Christian is gifted to play a role in leading others to Christ.

Another important spiritual action an on-mission man takes is to become a lifeline of prayer to intercede for the lost. We need to present the world's needs to God as we bring God's message to the world. God's plan for reaching the world depends on His power, and that power comes through prayer. Through prayer we can reach lives, even in countries where missionaries are not allowed to serve.[13]

An on-mission man passionately advocates the multiplication of on-mission Christians and churches. " 'The har-vest is plentiful, but the workers are few. Ask the Lord of the harvest, therefore, to send out workers into his harvest field' " (Luke 10:2, NIV).

The passion for on-mission men comes with the realization that leading people to Christ is not an unusual, occasional experience reserved for only a few Christians. They understand that they are a part of the game plan and long for the awakening of more and more on-mission Christians. "Each of us 'regular' Christians, with God's help, has to discover a personalized path to being *on mission*. Someone else's inspiring story, someone else's creative method, someone else's magazine article ... allow the mission to remain at arm's length. If we choose to be *on mission*, it is because God has intimately touched our hearts with the profundity of our salvation and opened our eyes to the personal way He created us to be *on mission* with Him."[14]

On-mission men understand that God did not create us to work alone. He intends for us to partner with others, whether in large groups or small, by cooperating, praying, volunteering, sending, sharing, or reproducing. They educate other men in mission principles, train men to apply those principles, promote mission activity, and involve as many men as possible in volunteer opportunities. On-mission Christians are passionate advocates for using men's unique makeup to reach other men for Christ.

❋ **Complete "Are You an On-Mission Christian?" on page 70 by marking the characteristics of an on-mission Christian you recognize in yourself.**

❋ **List five places you have frequented or five activities you have been involved in during the past 24 hours.**

1. _____

2. _____

3. _____

4. _____

5. _____

❋ **This list represents opportunities and places in which God can use an on-mission man. How aware were you of these opportunities? How willing were you to be used by God?**

❋ **Use this activity with the men in your ministry to illustrate the constant awareness that is necessary to be a man on mission for the Lord.**

ARE YOU AN ON-MISSION CHRISTIAN?[15]

An on-mission Christian is spiritually *awakened* (an upward process; see Isa. 61:1; Luke 4:18-19; Acts 4:13; Rom. 1:14-15).
- ❏ Lives in a personal relationship with Jesus Christ as Savior and Lord
- ❏ Obeys the Bible as a daily disciple and personally embraces the Great Commission
- ❏ Serves through a local church, using his unique gifts and experiences
- ❏ Faithfully gives of time, treasure, and talent to evangelistic mission efforts
- ❏ Responds to God's touch by praying for and caring about men who need to know Christ

An on-mission Christian is continually *adjusting* (an inward process; see Acts 8:35; 10:34-35; 1 Cor. 9:22-23; Col. 4:3-6).
- ❏ Seeks to understand and remove the barriers that keep men from hearing the gospel
- ❏ Discovers how God has uniquely created him to share Christ
- ❏ Inwardly changes the attitudes and behaviors that may hinder sharing the gospel
- ❏ Outwardly adapts to the variety of men to whom and settings in which Christ may be presented
- ❏ Plans ways and develops partnerships to help deliver the gospel message effectively

An on-mission Christian is evangelistically *active* (an outward process; see Acts 5:42; Rom. 10:13-15; 2 Cor. 5:11,20).
- ❏ Loves God and others, personally sharing Christ at every divine appointment
- ❏ Builds intentional relationships with men who do not yet know Christ
- ❏ Uses unique gifts, abilities, and vocational skills to serve and share Christ
- ❏ Invites men into settings where they will hear the gospel in personally relevant ways
- ❏ Cooperates with other believers who are purposefully sharing Christ with targeted groups
- ❏ Persistently prays for the lost

An on-mission Christian is a passionate *advocate* (a forward process; see Luke 10:2-3; Acts 13:2-3; Phil. 1:3-5; 4:15-17; 2 Tim. 1:8-10).
- ❏ Longs for the multiplication of on-mission Christians and churches
- ❏ Helps men discover their gifts and personal styles for sharing Christ
- ❏ Trains others in on-mission principles and promotes mission education in the church
- ❏ Mobilizes others to learn on-mission principles through active volunteer involvement
- ❏ Sends on-mission Christians to all people and all people groups of the world

In the right environment on-mission men who are awakening, adjusting, and discovering personal ways to share Christ will passionately advocate the process in other men. It is important that these on-mission men be supported by a men's ministry that advocates focused, deliberate, creative, versatile ways to empower its men to be on mission. "The reality is that even the heartiest *on-mission* Christian won't last long in isolation. The Bible is clear that to actively share Christ means to be attacked by many adversaries. And the inner strength God provides by His Spirit is augmented by the strength that comes from being active together with other *on-mission* Christians."[16]

✳ **Identify steps your men's ministry can take to support and encourage men who may have lost sight of the mission, are battling adversaries, feel they have failed, or feel weary and unappreciated.**

_____

_____

_____

_____

One way to support and encourage men is to have an on-mission pep rally during a Sunday-morning worship service, featuring men's testimonies about their discouragements and victories in mission service. Another possibility is to extend an altar call to all men in the church. Have the pastor or another man lead a commissioning prayer for men to remain true to their callings. Another idea is to play a segment of Franklin Graham's book on cassette, *Living Beyond the Limits* (see "Resources" on this page), encouraging men to keep their eyes on the Lord of the harvest and on those who need a witness.

Opportunities for on-mission Christians exist all around the world, but very few are prepared to go. In *The Man God Uses* Henry Blackaby writes, "If God has unconditional rights to your life, then you will accept that He has the right to send you anywhere, at anytime, for His purposes." Blackaby relates a personal experience supporting that statement: "I once asked a congregation if they believed this [statement] to be true. 'Amen' rang out from every corner of the auditorium. Then I asked how many of them had valid passports! Only a few nervous chuckles could be heard in response. Their actions indicated more about what they believed than their words."[17]

Something besides a passport might keep your men

from being sent by God; debt or other difficulties may make them unavailable for God's use. An on-mission Christian depends on God to meet his needs. He searches his heart to determine whether he has been seduced by things of the world, and he turns to God to seek freedom from slavery to the world's agenda.

An on-mission Christian won't allow himself to remain in bondage. He is ready to go at a moment's notice wherever the Lords sends him—across the street or around the world.[18]

Resources

Blackaby, Henry, and Tom Blackaby. *The Man God Uses.* Nashville: LifeWay, 1998.

The Commission (magazine). Richmond: The International Mission Board of the Southern Baptist Convention.

Graham, Franklin. *Living Beyond the Limits.* Nashville: Thomas Nelson, 1998.

Greenway, Roger S., and Timothy M. Monsma. *Cities: Missions' Final Frontier.* Grand Rapids: Baker Books, 1989. Out of print.

Nix, William. *Transforming Your Workplace for Christ.* Nashville: Broadman & Holman, 1997.

On Mission (magazine). Alpharetta: The North American Mission Board of the Southern Baptist Convention.

Perkins, John M. *Beyond Charity: The Call to Christian Community Development.* Grand Rapids: Baker, 1993.

Piper, John. *Let the Nations Be Glad!* Grand Rapids: Baker, 1993.

Robinson, Darrell. *People Sharing Jesus.* Nashville: Thomas Nelson, 1995.

Roesel, Charles, and Donald Atkinson. *Meeting Needs, Sharing Christ.* Nashville: LifeWay, 1995.

Rogers, Mike, and Debi Rogers. *The Kingdom Agenda: Experiencing God in Your Workplace.* Nashville: LifeWay, 1997.

Willis, Avery T., Jr. *MasterLife 4: The Disciple's Mission.* Nashville: LifeWay, 1997.

Notes

[1]Oswald Chambers, *My Utmost for His Highest*, ed. James Reimann (Grand Rapids: Discovery House, 1992), Nov. 10.

[2]Avery T. Willis, Jr., *MasterLife 4: The Disciple's Mission* (Nashville: LifeWay, 1997), 112.

[3]James S. Stewart, *Thine Is the Kingdom* (New York: Scribner's, 1957), 11.

[4]"Internationals Among Us," *Wonder-Working Power* (Richmond: The International Mission Board of the Southern Baptist Convention, 1998), 7.

[5]Ibid.

[6]Stewart, *Thine Is the Kingdom*, 14.

[7]Ibid., 11–15.

[8]Interview with Nate Adams, Vice-President, Mobilization and Mission Education, North American Mission Board of the Southern Baptist Convention, September 1998.

[9]Nate Adams, "Becoming an on-mission Christian," *On Mission*, premiere 1998, 23.

[10]Ibid.

[11]Ibid., 25.

[12]Ibid.

[13]Willis, *MasterLife 4*, 113.

[14]Adams, "Becoming an on-mission Christian," 26.

[15]Ibid., 24.

[16]Ibid, 26.

[17]Henry Blackaby and Tom Blackaby, *The Man God Uses* (Nashville: LifeWay, 1998), 127.

[18]Ibid.

POINT 5

◆

Provide Entry Points

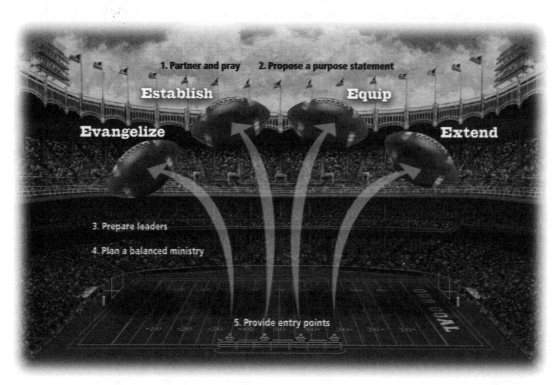

Paul's statement of his missionary strategy, recorded in 1 Corinthians 9:22-23, suggests an important concept for each men's ministry. Effective men's ministries recognize that not all men in their church and community are at the same point in their spiritual development. Different men are attracted to different things. Some want sports. Some like speakers. Some hate to sing, while others love it. Some like large groups. Others prefer small groups. It is vital for each men's ministry to offer a variety of entry points, making it easy for men to get involved. You won't be able to provide a lot of options all at once, but as you grow, make sure you create a good mix so that your ministry reaches as many men as possible and meets as many needs as possible.

In point 4 you examined the biblical foundation for developing men in four key areas: evangelizing men to salvation and church membership, establishing men to spiritual maturity, equipping men for ministry, and extending men on mission. You learned that different men have different

> *To the weak I became weak, that I might win the weak; I have become all things to all men, that I may by all means save some. And I do all things for the sake of the gospel.*
>
> 1 Corinthians 9:22-23, NASB

spiritual needs and that every man's greatest spiritual need lies in one of those four categories. In addition, men differ in such characteristics as their interest in in-depth Bible study and their willingness to share openly in a group. These differences illustrate the reason multiple entry points are important in men's ministry. One man may be reached through an intensive discipleship study, while another would consider attending only a large men's gathering. One might join a disaster-relief effort but would be uncomfortable sharing in a men's support group.

Points 5A, 5B, 5C, and 5D will present practical ways to begin and sustain ministry to men in each of the four primary areas of spiritual need: evangelizing men to salvation and church membership, establishing men to spiritual maturity, equipping men for ministry, and extending men on mission. Each category will introduce you to a variety of entry points that will appeal to men's individual needs and interests, helping them get off the sidelines and into the game.

POINT 5A

◆

Provide Entry Points: Evangelize Men to Salvation and Church Membership

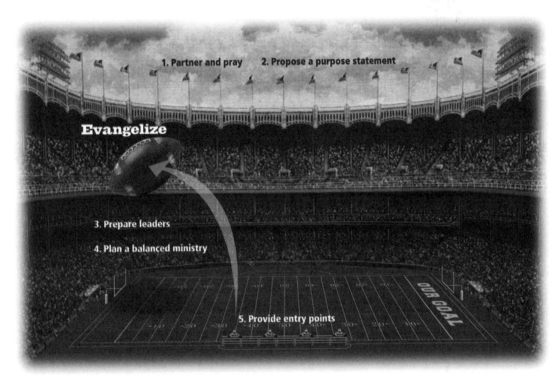

1. Partner and pray 2. Propose a purpose statement

Evangelize

3. Prepare leaders

4. Plan a balanced ministry

OUR GOAL

5. Provide entry points

Point 5A offers a variety of ideas for evangelizing men to salvation and church membership. Prayerfully consider ways your men's ministry can use or adapt the ideas to involve your men in reaching other men for Christ. A calendar and a timeline are provided at the end of the point to assist the leader with planning.

TESTIMONY WORKSHOP

Men want to share their faith with family members, neighbors, and coworkers. One way to prepare them for witnessing opportunities is to offer a testimony workshop. This experience will assist men with writing their personal salvation testimonies and will equip them to adjust their testimonies to fit the needs of seekers, self-satisfied persons, and skeptics they may encounter.

Use the following procedure to conduct the testimony workshop.

1. Teach men how to write their testimonies, using the outline presented in point 4A of this manual (p. 41) or a similar model.
2. Have men form pairs and practice giving their testimonies to each other. Give them copies of the following criteria for evaluating each other's testimony.

> *"I am the way and the truth and the life."*
>
> Luke 14:6, NIV

- Look for the story line. Avoid tampering with it, because it tells the way Christ entered the man's life. However, if the story line is missing or unclear, the testimony will not sound authentic.
  - Examine all parts of the testimony. Are they equally developed? Are doctrinal statements about the penalty of sin, Christ's payment for sin, and how to receive Christ presented accurately?
  - Evaluate the amount of detail in the testimony. Is it too sketchy or too detailed?
- Be sure the final sentence leads to further conversation.
- Search for church words and religious jargon. The testimony should not sound preachy.
3. Allow time for pairs of men to work together to revise their testimonies.
4. Have three men, enlisted before the workshop, play the roles of a seeker, a self-satisfied person, and a skeptic. Position them at different points in the meeting room and form three groups of men to gather around the three role players. Several men should

then take turns witnessing to the role players as the other men observe. (If your group is too large for this to be practical, ask three men to witness to the three role players in front of the entire group.)

5. Ask men to return to pairs to evaluate their experiences witnessing to the role players. They should discuss difficulties and make suggestions for improving their witnessing approaches and deliveries. (If you had three role plays before a large group, evaluate the experiences as a group.)

The facilitator should be available to counsel men when testimonies are being evaluated. It is common during such a workshop for a man to make a decision for Christ or to receive assurance of salvation.[1]

EVANGELISTIC EVENTS

Your men's ministry can utilize special evangelistic events to reach men. Men's evangelistic events have two objectives:

1. To involve new men who are not involved in your church's ongoing men's ministry
2. To reach unsaved men with the gospel

These events are planned to be intentionally evangelistic—to sow seeds of the gospel and to reap a harvest of saved souls. Every man should leave the event with a clear understanding of how to know Christ personally. Evangelistic events can also discover and cultivate men who may not be ready to make a decision or who may not yet understand the gospel.

Evangelistic events are—

- interesting—they excite men, draw them in, and hold their attention;
- creative—they encourage new, out-of-the-box thinking and planning;
- effective—they present the gospel in new and powerful ways.

Evangelistic events can be major entry points for men to come to Christ, because these events meet men where they are. This approach, called affinity ministry, develops a ministry targeted to a specific affinity group. Christian men who have a passion for fishing, hunting, and sports, for example, can use their gifts and abilities to reach other men who have the same interests.

A Formula for Event Evangelism

Prayer is the most important part of event planning. Only God can bring a soul from death to life. If we plan and promote, we get what these elements can give us—a well-planned and well-promoted event. But if we pray, we get what God can give us—men who hear and respond to the good news of Jesus Christ. Prayer is basic and essential to your strategy.

After the essential of prayer, planning your evangelistic event is as easy as A-B-C:

- *A* stands for *attraction*. Lost and unchurched men must be attracted to your event. Even if you have the most effective speaker, music, or evangelism strategy at your event, no one will respond to the claims of Christ unless you first attract those who do not know Him. The men's evangelistic events described later have a built-in attraction. Many men must work to invite and bring lost friends, neighbors, and coworkers to these events. Plan your event so well that Christian men who bring their lost friends will not be embarrassed but proud of its quality, impact, and image.
- *B* stands for *bridge*. A nonthreatening, relational climate for evangelism must be achieved. Use food, music, group-building activities, and other elements to create a warm, friendly atmosphere that is conducive to sharing the message of Jesus Christ.
- C stands for *communicate the gospel*. Evangelism cannot take place unless the gospel is communicated. Paul stated, "I am not ashamed of the gospel, for it is the power of God for salvation" (Rom. 1:16, NASB). Construct your event so that every element funnels men toward hearing and responding to the life-changing gospel of Jesus Christ.

Planning an Evangelistic Event

Every evangelistic event you plan for men should include these elements:

- Prayer—communicating with God
- Program—planning what will take place
- Procedure—making practical arrangements
- Promotion—getting the word out

Involvement is key to an evangelistic event. To fill a room that seats nine hundred men, give three hundred a job. Every man with a job will average bringing two more men. As you move through the preparation process for any event, involve as many men as possible.

Use the chart "Organization for an Evangelistic Event" on page 75 to establish an organizational structure for an evangelistic event.

After your organizational structure is in place, break down your plans for the evangelistic event into manageable bites. The chart "Evangelistic-Event Planning Sheet" on page 76 suggests an organizational timeline that can be used for any evangelistic event. Adapt the planning steps to meet your specific needs.

IDEAS FOR EVENT EVANGELISM

Use the following event descriptions as a guide for your planning. Only you know which events will work in your unique setting because only you know your church, its resources, its members' talents, its history, and its location. A wild-game supper may not work in an inner-city church in Philadelphia, and a sports clinic may not work in a south-Florida church composed mostly of retirees. The most effective event strategies

ORGANIZATION FOR AN EVANGELISTIC EVENT

Event: _____

Director of event: _____ Phone: _____

Program-team leader: _____ Phone: _____

Program-team members:

1. _____ Phone: _____
2. _____ Phone: _____
3. _____ Phone: _____
4. _____ Phone: _____

Procedure-team leader: _____ Phone: _____

Procedure-team members:

1. _____ Phone: _____
2. _____ Phone: _____
3. _____ Phone: _____
4. _____ Phone: _____

Promotion-team leader: _____ Phone: _____

Promotion-team members:

1. _____ Phone: _____
2. _____ Phone: _____
3. _____ Phone: _____
4. _____ Phone: _____

Prayer-team leader: _____ Phone: _____

Prayer-team members:

1. _____ Phone: _____
2. _____ Phone: _____
3. _____ Phone: _____
4. _____ Phone: _____

EVANGELISTIC-EVENT PLANNING SHEET

Event: _____ Purpose: _____

What	Who	When	Where
1. Secure program personalities.	Pastor/event director	6–12 months before	
2. Select and enlist preparation committees.	Pastor/event director	6 weeks before	
3. Arrange for food, equipment, decorations.	Procedure team	4 weeks before	
4. Order follow-up materials.	Program team	4 weeks before	
5. Promote prayer in departments, organizations, committees.	Prayer team	4 weeks before	
6. Make hospitality arrangements: motel, meals, transportation.	Procedure team	4 weeks before	
7. Make publicity plans. Secure promotional tickets, response cards/envelopes.	Promotion team	4 weeks before	
8. Promote event in newsletter and bulletin.	Promotion team	4 weeks before	
9. Secure print, radio, TV, sign, and marquee space.	Promotion team	4 weeks before	
10. Mail attendance-plan letters to members.	Promotion team	3 weeks before	
11. Enlist commitment counselors.	Program team	3 weeks before	
12. Distribute promotional items.	Promotion team	3 weeks before	
13. Distribute tickets to members.	Promotion team	3 weeks before	
14. Call prospects.	Church members	2 weeks before	
15. Train counselors in counseling, follow-up.	Pastor/program team	1 week before	
16. Reconfirm hospitality arrangements.	Procedure team	1 week before	
17. Pick up program personalities.	Procedure team	Day before	
18. Complete final physical arrangements.	Procedure team	Day of event	
19. Follow up on new converts.	Commitment counselors	Immediately after event	
20. Visit prospects.	Church members	Immediately after event	

emerge where your church (with its unique gifts and abilities) intersects with your community (with its unique interests and needs).

Evangelistic Social Events
An evangelistic social event brings Christians and non-believers together in a relaxed, nonthreatening setting for fun, fellowship, and a low-key presentation of the gospel. These can be great opportunities to communicate the good news of Christ to friends and associates in a meaningful way. Here are ideas for how to begin.

1. Start with prayer. Commit to the Lord the details for the event, everyone who will be involved, and the eternal results God will bring about.
2. Establish a small team to share the workload. This will not only reduce your stress level but also utilize more gifts in the body of Christ to make the event the best it can be. Delegate responsibilities according to gifts and abilities.
3. Select a suitable setting. The gathering should be hosted in someone's home where men's neighbors and friends will feel most comfortable. Create the relaxed atmosphere of a backyard barbecue.
4. Agree on a program. A businessman or a professional athlete could give a testimony. This in-person life story can have an incredible impact as the Holy Spirit works in men's hearts. A quality Christian evangelistic video, such as the *Jesus* film, is a good alternative.
5. Decide on refreshments. You could offer a complete meal or only dessert. Keep it simple if possible. Jesus Christ is the attraction, not the food.
6. Pray about whom to invite, make a list, and offer invitations either in person or by mail. Call to confirm who will be able to attend.
7. Plan a way to get responses from men after the program. One nonthreatening way is to distribute response cards similar to the following.

RESPONSE CARD
Name: _____
Address: _____
City: _____
State: _____ ZIP: _____
Home phone: _____ Work phone: _____
❏ I have prayed to receive Christ.
❏ Please send additional information about the Christian life.
❏ I would like for a church member to visit me.
❏ Please send information about future events.
Comments: _____
_____
_____

8. Be prepared to follow up on men who attended. Sometimes the response to an evangelistic program is a sincere commitment, other times a cry for help. In either case it would be a disservice not to offer to help a man take one step closer toward a growing relationship with God.

Wild-Game Dinner
An exciting evangelistic event for men is a wild-game dinner. The hunters and fishermen in a local church bring their wild game to be cooked and served either at the church or at a neutral site in town. These men invite their unsaved hunting and fishing buddies to come with them, and all of the men wear their camouflage hunting clothes. An inspirational speaker is enlisted who can communicate the gospel message in terms a hunter or a fisherman can relate to. Specialized conferences may also be offered, such as turkey hunting, deer hunting, or bass fishing. These three conferences attract three different groups of men. Men are given an opportunity to respond by indicating their decisions on response cards like the sample shown on this page. Church members are encouraged to reserve tables for 12 men each for one hundred dollars.

Many men's ministries incorporate the hunting theme with games and group builders, which are designed to create an informal, friendly atmosphere. For example, one men's ministry had different tables of men swapping hunting stories. Each table then selected the man with the most unusual or interesting story, who shared it with the whole group. The whole group then selected the winner by applause. The winner was given a hunting video.

Here's how to plan and conduct an evangelistic wild-game dinner.

1. Attend a wild-game dinner to observe the way it is done.
2. Start where your men's ministry is ready to start.
3. Be prepared to work. Planning this event takes four or five months. It is advisable to set up a week-by-week schedule of what needs to be done. The following teams are suggested.
   - Service team helps organize individuals to serve the food.
   - Cooking team prepares the wild game.
   - Ushers direct participants to their reserved tables.
   - Clean-up team cleans up after the event.
   - Security and crowd-control team helps direct traffic and monitor the crowds.
   - Follow-up team follows up on the decisions made.

Sports Events
Another ministry that attracts lost men is a sports event—anything from NASCAR races to T-ball leagues for their children. When the Southern 500 takes place

in Darlington, South Carolina, each year, the Welsh Neck Baptist Association sponsors an event called "Bring a Boy" at the race track on the Saturday prior to the big race on Sunday. In 1997 more than 10,000 men and boys had an opportunity to hear testimonies from several race-car drivers. Even though you may not have a major race track in your backyard, you can develop other sports ministries like T-ball leagues, soccer leagues, and baseball leagues or clinics. These outreach ministries could be staffed and coached by volunteers. You might begin with a one-day sports clinic for the community and then progress to a full league. Always remember that the focus is to reach men and their families for Christ. The coaches must have more passion for ministry than for winning the league championship.

Golf Tournament

Golf is a wonderful tool for evangelism because many men love it. The men in your church invite lost and unchurched men to a golf tournament, which is usually played in a scramble format. At least one of the men in each foursome should be a prospect. Before the tournament begins, some churches hold a golf demonstration or clinic, using either a Christian golf-tour professional or club pro as a draw for the tournament and the demonstration. Other churches have an event with a meal and a speaker after the tournament is over.

If a golf demonstration or clinic is held before the tournament begins, the gospel can be shared by the clinician. In some cases the golf expert cannot share the gospel (in some cases he may not even be a Christian). In this case the pastor may relate the good news, or a member may share an evangelistic testimony. Response to the gospel can be facilitated through the use of a response card like the one on page 77. In other cases the Christian men in each foursome can discuss what the speaker has shared during breaks in the tournament action. If the church chooses to have a meal with a speaker after the tournament, the gospel would be shared as it would be during a wild-game dinner. Make sure your speaker is experienced in inviting men to make a commitment to Christ.

Businessmen's Power Breakfast or Luncheon

Networking is the watchword of our age. An evangelistic businessmen's breakfast or luncheon gives networking an eternal twist. A delicious meal is served for businessmen at a local restaurant. Sometimes one or two musical numbers are presented. On occasion a short, nonreligious segment deals with an aspect of business or personal growth. Finally, the special speaker is introduced. He may be a politician, war hero, author, or famous figure in the business or entertainment industry. His talk is personal and always includes a testimony of the way he came to faith in Jesus Christ.

The speaker also says a prayer to receive Christ as the men pray silently. At the end of his talk the speaker calls attention to a response card that is at each place setting, is under each plate, or is distributed at this point (see the sample on p. 77). Everyone is invited to fill out the card and to make a comment or a suggestion about the program. "Oh, by the way," the speaker explains, "if you prayed with me earlier to receive Christ, please check the box. I want to rejoice with you in your decision and send you some material on how you can grow as a new believer."

Needs-Based Seminars

Evangelistic needs-based seminars usually target adults by addressing their needs while contagiously communicating the claims of Christ. North America is filled with men who are hurting. Millions of men have climbed the ladder to success only to find that it was leaning against the wrong wall. Others have lost jobs or are experiencing family crises, while still others are experiencing depression and isolation. Men's ministries that offer practical help for hurting men have many opportunities to introduce them to Jesus Christ.

Potential topics for needs-based seminars include marriage, parenting, job fair, money or time management, health fair, divorce recovery, and single parenting. Here are suggestions for conducting a seminar.

- Choose the most convenient time and place for the men targeted by the event.
- Promote the event through the theme, subject matter, and instructor. Present seminars in ways that attract men. Use titles that attract men, like "How to Succeed in Fathering," "Life After Divorce," or "Making a Good Marriage Better." LifeWay Christian Resources sponsors marriage-enrichment weekends nationwide (see "Resources," p. 80). If an event is held in your area, promote attendance by using the title "How to Make Every Day Valentine's Day."
- Build attendance by having Christians give free tickets to men who may be interested.
- Register participants by giving them response cards (see the sample on p. 77). Provide them an opportunity to receive Christ and to mark their cards.

Excellent resources suitable for evangelistic needs-based seminars can be ordered (see "Resources," p. 80).

Father-Child Winter Beach Party

Plan a wintertime fellowship for fathers and their children. Use a beach-party theme by creating beach scenes in the fellowship hall or the family-life center. Invite everyone to attend dressed in summer clothes. Have a beachball volleyball game. Fill children's plastic swimming pools with sand and let fathers and children build sandcastles. Play beach songs in the background.[2] After refreshments, read Matthew 7:24-27 and emphasize the importance of building our lives on the firm foundation of Jesus Christ.

Kite Day and Hobby Day

Allow fathers opportunities to be with their children by holding a Kite Day or a Hobby Day.[3] Announce a location for flying kites. Or invite fathers and children to display their model airplanes, trains, and cars at church. Have a demonstration at either event and use it as an opportunity to present a witness. For example, after a kite-flying demonstration relate the tug of the kite to God's tugging on our hearts. At a model plane, train, or car fair ask, Where is your life taking you?

Pay-per-View Boxing

Order a pay-per-view boxing match to be viewed at a man's home and publicize the event in your church and in local neighborhoods. Provide snacks and soft drinks. Point out that the Bible often uses sports analogies to convey spiritual truths. Read and briefly discuss 1 Corinthians 9:24-27, making the point that many men are "running aimlessly" (v. 26, NIV). Rather than seek things that do not last, we can receive God's gift of eternal life, "a crown that will last forever" (v. 25, NIV). Invite men to attend a worship service, a men's ministry event, or a men's small group.

EVANGELISTIC MINISTRIES

Approaches other than evangelistic events can be used to connect with lost men.

Men's Fitness Plan

One idea is to develop a wellness plan for the men in your church. Men in your church would begin by connecting with their friends and acquaintances through regular walking or jogging, basketball before or after work or during lunch, or tennis or golf once a week. Men should begin the exercise period with prayer.

As the relationship develops, men should invite other men to participate in a seminar on men's health issues, such as reducing the risks of diabetes, high blood pressure, high cholesterol, obesity, and heart disease. These subjects are addressed in *Fit4: A LifeWay Christian Wellness Plan*, an excellent resource that helps men understand the importance of a healthful, balanced lifestyle (see "Resources," p. 80). By combining daily spiritual-growth opportunities, weekly health information on proper nutrition and exercise, direct application of new information to daily life, and written and group accountability, *Fit4* helps men take the next step toward developing healthful habits that will benefit them in all areas of life.

At the seminar a man should share a personal testimony about the *Fit4* wellness plan. Some testimonies will relate to how being part of a fitness group helped him lose weight and keep it off. Other testimonies will be about how regular exercise helped a man reduce his stress level. The testimonies should also explain that *Fit4* is a way for men to improve their relationships with God and develop strong relationships with other men who share their concerns. A *Fit4* group can be started as an outgrowth of the sporting activities or the discovery of common health concerns.

Fishers of Men National Tournament Trail

Fishers of Men National Tournament Trail is a ministry that reaches hard-core weekend bass fishermen. These men usually fish in tournaments for prize money each weekend six to nine months a year. They have little or no desire to go to church, because they are usually fishing every Sunday. You can reach men like this by inviting them to fish in a Fishers of Men National Tournament Trail. Watch what God can do as the lost men listen to an inspiring message at the pretournament meeting on Friday night before the Saturday tournament.

Lost men are attracted to this tournament by the payback and the professional way it is run. However, something is different from the tournaments they have fished in before. The contestants do not drink or use bad language, and a prayer is offered before and after the tournament. The gospel message is communicated in terms fishermen can understand.

How does a local church conduct a bass tournament?

1. Begin your preparation from six to eight months in advance of the opening weekend. Events usually run one weekend a month, March through August.
2. Conduct the tournament from a bass-club format. The job is too big for one man.
3. Make sure you have a quality speaker who can communicate with the competitive non-Christian fishermen who attend the pretournament meeting.
4. Provide a motel list for out-of-town participants.
5. The launch site and permits must be in place six months prior to the tournament.
6. Print a minimum of three thousand brochures to ensure that you include non-Christians. Place these at all boat shows, in bait and tackle stores, at landings, and in discount stores that sell fishing gear within a 75-mile radius. Preferably, distribute brochures at every landing around the lake every weekend before your tournament for a couple of months. Work with your Baptist association to mail brochures to churches. Your state men's ministry director can possibly assist.
7. Fishing pros, especially the good ones who draw competitive fishermen, need to come from the Bass Anglers Sportsman Society (BASS) top one hundred trail and the Forrest L. Woods (FLW) tour. Remember, the better the pro you bring, the better the sponsors he has and the better the door prizes

he will bring with him. His job is to promote the companies that support him.

8. Payback should be in the 85 to 90 percent range in order to draw non-Christians. A minimum of one thousand dollars for the first prize is expected for most secular tournaments.

9. The Friday-night event can be fun, but the message needs to be the centerpiece of the evening. Limit the evening's activities to two hours, including the following elements.
   • A meal, though an elaborate one is not necessary
   • A couple of songs
   • A short, 20- to 25-minute message that is not preachy but clearly communicates the gospel
   • Door prizes

10. Consider insurance for your protection, as well as the protection of the church and individuals involved. This is why conducting the tournament through a bass club is advisable.

11. Additional items that will be needed: digital scales, at least one $25 door prize for every three participants, an outdoor sound system, a bullhorn to announce the start, water tanks with live fish, bags for fish transport, and tape to mark trolling motors after live well check.

For more information about this tournament trail, email *fishersofmen@fishingworld.com;* visit the Web site at *www.fishingworld.com/fishersofmen;* or call (803) 481-0802.

Ministry to Deer-Hunting Clubs

A significant number of men are involved in deer-hunting clubs. Most clubs consist of men who never attend church. They usually spend most of their free time either hunting deer or hanging around the deer club in season and out of season. This three- to five-year strategy is to have a committed Christian deer hunter actively attempting to influence his club for Christ. Through his influence men in the club are saved and begin studying the Bible and praying together. Many of these men will not attend church, but through this ministry their deer-hunting clubs gradually take on the characteristics of small mission churches.

OTHER IDEAS FOR EVANGELIZING MEN TO SALVATION AND CHURCH MEMBERSHIP

1. Start an annual chili cook-off.
2. Offer nonthreatening family activities like a father-son camp out or a father-daughter banquet.
3. Provide support groups for divorce recovery or addictive behaviors.
4. Offer weekend activities for single fathers and their children.
5. Present testimonies of Christian athletes via video at a neighborhood bowl-game party.

6. Invite friends over for dinner and a movie—the *Jesus* video!
7. Hold a steakout to which men invite lost friends for a steak meal, motivation, and music.
8. Sponsor hunting or fishing camps.
9. Sponsor an event such as a walk/run or a softball tournament.
10. Offer exercise, competition, fellowship, and a Christian witness through team sports.
11. Provide Christian literature and fellowship at truck stops.

✳ Use the one-year calendar on page 81 to schedule ministries for evangelizing men to salvation and church membership during the next year. Be sure to check the church's calendar so that you do not double book with any key church activities.

✳ Use the ministry timeline on page 82 to list each task needed to establish each ministry action. Also include a projected beginning date for each task.

✳ Step back and consider:
   • **Are your goals realistic?** ❑ Yes ❑ No
   • **Are your goals measurable?** ❑ Yes ❑ No
   • **Are your goals open to evaluation?** ❑ Yes ❑ No
   • **Are your goals flexible?** ❑ Yes ❑ No

Resources

Atkinson, Donald A., and Charles L. Roesel. *Meeting Needs, Sharing Christ.* Nashville: LifeWay, 1995.

Christian Financial Concepts and Life Pathways, Inc. (800) 722-1976.

Fay, Bill, and Ralph Hodge. *Share Jesus Without Fear.* Nashville: LifeWay, 1997.

Fit4: A LifeWay Christian Wellness Plan. Nashville: LifeWay, 2000.

Focus on the Family. (800) 232-6459.

How to Have a Full and Meaningful Life (tract). Nashville: LifeWay, 1971.

LifeWay Christian Resources. Inquire about or order resources by writing to Customer Service Center, MSN 113; 127 Ninth Avenue, North; Nashville, TN 37234-0113; by calling toll free (800) 458-2772; by faxing (615) 251-5933; by visiting *www.lifeway.com;* by emailing *customerservice@lifeway.com;* or by visiting a LifeWay Christian Store. Inquire about marriage-enrichment events by calling (800) 254-2022.

McGee, Robert S. *Search for Significance* LIFE Support Edition. Nashville: LifeWay, 1992.

Robinson, Darrell. *People Sharing Jesus.* Nashville: Thomas Nelson, 1995.

Sledge, Tim. *Making Peace with Your Past.* Nashville: LifeWay, 1992.

Smith, Jack R., and Jennifer Kennedy Dean. *Witnessing Through Your Relationships.* Nashville: LifeWay, 1994.

Springle, Pat. *Conquering Codependency: A Christ-Centered 12-Step Process.* Nashville: LifeWay, 1993.

Welch, Bobby H., and Doug Williams with David Apple. *A Journey in FAITH.* Nashville: LifeWay, 1998.

Notes

[1] Adapted from Avery T. Willis, Jr., *MasterLife Leader Guide* (Nashville: LifeWay, 1997), 117–20.
[2] Richard E. Dodge, *Ideas for Reaching Adults* (Nashville: Convention, 1992), 4.
[3] Ibid., 5.

EVANGELIZING MEN TO SALVATION AND
CHURCH MEMBERSHIP: ONE-YEAR CALENDAR

SEPTEMBER	OCTOBER	NOVEMBER
DECEMBER	**JANUARY**	**FEBRUARY**
MARCH	**APRIL**	**MAY**
JUNE	**JULY**	**AUGUST**

EVANGELIZING MEN TO SALVATION AND
CHURCH MEMBERSHIP: MINISTRY TIMELINE

1. Ministry	Tasks	Beginning Date	Date Completed
2.			

3. Ministry	Tasks	Beginning Date	Date Completed
4.			

POINT 5B

◆

Provide Entry Points: Establish Men to Spiritual Maturity

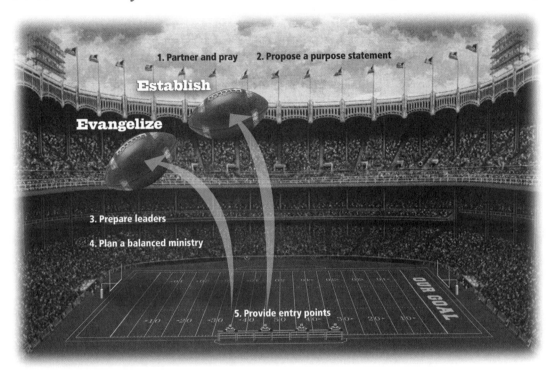

Point 5B offers a variety of ideas for establishing men to spiritual maturity. Prayerfully consider ways your men's ministry can use or adapt the ideas to involve your men in spiritual-growth opportunities. A calendar and a timeline are provided at the end of the point to assist the leader with planning.

MEN'S PRAYER TEAMS

Prayer is a key element in establishing men to spiritual maturity. Praying with partners or with a group will convince your men that God understands their needs and circumstances and is willing and able to heal, transform, or strengthen them in their difficulties. Here is a way to establish prayer teams among your men.

1. Ask men to decide on specific requests. Ask: What need in your life concerns you most? With which problems do you need God's help? Have men write their specific thoughts.
2. Ask men to commit themselves to pray every day. Men should set aside at least five minutes each day when they can fully concentrate on God and their requests. Encourage them to record the time on their calendars. Challenge them to pray whenever and wherever this need comes to mind.
3. Help men find prayer partners. Link each man with another man or a group of men who will pray for him and his request every day. He should commit to pray for their requests, as well.
4. Men must take time to listen, giving God the opportunity to speak to their hearts as they are quiet before Him. Encourage them to write down any new thoughts or insights. They should be obedient to do anything they know God asks them to do.
5. Men must leave the results to God, believing that He is at work even if they cannot see anything happening. They should tell God what they honestly want but let Him choose the solution.
6. Help men review the results of prayer by asking: What has happened? Has the circumstance changed? Has your attitude changed? Do you have a new perspective?[1]

Make copies of "Prayer Log" on page 84 for men to use as they pray for themselves and for other men.

> *The things you have heard me say in the presence of many witnesses entrust to reliable men who will also be qualified to teach others.*
>
> 2 Timothy 2:2, NIV

PRAYER LOG[2]

Month: _____

My needs: _____   My partner's needs: _____

_____   _____

_____   _____

Check the days you pray. Record answers or insights.   Check the days you pray. Record answers or insights.

❏ 1. _____	❏ 1. _____
❏ 2. _____	❏ 2. _____
❏ 3. _____	❏ 3. _____
❏ 4. _____	❏ 4. _____
❏ 5. _____	❏ 5. _____
❏ 6. _____	❏ 6. _____
❏ 7. _____	❏ 7. _____
❏ 8. _____	❏ 8. _____
❏ 9. _____	❏ 9. _____
❏ 10. _____	❏ 10. _____
❏ 11. _____	❏ 11. _____
❏ 12. _____	❏ 12. _____
❏ 13. _____	❏ 13. _____
❏ 14. _____	❏ 14. _____
❏ 15. _____	❏ 15. _____
❏ 16. _____	❏ 16. _____
❏ 17. _____	❏ 17. _____
❏ 18. _____	❏ 18. _____
❏ 19. _____	❏ 19. _____
❏ 20. _____	❏ 20. _____
❏ 21. _____	❏ 21. _____
❏ 22. _____	❏ 22. _____
❏ 23. _____	❏ 23. _____
❏ 24. _____	❏ 24. _____
❏ 25. _____	❏ 25. _____
❏ 26. _____	❏ 26. _____
❏ 27. _____	❏ 27. _____
❏ 28. _____	❏ 28. _____
❏ 29. _____	❏ 29. _____
❏ 30. _____	❏ 30. _____
❏ 31. _____	❏ 31. _____

EVERY MAN A MENTOR

Any man who claims to have achieved something by himself is not being totally honest. In every man's life are others who have helped him along the way. Speaking at a 1993 Promise Keepers conference in Boulder, Colorado, Howard Hendricks said:

> Every man needs to have three individuals in his life: You need a Paul, you need a Barnabas, and you need a Timothy. You need a Paul, that is, you need an older man who is willing to build into your life. … You need somebody who's willing to share with you not only his strengths but also his weaknesses, not simply his successes but his failures and what he learned in the laboratory of life. You need a Barnabas, somebody who loves you but is not impressed by you. Have you got anybody in your life that's willing to keep you honest, that's willing to say to you, "Hey, man, you're neglecting your wife. I know it. Everybody else knows it. It's about time you know it"? … And third, you need a Timothy. You need a younger man into whose life you are building yours.

Today men are not involved in vital relationships as they once were. Men reach adulthood with no concept of what it means to be a man in Christ. Mentoring brings older and younger men into relationship in such a way that younger men grow as older men guide. That is the historical pattern; it is also the biblical pattern.[3] The changes produced in a man's life through mentoring can have a ripple effect in his family, church, workplace, and community.

Who Is a Mentor?

No man automatically grows in Christlikeness. A mentor begins where an evangelist leaves off by discipling a man one-to-one. A mentor walks alongside another man, saying, "You can do it!" He is a guide, like taillights on the car ahead, showing the way through the darkness. He offers encouragement and support. Caring enough to spend time with someone is a powerful witness for Jesus Christ.

A good mentor is a good listener, allowing the other man to share struggles and pain, as well as victory and joy. A mentor can help another man identify and develop needed life skills like dealing with anger and stress. He can also identify and find resources for improving job skills, parenting skills, marriage enrichment, financial and home management, and relationship skills. Above all, a mentor is committed to helping a man develop an intimate walk with Jesus Christ, someone God can use to help him take the next steps in character building and spiritual development. A mentor

agrees to be a role model in such areas of the Christian life as prayer, Scripture reading, and Scripture memorization. Two men may choose to meet together for six weeks, three months, or three years. But the primary goals are to support each other and to grow in Christ.[4]

A mentor cannot be God in someone's life. Human beings are fallible. Therefore, both men in the mentoring relationship must seek to grow closer to God and His truth with each encounter. The mentor is not afraid to respond to certain questions by saying, "You need to go to God on that one." His primary goal is to teach and encourage another man to hear God rather than to depend on the mentor. Resources like *Experiencing God, The Seven Seasons of a Man's Life, Living God's Word, When God Speaks,* and *In God's Presence* are excellent tools to help a man recognize how God is speaking to and leading him (see "Resources," p. 95).

Why Have Mentors?

Mentoring has evolved for the following reasons.

- Mentoring is biblical. Paul instructed older men to mentor younger men (see 2 Tim. 2:2).
- Jesus modeled mentoring in the way He related to His disciples (see John 1:35-39). "The principles that were important to Jesus and lived out in His own life became important to the disciples."[5]
- Mentoring has been the primary way knowledge and skills have been handed down through the ages. Men trained their sons to follow in their professions. Apprentice programs are expressions of mentoring.
- Mentoring works. One-to-one or small-group mentoring is an effective teaching method that has been proved in schools, churches, and businesses around the world.[6]
- We are brothers and members of the same body. Consider the many one-another passages in Scripture.
- There is a shortage of spiritual leaders. The work of the average church in America is done by 20 percent or less of its membership.
- Many men did not receive the fathering they needed. Only half of America's children live in stable homes with their biological fathers and mothers.[7] The absent-father syndrome devastates children, and its effects last a lifetime. When Dad is physically or emotionally absent, boys either depend on their mother or are forced to look to the world for a role model. The world teaches, "Become a macho man," which is often only an act to hide insecurity in being unable to identify with men. If the boy looks to his mother for a role model, the results may be a loss of masculinity and the potential for homosexuality. He will tend to marry a dominant woman, respond passively, have great dif-

ficulty trusting the Heavenly Father, and become one of the next generation of emotionally absent fathers. Girls without adequate fathering often reject their appearance and sometimes their femininity, crave attention, feel that they can never be loved, and can be attracted to older men or men who offer little intimacy.[8]

- The prospect of revival demands it. Many of those who pray for and predict revival in America express concern over not having enough leaders in place to minister to new Christians.

In *As Iron Sharpens Iron* Howard and William Hendricks write: "The most compelling question that every Christian man must ask is this: 'What am I doing today that will be an influence for Jesus Christ in the next generation?' There are only two things God is going to take off this planet. One is His Word, the other is His people. Therefore, if you are building His Word into people, you can be confident that you are building a legacy that will last into eternity."[9]

Who Should Be a Mentor?

The role of mentor is mentally, emotionally, and spiritually challenging. Mentors must have these qualities.

- Mentors should be authentic. Only Christ-centered lives can pass another man's scrutiny.
- Mentors should be transparent. Mentors must allow themselves to be known, for they establish credibility by revealing their mistakes and by sharing what they have learned from them.
- Mentors should be growing, not grown. They are willing to admit that they do not know everything. However, they have a disciple's heart.
- Mentors should be committed. In 1 Timothy 4:12 Paul wrote to Timothy, "In speech, conduct, love, faith, and purity, show yourself an example of those who believe" (NASB). Mentors are committed to a godly lifestyle.[10]

What Do Mentors Do?

Mentoring can be more than a once-a-week visit. It means maintaining contact throughout the week, serving as a liaison to the man's family, answering job-related questions, or standing by his side during difficult times.

The man being mentored controls the degree of involvement with the mentor. Therefore, it is most important that the two agree to be faithful and committed to meeting with each other.

The best way to become a mentor is first to experience mentoring. Consider enlisting someone to be your mentor. Identify an area of your life in which you need to grow. Be honest with yourself. The area could be anything from a disciplined prayer life to managing money or overcoming a bad habit. Look for a man who has the character traits you need to develop. Ask him to become your mentor and help you grow in your specific area of need. As you mentor other men, you will need to return to your mentor to process what you are experiencing. Your mentor becomes your source of encouragement and objectivity for mentoring another man.[11]

Guidelines for Mentoring

Establish clear expectations and boundaries with your mentor and with the man you mentor. How long will you meet? How often? What is your purpose? Mentors do not sign on to manage a person's entire life. Begin by clearly establishing what you will and will not provide.

Adopt a structure for the mentoring experience. Consider using a discipleship course to get from point A to points B, C, and D. For example, you might study together *The Seven Seasons of a Man's Life: The Season of Rebuilding* (see "Resources," p. 95).

Combine transparent sharing with active listening. Above all, mentoring involves relationships. Place primary emphasis on being a friend rather than on giving advice. Share some of your own struggles. Then listen carefully to understand the struggles of the man you are mentoring. He needs your wisdom, but he will be able to receive it only to the degree that you have established a caring relationship.

Be flexible while retaining a sense of purpose. Every mentoring experience is different. The man you are mentoring is likely dealing with complex problems as varied as money, sex, addiction, guilt, and relationships. Each man's situation is unique.

Resist the urge to solve, or even address, all of the man's problems. Often a person just needs to talk about a problem to find the solution. Experienced mentors listen to secondary issues, but they expend their energy on the real purpose of the relationship. Keep the main thing the main thing.

Don't just talk; do something! If you were coaching someone on throwing and catching a football, you would play catch. If you are mentoring a man about spiritual growth, pray together and study the Bible together. If you are mentoring about money, plan a budget together. If addiction is the issue, work through the 12 steps together. LIFE Support resources offer help for dealing with chemical dependency, codependency, sexual addiction, and other life issues (see "Resources," p. 95). Translate your purpose into action.

Don't try to do the job alone. View yourself as part of the discipling team. Encourage and sometimes require the man you mentor to get other appropriate help through counseling, support groups, church attendance, or classes. Never let your ego lead you to believe that you can provide all the man needs.

Celebrate small steps of success. Break the journey toward Christlikeness into manageable bits. When the man you mentor makes progress, give God the credit, rejoice, and celebrate. Reinforce positive behavior by congratulating him when he does well. We all need a lot of encouragement when we seek difficult life change.

Trust God for the results. "Cast your bread upon the waters, for after many days you will find it again" (Eccl. 11:1, NIV). A little boy watching a parade wouldn't stop squirming. His father scolded him, unaware that his son was standing on an ant bed. Finally the boy said, "Dad, things are going on here that you don't know nothing about." When you mentor, recognize that God is at work. Be patient. You may pour yourself into a man who seems to gain nothing, but over the long term you will see God work miracles. A mentor cannot be responsible for what only God can do. Maintain your walk with God and trust Him for the results.[12]

Identifying Mentors
1. Before launching a formal mentoring ministry, ask your men's ministry leadership team to take the following steps.
   - Examine parallels to Paul-Barnabas-Timothy relationships. For peer mentoring, study Jonathan and David. For an older-younger combination, look at Jethro and Moses. For a younger-older pair, consider Elisha and Elijah.
   - Think of a young man who has promising gifts but who experienced a troubled past. Divorce leaves behind effects on children such as insecurity, anger, underachievement, and low self-esteem. Abuse and neglect contribute to similar problems. How might your mentoring transform these liabilities into strengths?
   - Analyze your negative attitudes about mentoring. Don't feel condemned by these feelings, but rather, assess the degree of and reasons for the following attitudes that may exist in you: lack of concern, skepticism, indifference, inadequacy, isolation, and ignorance. Think and pray about a strategy to eliminate or minimize these obstacles.
   - Overcome your feelings of inadequacy by taking time to write in detail what you may have that a younger protégé may need: experience, knowledge, access, money, resources, friendship, time, or uniqueness. Don't be modest, but rather, acknowledge God's blessings and approach Him with a willingness to share with those less fortunate than you.
   - Mentoring happens in various degrees all around you. Identify three examples of one man's influencing another. The type and degree may vary. It may not immediately be apparent that they are mentoring. Don't focus on the grandiose but on humble, simple acts of service. Could you relate to another man in a similar way?[13]
2. Ask for your pastor's input. Inform him that you are

in the process of identifying men who can serve as mentors for other men.
3. Recruit deacons and male Sunday School teachers as mentors.

Identifying Men to Mentor
1. Pray for God to point out men who need to be mentored: "Lord, who is someone who could use what I have to offer? Open my eyes to see that man." If you pray for a man to mentor, sooner or later God will probably bring one into your life. Pray that you will recognize the man God sends your way.
2. Start with your area of expertise. When you see a younger man with deficiencies in an area in which you have ability or training, offer to help. For example, maybe a man at church is struggling with his taxes, and you are an accountant. Offer to stop by his house and give him suggestions. You don't have to do his taxes for him. Simply support him as he works through the situation.
3. Place yourself in proximity to younger men. Coach a church or community sports team or teach a young men's Sunday School class. If you work with boys in Royal Ambassadors, coach a boys' basketball or soccer team, teach a boys' Sunday School class, assist with a church youth group, or volunteer at a school, you may have opportunities to meet young fathers.
4. Create low-risk opportunities for interaction. Low risk means that no one has to perform and no one will be judged. The purpose is to have a good time and enjoy each other's company. You might invite a group of men to your house for a cookout, take several hunting or fishing, organize a men's night out to the ballpark, or schedule a workday at church to tackle special projects. End the day with something relaxing, such as eating ice cream or swimming.
5. After you select a man as a prospect for mentoring, give him one-to-one attention through a low-risk activity. Buy him lunch, play golf with him, invite him to a special event or convention you plan to attend, or ask him to lend a hand with a project you are doing. By initiating these kinds of offers, you invite the man onto your turf with no strings attached and with no, or at least low, expectations.[14]

DISCIPLING MEN THROUGH SMALL GROUPS
As Jesus was ascending to His Father, He left us the command to disciple believers, " 'teaching them to obey everything I have commanded you' " (Matt. 28:20, NIV). When we disciple believers, we obey a direct command of Christ. We are expected to disciple believers intentionally and systematically.

One way to help men become better disciples of Christ is through small groups. A small group can be defined as an intentional gathering of from 3 to 12 men who commit themselves to work together to become better disciples of Jesus Christ. Small groups assume a variety of formats and focuses: prayer groups, Bible studies, mission fellowships, evangelistic teams, ministry teams, new-member groups, house churches, Covenant Groups, and many others. All are good examples of small groups because they are marked by a commitment to a shared process of growth as disciples.

How Small Groups Function

Three principles operate to make small groups effective for growing disciples.

The goal is discipleship. The primary purpose of small groups is to make disciples, in obedience to Christ's command in Matthew 28:19-20.

The foundation is leadership. Disciples are not made unless disciple makers help them learn about and live the Christian life. Therefore, leadership is essential to small-group ministry. One goal of small groups should be to help equip effective leaders who can make disciples through small groups. So while the goal of small groups is discipleship, the foundation of small groups is leadership.

The structure is community. People can learn and grow only in an atmosphere of love and acceptance. Community is not one aspect of group life; it is the very structure within which the group operates. That atmosphere is Christian community. A healthy community produces healthy disciples.[15]

The church is intended to be a growing, dynamic organism, a community of growth. Small groups perfectly lend themselves to growth in discipleship because men learn best when they are part of a caring and committed community. They grow in understanding and obedience when—

- they share experiences with other learners;
- they are held accountable to one another for continued growth;
- they are affirmed and loved;
- they are part of a structure that allows for and reinforces growth.

Good small groups can provide each of these benefits and much more by allowing men to learn through both affirmation and challenge. In a small group, men regularly meet with committed fellow disciples. They learn together, formally and informally. They have opportunities to get to know one another better, to pray for one another, and to help meet needs. They can look for opportunities to reach out to others outside their group, either in the church or the community. Their shared experiences reinforce what they are learning together.

As their knowledge of one another deepens, men challenge one another to take new steps in growth. Through this process they each become a source of encouragement to the others in life's difficulties. As their commitment to obeying Christ and their gratitude for His work in their lives increases, men find new reasons to worship and thank God together. From this kind of community comes a sense of joyful challenge that draws other men to join them as they seek opportunities for growth. The possibilities are limitless.[16]

Benefits of Small Groups

Men's small groups are important for the following reasons.

1. Small groups allow men to share their lives (see 1 Thess. 2:8-9).
2. Small groups provide a place to function as genuine Christians in the following ways.
   - Accept one another (see Rom. 15:7).
   - Love one another (see John 13:34-35).
   - Encourage one another (see 1 Thess. 5:11).
   - Build up one another (see 1 Thess. 5:11).
   - Carry one another's burdens (see Gal. 6:2).
   - Confess sins to one another (see Jas. 5:16).
   - Pray for one another (see Jas. 5:16).
   - Instruct one another (see Rom. 15:14).
3. Small groups are a means to grow men in Christ (see Col. 1:28).
4. Small groups maintain the momentum of a large event.
5. Small groups offer accountability in the following areas.
   - In the past week have I been with a woman in a compromising situation?
   - Have all of my financial dealings been filled with integrity?
   - Have I viewed or read sexually explicit material?
   - Have I achieved the goals I set for Bible study and prayer?
   - Have I spent quality time with and given priority to my family?
   - Have I fulfilled the mandates of my calling?
   - Have I just lied to you?

Leader Qualifications

A men's small-group leader should have the following characteristics.

- Personal commitment to discipling men in Christlikeness.
- Reliance on the Holy Spirit for power to equip men to live biblical teachings in every area of life. Discipleship seeks to transform a man's innermost being. This change is possible only as God works in and through him.
- Commitment to growing personally through prayer and Bible study. Small groups are only one element of personal discipleship. A group leader must model personal discipline if he is to guide others to walk with Christ.

- Trainable nature. Group leaders are constantly aware of their weaknesses and seek to strengthen them through personal development.
- Leadership qualities. Group leaders need the abilities to see the big picture of ministry and to encourage others to become a part of that picture.
- Vision. A group leader needs a vision of the radical transformation men's small groups can make.
- A love for others. A group leader needs to love men and to want to see them grow in their relationships with Christ.
- Applicable gifts and interests.
- Ability and desire to work with others as a team.[17]

Starting Small Groups

1. Enlist a coordinator whose spiritual gift is administration. He is responsible for training leaders, conducting monthly leaders' meetings, and enlisting men for groups.
2. Enlist small-group leaders.
3. Provide leader training.
4. Create windows for group start-ups:
   - Following a conference, retreat, or seminar
   - Following a wild-game dinner
   - Following a sports league
5. Find a convenient location for your meetings and, if possible, plan to meet weekly to ensure continuity of learning and enthusiasm.
6. Plan the meetings for 1½ to 2 hours to allow time for discussion. Often, more insights are gained through interaction than through the material itself.
7. In choosing men for the group, pray that God will lead you to men He is giving hearts for investing their lives in others. Men with whom we desire to share Christ's love are not projects but special individuals with unique needs and concerns. Ministering to them takes time and effort. Personally invite men to join. Here are criteria you can use for placing interested men in men's small groups.
   - Men who have already developed relationships with one another
   - Men who are in similar stages of life or who have common backgrounds
   - Men in different stages of life or with different backgrounds
   - Men who live or work close to one another or who share a common time to meet
   - Men who are interested in the same topic
   - Men who share a common spiritual focus: relationships, Bible study, evangelism training, accountability, discipleship, and so on
8. From the start, make clear that the group's primary goal is not fellowship, although that is an enjoyable by-product. The purpose is to prepare men to take an active part in fulfilling Jesus Christ's Great Commission and in living the Great Commandment.
9. In addition to regularly scheduled group meetings, consider a special outreach event in conjunction with it. This would provide an opportunity to bring together men with whom God has given you a special relationship, either to introduce them to Christ or to help them grow in their faith.
10. Publicize effectively.
    - Ask the pastor to promote men's small groups.
    - Feature testimonials from men who have participated in small groups.
    - Use personal invitations and visits.
    - Plan a kickoff event.
    - Show promotional videos.
    - Include a men's small-group informational brochure in new-member packets.
    - Place announcements in the church newsletter.
    - Distribute "Small-Group Enrollment Sheet" (p. 90) at men's gatherings.
11. Stay flexible.
12. Form groups from existing ministries.
    - Working committees in men's ministry
    - Existing groups that meet monthly
13. Throughout the group experience, impress on the men that evangelism and discipleship are long-term processes and that when the series concludes, it does not mean the end of their involvement in these biblical callings. In fact, it will probably be just the beginning of a fulfilling, fruitful new ministry.

Leading a Small-Group Study

Discipleship courses are small-group studies offered anytime during the day, on weeknights, or on weekends. The day and time are usually set in cooperation with the men's ministry group leader, who coordinates with the church staff. Be flexible and work with others to find a time that is convenient for all. Sunday and Wednesday work best for men who are regular church attenders, because it means one less night away from home. Home discipleship groups can meet anytime.

A men's small-group leader should keep these points in mind when leading a men's study.

1. Men come and go. If you begin a 12-week study, be prepared to lose participants during the course. Men go on business trips and juggle their schedules to attend their children's school programs or ball games. Don't let the fact that someone might be able to attend only six or eight sessions keep you from letting him enroll. The man may be motivated to finish the study independently. Direct him to another group if one meets at a time that better fits his schedule. Teach whomever the Lord gives you.
2. Be flexible. You may have to change locations or dates to accommodate a church emphasis, such as a revival, or to swap rooms with another group.

SMALL-GROUP ENROLLMENT SHEET

Name: _____

Address: _____

Home phone: _____ Work phone: _____

Times you can meet:

	Morning	**Evening**
Sunday	_____	_____
Monday	_____	_____
Tuesday	_____	_____
Wednesday	_____	_____
Thursday	_____	_____
Friday	_____	_____
Saturday	_____	_____

What kind of men's small group would you be interested in?

❑ Relationships   ❑ Accountability

❑ Bible study   ❑ Discipleship

❑ Evangelism training   ❑ Covenant

❑ Other: _____

What topics would you be interested in discussing in a men's small group?

_____

_____

_____

_____

What are some of your personal interests and hobbies?

_____

_____

_____

_____

Are you already in a men's small group? ❑ Yes ❑ No

If so, when and where does it meet, and what topic are you discussing?

_____

_____

_____

3. All men have different learning skills. Do not turn group sessions into minilectures. Do not simply rehash what men read in their workbooks during the week. Use a variety of teaching techniques. Encourage discussion, use audiovisuals, and involve men in reading and praying. Use role plays, case studies, art projects, and games.

4. Avoid church talk or church words. Use simple words. Always define Bible terms. Use analogies and illustrations that are relevant to men's circumstances.

5. Some men talk more than others. Do not let anyone monopolize the session. Tell the talkative man that you would like to hear from the others and that you need his cooperation to do so. Consider assigning the man extra reading to present at a later session.

6. Be a credible leader. Genuineness and sincerity build credibility. Demonstrate concern and compassion.

7. Set aside 1½ to 2 hours for the group session.

8. Supply resource materials. Discipleship courses produced by LifeWay Christian Resources include leader guides that can be used with little or no modification (see "Resources," p. 95). Prepare handouts ahead of time. Encourage each man to purchase a workbook. Check with the church to learn whether budget money is available to supplement the cost. Also provide necessary supplies and equipment.

9. Use the following ideas to encourage men to complete reading assignments between group sessions.
   • Suggest a buddy system. Encourage pairs of men to hold each other accountable during the week.
   • Have men discuss their daily work together in pairs or small groups.
   • Do not shame a man who does not complete daily work. On some days he may be doing well just to attend the session. The fact that he wants to have fellowship with believers and to hear God's Word may have to suffice. Explain that participation in discussion is enhanced by doing the homework. Other types of men's small groups are more suitable for men who want only to talk and pray.[18]

Dealing with Conflict in a Small Group

Because we are human, interpersonal issues complicate relationships in a men's small group. Think of these complications as a great way to work on Christlike relationships and to help the group leader grow.

Colossians 3:12-14 tells us how to deal with conflicts among believers: "As God's chosen people, holy and beloved, clothe yourselves with compassion, kindness, humility, gentleness and patience. Bear with each other and forgive whatever grievances you may have against one another. Forgive as the Lord forgave you. And over all these virtues put on love, which binds them all together in perfect unity" (NIV). The group leader must

be sensitive to each man's needs and must lead group members to work together to make peace. He should follow these strategies for peacemaking.
• Give up your rights, just as Jesus did.
• Don't be afraid to confront.
• Avoid arguments. If a man wants to argue about doctrine, direct the conversation to walking in the Spirit, which brings self-control. Explain that the Holy Spirit is our Teacher, and we should respect what God is teaching each man. Ask two or three in the group to do additional study and to be prepared to lead a discussion in the next session. It is not who wins the argument that counts but who wins a brother and how the discussion affects each man's lifestyle over the long haul.
• Try your best not to be partial to anyone.
• Above all, do everything in love.[19]

Concluding a Men's Small Group and Beginning a New One

As the quarter (three months) comes to an end, discuss with your group what to do next. Keep in mind the goals of a small group: to provide a circle of ongoing support and accountability for applying biblical teachings to life and to use the strength gained from accountability to develop disciples. With these purposes in mind, decide together whether you should expand, continue, or begin new small groups. Schedule training sessions for new group leaders.

DISCIPLING MEN THROUGH SUPPORT GROUPS

Every man has experienced some type of dysfunction in his past. Support groups help men heal emotional scars and past memories that interfere with their growth in Christ. Support groups help men deal with issues like low self-esteem, grief, divorce, codependency, and addiction. Relationships with others greatly improve when men learn why they behave as they do and how their behavior affects others.[20]

Men's support groups help men fulfill the mandate given in Galatians 6:2, to "bear one another's burdens" (NASB), in the following ways.
• By touching an undercurrent of hurt that exists in men's lives. Men look for and need support in times of divorce recovery and job loss, in their search for meaning and purpose in life, and in their efforts to recover from addictions.
• By touching unchurched men where they hurt, such as ministering to single fathers who have custody of their children only on weekends or holidays
• By leading group members to faith in Christ
• By helping men through life crises
• By building strong church leaders
• By encouraging men to stop running from problems and start facing them in God's strength

Here are steps for beginning a men's support-group ministry.

1. Pray at every point.
2. Make a commitment to train.
3. Secure church approval.
4. Select a support-group coordinator.
5. Train leaders and facilitators.
6. Determine men's needs, both churched and unchurched.
7. Order materials (see "Resources," p. 95).
8. Decide on child care.
9. Set a time, date, and place.
10. Set fees.
11. Publicize.
12. Get started.
13. Schedule an introductory meeting.
14. Commit to a group covenant.
15. Provide sabbaticals, ongoing training, and support.
16. Evaluate the process.
17. Continue the process of prayer, preparation, and ministry.

A support-group facilitator is not a teacher in the usual sense; instead, he assists and guides participants to discover solutions. His primarily roles are to provide encouragement and support for group members, to guide the group to stay focused on the topic, to nurture a sense of openness and inclusiveness in the group, and to refer an individual who needs professional help. The facilitator has an added advantage when he has had firsthand experience with the issue being addressed.[21]

LifeWay Christian Resources produces the LIFE Support Series, which offers resources suitable for helping men both inside and outside the church (see "Resources," p. 95).

DISCIPLING MEN THROUGH COVENANT GROUPS

A Covenant Group provides men a context for experiencing discipleship and accountability. A Covenant Group is composed of seven men who have made a commitment to the Covenant and desire accountability in living it. A Covenant Group has two main purposes.

1. To provide men a circle of ongoing relationships for support and accountability in applying the Covenant to life
2. To use the strength gained from accountability to develop disciples

The Covenant

At the heart of the Covenant Group discipleship process are six Covenant points.

I will be a person of integrity (see 2 Tim. 2:15). My attitudes and actions reveal my commitment to live the life Christ modeled—to speak the truth in love, stand firm in my convictions, and be honest and trustworthy.

I will pursue consistent spiritual growth (see Col. 2:6-7).

The Christian life is a continuing journey, and I am committed to a consistent, personal relationship with Jesus Christ, to faithful study of His Word, and to regular corporate spiritual growth through the ministry of a New Testament church.

I will speak and live a relevant, authentic, and consistent witness (see 1 Pet. 3:15). I will tell others how Jesus changed my life, and I will seek to live a radically changed life each day.

I will seek opportunities to serve in Christ's name (see Luke 4:18-19). I believe that God desires to draw all men into a loving, redeeming relationship with Him. As His disciple, I will give myself to be His hands to reach others in ministry and missions.

I will honor my body as the temple of God, dedicated to a lifestyle of purity (see 1 Cor. 6:19-20). Following Christ's example, I will keep my body healthy and strong, avoiding temptations and destructive personal vices. I will honor the gift of life by keeping myself sexually pure and free from addictive drugs.

I will be godly in all things, Christlike in all relationships (see Col. 3:12-14). In every relationship and every situation I will seek to live as Christ would. I will work to heal brokenness; value each person as a child of God; avoid petty quarrels and harsh words; and let go of bitterness and resentment, which hinder Christian love.

The Covenant Group

Participation in a Covenant Group may establish a life-long desire to be part of a biblically based, mutually supportive discipleship group. Men who have committed to be growing disciples are encouraged to participate in a Covenant Group.

Covenant Groups differ from other groups in the following ways.

1. Covenant Groups are Covenant-based.
2. Mutual accountability is included to encourage living the Covenant.
3. Covenant Groups are characterized by trust and confidentiality.

A Covenant Group can meet whenever it is convenient for its members. What is important is that the group makes a mutual agreement to be faithful in meeting regularly. Sporadic meetings and occasional attendance will not build the trust and spirit that lead to growth and continual support.

Covenant Groups should not compete with the church's ongoing ministries. They are tools to strengthen, enlarge, and add depth to your men's ministry and your church.

How long should a Covenant Group last? Committing to one quarter (three months) may be best. At the end of that time members can recommit and continue, divide and start new groups, or form different groups. Designating an ending time will avoid slow death by attrition. It may also encourage other men to commit to accountability through a Covenant Group.

Becoming Involved in a Covenant Group

Any man who desires and makes a commitment to become Christlike can become involved in a Covenant Group by embracing the Covenant and by seeking to live the Covenant daily. A man can be introduced to a Covenant Group through different discovery experiences. Discovery experiences allow men the opportunity to explore making a commitment to the Covenant. A leader may freely share from his own experiences about applying different aspects of the Covenant in his daily life, but he does not impose expectations on interested men. The leader should challenge men to a positive response to follow Christ in discipleship, but the challenge should come in the form of a better understanding of the biblical meaning of Covenant living and by exposure to the leader's life and spiritual journey.

If it is not practical or advisable to offer a group event to introduce men to this concept of discipleship, meet with them on a one-to-one basis and share the basic ideas of the Covenant and the Covenant-Group process. Then invite them, either individually or as part of a small group, to learn more about the Covenant and to begin applying its principles in their lives.

Covenant-Group Leaders

Seeking the cross of Christ is a commitment that is almost impossible to implement without partnership with others on the same journey. A leader of a Covenant Group is called a champion. A champion seeks to follow Christ; yet he has a sense of the right direction to go, and he can invite other men to come along with him. A secondary goal of Covenant Groups is to help men develop leadership character and skills that will prepare them for a lifetime commitment of seeking Christ. Therefore, identifying and supporting champions are key elements to successful Covenant Groups. As a Covenant-Group ministry grows, it becomes increasingly important to recruit, train, and support champions within the groups. The first champions will need to be recruited directly. However, as Covenant Groups begin functioning, the group leader will want to seek other potential champions within the group.

The champion's role is like that of a guide. He sets the tone for the importance and urgency of seeking Christ together. His willingness to be committed, open, encouraging, and attentive is crucial to the group's progress. He should ask the Lord what He wants for the group and should be committed to carrying it out.

Another important function of a champion is to encourage relationship building among group members. During meeting times he must try to balance the time given to each man, asking the quiet ones questions and

finding issues all of the men have in common. Outside the weekly meeting the champion should commit to build relationships with group members. He should eat lunch with them, pray for them, or leave a verse on their answering machines or email. Relationships within the group will continue to grow as others follow his example. Lifelong friendships frequently develop through Covenant-Group experiences.

It is helpful for leaders to have orientation before beginning. Champions of Covenant Groups need orientation about the content of the Covenant, the purpose of the group, how to encourage and motivate fellow group members to greater obedience to Christ, and what to do if problems develop. Orientation should be conducted in the context of a formal training process. Key orientation elements include—
* elements of the Covenant and living the Covenant daily;
* Covenant-Group process from entry point to lifelong discipleship;
* expectations for the champion, including accountability for the development of the Covenant Group and support he can expect as he guides the group;
* confidentiality;
* group-facilitation skills—not providing answers but facilitating dialogue and discussion that lead to members' discovery of God's truth. Champions should be prepared to lead this process from love and respect for men under the Holy Spirit's guidance and direction.

Champions also need regular support. Only when they begin to function in their leadership roles will they identify areas in which they need assistance. One way to provide this support is through a weekly meeting with champions. This time may be spent—
* renewing commitments to Covenant Groups as a discipleship process;
* studying a particular aspect of the Covenant;
* planning together;
* developing skills in areas such as facilitating groups, dealing with difficult people, finding and befriending persons without relationships with Christ, introducing Covenant Groups to others, using questions to facilitate discussion, and developing Covenant Groups.

Leadership development is a key element in the success of continued Covenant Groups. As you identify, recruit, and train leaders, recognize that your role is that of a discipler. Only as you develop a personal commitment to the Covenant will you develop rich relationships with champions. Preparing a champion is a process of modeling for him a growing disciple's lifestyle, mentoring him to develop a similar lifestyle, and multiplying new disciples through him.

How to Begin a Covenant Group

First, you need seven men who are committed to living the Covenant. You can find existing disciples or develop new ones at church or in your community. You will be walking in accountability and friendship with these men, so carefully consider who should be in the group. Do not limit yourself only to close friends, but including complete strangers could hinder honesty and openness. It takes time to build relationships to the level of true accountability. Seek men who trust one another and who feel comfortable together.

In the first couple of meetings plan an orientation to the Covenant, as well as a getting-to-know-you time. Many men in your group may be familiar with Covenant Groups through a discovery experience. Review the Covenant. At your first meeting you may want to use a creative commitment ceremony for the Covenant, such as having members recite it together and sign their names. Set basic guidelines and goals for the time you spend together, such as expectations for confidentiality and communication during group meetings.

Find ways to serve outside your weekly meetings. Discuss possible ministry opportunities and choose a specific target group to serve and witness to. Adopt a ministry together, and serve and pray for those people.

What Takes Place in a Covenant Group?

Men in a Covenant Group should meet regularly to hold one another accountable to the Covenant. Your group will share personal faults, struggles, and temptations, as well as joys and victories. The group should encourage members to seek repentance and forgiveness in areas of weakness, as well as celebrate in times of victory. To accomplish these goals, include time for prayer and encouragement. Never forget to emphasize the importance of confidentiality in the group. Men will not be open and honest if they cannot trust that what they share will be kept within the group.

The following are important components of a Covenant-Group meeting.

Accountability. "Speak the truth in love" (Eph. 4:15, NIV). Love one another enough to speak the truth to one another, "as iron sharpens iron" (Prov. 27:17, NIV). Whenever you see a group member outside the group meeting, ask how he is doing with the Covenant points that day. During the Covenant-Group meetings, share your struggles and triumphs of the week.

Prayer. "Pray without ceasing" (1 Thess. 5:17, NIV). Being a growing disciple involves prayer. Individually and as a group, commit to pray for one another, your friends, your family, your city, your church, your leaders, and other Covenant Groups. As group members share their concerns and praises, make a prayer list to guide your prayers for one another during the week.

Encouragement. Encouragement goes hand-in-hand with accountability. As you keep one another accountable, speak uplifting verses, give testimonies of God's faithfulness, and thank one another for being supporting and loving. As a Covenant-Group leader, particularly be devoted to encouraging group members. Build relationships. Devote yourself to being a resource for the men.

As you decide together how to use the time during Covenant-Group meetings, carefully consider the group's needs. Try to challenge the men at the end of each meeting with something practical they can do to exercise a Covenant point. One recommended activity is to memorize the six Scriptures of the Covenant points. Take one verse at a time and say it together several times in the meeting. Have each man write it on a piece of paper and tape it on his mirror or next to his bed. Encourage the men to live with the verse for a week and to meditate on it as they try to memorize it.[22]

GROWING DISCIPLES WEEKEND

Not all men are motivated to join a discipleship group. One way to motivate men for discipleship is to offer a Growing Disciples Weekend, which provides men a brief but meaningful and challenging discipleship experience and previews a discipleship course they may wish to study after the weekend. Growing Disciples Weekends may be offered to preview the following discipleship courses.

- *Experiencing God*
- *MasterLife*
- *Life in the Spirit*
- *The Kingdom Agenda*

Administrative materials are available for church leaders who wish to offer Growing Disciples Weekends (see "Resources," p. 95).

SPIRITUAL-GROWTH RETREATS

Consider an annual spiritual-growth retreat or workshop to disciple men. Although improved technologies have increased our capacity to stay in touch, men sorely lack close relationships. A retreat provides an uninterrupted time to experience community and personal relationships. The male context at a retreat allows men to process truths and challenges that apply uniquely to men, affirming their gender-role distinctives.

Marriage, parenting, sexual purity, serving Christ at work, personal finances, and anger are just some topics of concern for men today. An excellent retreat for men is Legacy Builders, which teaches the biblical basis of manhood. Men learn how to apply the principles of being God's man to home, church, and marketplace. *Legacy Builders* materials are available for study, including guidance for retreat leaders (see "Resources," p. 95).

Continue the momentum God created at the retreat by beginning a small-group study of *The Man God Uses*, *The Kingdom Agenda: Experiencing God in Your Workplace*, *Faithful and True*, or *The Seven Seasons of a Man's Life* (see "Resources," p. 95).

BIBLE STUDIES

Regularly plan special Bible studies to give a boost to men's spiritual lives and to reach those who do not attend ongoing discipleship groups or Sunday School classes. Consider Bible studies on these occasions.

• Monday night, followed by football on TV
• Men's luncheons or breakfasts at a restaurant
• Men's prayer meetings and leadership meetings

Make sure the leader presents a lesson that is practical, relatively brief, and complete within itself. Ideal resources that could be adapted are *The Kingdom Agenda: Experiencing God in Your Workplace, The Seven Seasons of a Man's Life, The Man God Uses, In God's Presence,* and *Living God's Word* (see "Resources" on this page). You might also consider teaching a book of the Bible through a series of self-contained Bible studies. Men should feel free to follow the entire series or to drop in as their schedules allow.

✷ Use the one-year calendar on page 96 to schedule ministries for establishing men to spiritual maturity during the next year. Be sure to check the church's calendar so that you do not double book with any key church activities.

✷ Use the ministry timeline on page 97 to list each task needed to establish each ministry action. Also include a projected beginning date for each task.

✷ Step back and consider:
• Are your goals realistic? ❏ Yes ❏ No
• Are your goals measurable? ❏ Yes ❏ No
• Are your goals open to evaluation? ❏ Yes ❏ No
• Are your goals flexible? ❏ Yes ❏ No

Resources

Arnold, Jeffrey. *The Big Book on Small Groups.* Downers Grove: InterVarsity, 1992.

Bailey, Waylon, and Tom Hudson. *Step by Step Through the Old Testament.* Nashville: LifeWay, 1991.

Biehl, Bobb. *Mentoring: Confidence in Finding a Mentor and Becoming One.* Nashville: Broadman & Holman, 1996.

Blackaby, Henry, and Richard Blackaby. *When God Speaks.* Nashville: LifeWay, 1995.

Blackaby, Henry, and Tom Blackaby. *The Man God Uses.* Nashville: LifeWay, 1998.

Blackaby, Henry T., and Claude V. King. *Experiencing God: Knowing and Doing the Will of God.* Nashville: LifeWay, 1990.

Bright, Bill, et al. *Seven Promises of a Promise Keeper.* Nashville: Word, 1994.

Burton, Jim. *Legacy Builders Retreat Preparation Manual.* Memphis: The Brotherhood Commission of the Southern Baptist Convention, 1995.

_____. *Legacy Builders Retreat Participant Workbook.* Memphis: The Brotherhood Commission of the Southern Baptist Convention, 1995.

Dalbey, Gordon. *Healing the Masculine Soul.* Nashville: Word, 1991.

Edgemon, Roy T., and Steve Williams. *Leading Discipleship in a Church.* Nashville: Convention, 1998.

Experiencing God Weekend Manual. Nashville: LifeWay, 1997.

Getz, Gene A. *Men of Character.* Nashville: Broadman & Holman, 1995.

Gorsuch, Geoff, and Dan Schaffer. *Brothers: Calling Men into Vital Relationships.* Colorado Springs: NavPress, 1994.

Growing Disciple Weekend Administrative Guide. Nashville: LifeWay, 1997.

Hassler, Betty, comp. *Leading Criminal Justice Ministry: Bringing Shalom.* Nashville: LifeWay, 1998.

Hendricks, Howard, and William Hendricks. *As Iron Sharpens Iron: Building Character in a Mentoring Relationship.* Chicago: Moody, 1995.

Hunt, T. W., and Claude V. King. *In God's Presence.* Nashville: LifeWay, 1994.

_____. *The Mind of Christ.* Nashville: LifeWay, 1994.

The Kingdom Agenda Weekend Manual. Nashville: LifeWay, 1997.

Laaser, Mark. *Faithful and True: Sexual Integrity in a Fallen World.* Nashville: LifeWay, 1996.

Lea, Thomas D., and Tom Hudson. *Step by Step Through the New Testament.* Nashville: LifeWay, 1992.

Life in the Spirit Weekend Manual. Nashville: LifeWay, 1997.

MasterLife Weekend Manual. Nashville: LifeWay, 1997.

McQuilkin, Robertson. *Life in the Spirit.* Nashville: LifeWay, 1997.

Moore, Waylon B. *Living God's Word.* Nashville: LifeWay, 1997.

Morley, Patrick. *The Seven Seasons of a Man's Life.* Nashville: LifeWay, 1996.

Neighbour, Ralph, and Bill Latham. *Survival Kit: Five Keys to Effective Spiritual Growth.* Nashville: LifeWay, 1996.

Rogers, Mike, and Debi Rogers. *The Kingdom Agenda: Experiencing God in Your Workplace.* Nashville: LifeWay, 1997.

Stand Firm (magazine). Nashville: LifeWay Christian Resources.

Weber, Stu. *Four Pillars of a Man's Heart: Bringing Strength into Balance.* Sisters: Multnomah, 1999.

Wilkinson, Bruce. *The Seven Laws of the Learner.* Nashville: LifeWay, 1994.

_____. *Teaching with Style: Applied Principles of Learning.* Nashville: LifeWay, 1988.

Willis, Avery T., Jr. *MasterLife.* Nashville: LifeWay, 1996–97.

Notes

[1]Adapted from William Carr Peel, *What God Does When Men Pray* (Colorado Springs: NavPress, 1993), 89–90.

[2]Ibid., 91.

[3]Adapted from Howard and William Hendricks, *As Iron Sharpens Iron: Building Character in a Mentoring Relationship* (Chicago: Moody, 1995), 183. Used by permission.

[4]Adapted from Betty Hassler, comp., *Leading Criminal Justice Ministry: Bringing Shalom* (Nashville: LifeWay, 1998), 27–28.

[5]Michael Rickenbaker, *Breaking into Prison* (Nashville: Spirit & Truth, 1993), 125.

[6]Adapted from Hassler, *Leading Criminal Justice Ministry,* 28.

[7]Hendricks, *As Iron Sharpens Iron,* 131. Used by permission.

[8]Adapted from Robert S. McGee, et. al., *Breaking the Cycle of Hurtful Family Experiences* (Nashville: LifeWay, 1994), 22–23.

[9]Hendricks, *As Iron Sharpens Iron,* 139,153. Used by permission.

[10]Adapted from Hassler, *Leading Criminal Justice Ministry,* 28.

[11]Ibid., 28–29.

[12]Ibid., 29–30.

[13]Adapted from Hendricks, *As Iron Sharpens Iron,* 255–56. Used by permission.

[14]Ibid., 184–87. Used by permission.

[15]Adapted from Jeffrey Arnold, *The Big Book on Small Groups* (Downers Grove: InterVarsity, 1992), 15–17.

[16]Ibid., 23–24.

[17]Adapted from *CrossSeekers: Covenant Living, Leader's Guide* (Nashville: LifeWay Christian Resources, 1998), 13.

[18]Adapted from Hassler, *Leading Criminal Justice Ministry,* 30–31.

[19]Adapted from *CrossSeekers,* 13.

[20]Adapted from Hassler, *Leading Criminal Justice Ministry,* 31.

[21]Roy T. Edgemon and Steve J. Williams, *Leading Discipleship in a Church* (Nashville: Convention, 1998), 18.

[22]Adapted from *CrossSeekers,* 11–12.

ESTABLISHING MEN TO SPIRITUAL MATURITY: ONE-YEAR CALENDAR

SEPTEMBER	OCTOBER	NOVEMBER
DECEMBER	JANUARY	FEBRUARY
MARCH	APRIL	MAY
JUNE	JULY	AUGUST

ESTABLISHING MEN TO SPIRITUAL MATURITY:
MINISTRY TIMELINE

1.

Ministry	Tasks	Beginning Date	Date Completed

2.

3.

Ministry	Tasks	Beginning Date	Date Completed

4.

POINT 5C

◆

Provide Entry Points: Equip Men for Ministry

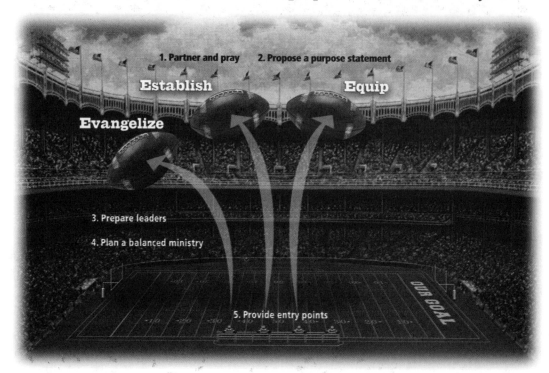

Point 5C offers a variety of ideas for equipping men for ministry. Prayerfully consider ways your men's ministry can use or adapt the ideas to involve your men in meaningful Christian ministry. A calendar and a timeline are provided at the end of the point to assist the leader with planning.

START A HANDYMAN MINISTRY

"I thought everybody had forgotten about me," said the 87-year-old man. He lived alone and had no close family to care for him. Living on a fixed income with no one to help him around the house had taken its toll. His roof leaked, the ceiling was falling, and a myriad of smaller things needed repair. The man called a local church, and his needs were relayed to the men's ministry coordinator.

The men's handyman ministry came to the rescue. Some men came and looked at the man's home, arranged funds to buy roofing materials, and completed the work. Twenty-four hours later the man was in a dry home once again. This help was a meaningful testimony to an elderly man who thought he had been forgotten. This is only one exam-

ple. Many elderly, disabled, and single-parent households need help. A handyman ministry can be an excellent way to bear witness of God's love. Ministering to the physical needs of people allows you an opportunity to minister to their spiritual needs as well. A handyman ministry is a physical way to minister to persons who need to see God's love in action.

Your men's ministry can implement a handyman ministry in your community by following these steps.

1. Check your church's insurance policy to make sure it covers this type of activity.
2. Survey your men to discover how many are willing to take part. You can start with as few as two or three. Select a leader.
3. Determine what kinds of skills the volunteers have. It is not required that everyone know how to make home repairs. Volunteers who know how to do a given job can guide others.
4. Find persons in your community who need help. Check with your Baptist association's director of missions or your local department of social services for names. Sometimes county health departments also know needs.

Each one should use whatever gift he has received to serve others, faithfully administering God's grace in its various forms.

1 Peter 4:10, NIV

5. Hold a volunteer meeting to discuss each project before you commit to do it.
6. Schedule a time with the person needing help and do the work. Don't be discouraged if you must start with a small number of volunteers and no money. Often, persons who cannot work can support the handyman ministry with money or tools. Members from other churches may also want to join in the work.

Focus on meeting spiritual as well as physical needs. When you have finished a job, present a Bible signed by all team members and have prayer with the recipient of your help. Make sure the person knows that you have helped in Jesus' name. Invite the person to your church and seek other ways to minister to his or her spiritual needs.

START A FIREWOOD MINISTRY

Andrea was both frightened and ashamed. Her husband lived with her and their four children, but he abused alcohol and refused to supply even their most basic needs. Winter was coming, and they had no firewood to heat their home, which also needed repairs. A woman in a local church told the men's ministry team leader about Andrea's circumstances and asked whether the men would be willing to assist. A mission project was born. The men provided the needed fix-up touches and five cords of wood. Andrea's home, as well as her heart, was warmed. Her self-image had been so poor that it was difficult for her to believe that anyone would care about her, a stranger in desperate need of help. Because of the men's compassion, Andrea found God's love and committed her life to Christ.

That was almost two years ago. Since then, the men have learned about a number of families who need firewood. What began as a one-time mission project blossomed into a number of similar projects. So far, the men have provided wood for nearly two dozen families in the area.

If your men's ministry has men who are willing to volunteer, a few chain saws, and the use of a truck, you have the resources to help persons like Andrea. As you make homes warmer through your labor, you will find abundant opportunities to share Christ. The time and effort you expend to provide for physical needs will open hearts to Jesus' provision for spiritual needs. When someone asks why anyone would make the effort to help, you have an open door to share the gospel.

Warm months are an excellent time to stockpile wood for use in wintertime. If you have a ready stockpile, you will be able to begin making deliveries as soon as you learn about someone who needs help. Organize a volunteer schedule so that you can keep a supply of wood available for use as needed. You might also want to begin a tree-removal service as a secondary ministry.

People gladly donate usable wood in order to have a tree removed.

You can implement a firewood ministry in your community by following these steps.
1. Recruit volunteers who share your desire to provide firewood to those who need it. Select a leader. Establish a monthly meeting time to discuss needs and to pray for God's guidance in projects.
2. Look for church members and community residents who need assistance. Likely prospects include single, physically disabled, sick, elderly, unemployed, homebound, and financially disadvantaged persons or families; widows; and newcomers to your area. County agencies may be able to provide names of persons who need help.
3. Obtain the consent of the person or family needing help.
4. Watch for other ways to minister to families you discover. Some persons desperately need help with things other than heat. Some also need home repairs or transportation to medical appointments. If other groups of volunteers in your church are willing to help with additional needs, share with them the needs you find.
5. Meet spiritual needs by visiting and praying with the recipients of the work.

START A GARDEN MINISTRY

Bernice was a disabled woman who had three children to care for. Because her government check wasn't enough to make ends meet, a Sunday School class at a nearby church had been helping the family. When the men of the church offered to help Bernice grow her own food, she eagerly accepted the opportunity. Even though she was disabled, she would get down in the dirt on her hands and knees and inch along the furrows of her garden plot. Her children were not yet in their teens, but they helped too. The family members were much happier to grow the food themselves than to accept a financial handout.

The men of the church decided that they could help feed the hungry by planting small garden plots the disadvantaged could use to grow food. Instead of giving persons a handout, the church members taught them how to produce vegetables and to preserve the fruits of their labor for later use.

A retired physician who owned a farm on the outskirts of town offered an acre for the project and tilled the land. The men's ministry divided the land into smaller plots for individual gardens. Sunday School classes and mission groups located those needing assistance. Church members helped the recipients plant, weed, harvest, can, and freeze the produce.

Hungry and malnourished persons are all around us. Although America is one of the wealthiest nations in the world, 1997 U.S. Census statistics report that more than 35 million of its residents (13.3 percent of the population) live below the poverty level. Your men's ministry can help meet the needs of hungry persons in your community by following these steps.

1. Select a coordinator who is willing to give time and energy to the project.
2. Determine your resources. Is someone in your church willing to donate the use of land? Do some members of your congregation have tillers or garden tools they will let you use? If no one in your church has land you can use, contact local farmers. In the city you might have a rooftop or container garden. Contact your county-extension service for more information about alternative gardening techniques.
3. Recruit volunteers to labor with, advise, and provide transportation for the needy.
4. Find persons who need help. Your Sunday School organization may be able to locate the needy, or you can contact your county's social-services department. Carefully select the recipients.
5. Start the project. Make sure an experienced gardener is on hand to tell the volunteers when to plant, fertilize, weed, and so on.
6. Watch for additional opportunities to minister. Your men's ministry might see that it needs to offer additional ministries, such as nutrition or budgeting classes. Perhaps certain groups in the church might "adopt" a recipient family.
7. Meet spiritual and physical needs that become evident.

Do not wait until spring to begin a garden ministry. This project requires planning and coordination. Begin the project in the fall so that you will have time to find available land.

SUPPORT A HABITAT-FOR-HUMANITY MINISTRY

Juanita, a single mother of two children, was paying $350 for an apartment grossly inadequate for her family's needs. Her income was enough to get by on but not enough to save money for a down payment on a home of her own. Three years ago Juanita and her children moved into a new, immaculate three-bedroom house, for which she pays $250 a month. Best of all, it will one day be hers. Who made Juanita's dream of home ownership possible? Habitat for Humanity and many volunteers from churches.

Habitat for Humanity builds houses for low-income persons who qualify for help. The pride of home ownership is a new, empowering feeling for persons who buy the houses with interest-free, 20-year mortgages, as is knowing that they helped build their own homes. The recipients must contribute at least five hundred hours of labor on their own homes or on other Habitat houses. They must also have adequate income to make

house payments and must have been steadily employed for the past two years.

Thousands of families in your state desperately need houses in which to rear their children, but they cannot get started without assistance. Your men's ministry can help one of these families by providing financial resources and volunteers to build a house in partnership with the local Habitat for Humanity organization. Larger churches can sponsor a single house with their own resources or can join others already involved in a project. Smaller churches can work together with several other churches to build a Habitat house.

Because building a house through Habitat for Humanity is a large project, it requires the cooperation of many men. Following is a brief outline of how your men's ministry can get started. The Habitat serving your area can provide more detailed instructions.

1. Survey your church for interested volunteers. Also find out whether any volunteers are professional plumbers or electricians and would be willing to work free or at cost. Habitat will give them a receipt for an in-kind, tax-deductible contribution.
2. Discuss the possibility of getting involved in a Habitat project with your church's appropriate committee (missions, ministry, benevolence, etc.). Follow your church's procedure for bringing recommendations to the congregation.
3. Designate an individual or a committee as the Habitat contact. If you don't know whether a Habitat for Humanity serves your area, call the headquarters (see "Resources," p. 103).
4. Divide the various tasks: funding, coordinating volunteers, scheduling, providing food, and so on.

Habitat for Humanity can provide materials to distribute in your church. Habitat also provides speakers and resource persons to churches on request.

Many state Baptist conventions sponsor Baptist Builders, which organizes men to construct churches. Contact your state Baptist-convention office for information.

SUPPORT A MEALS-ON-WHEELS MINISTRY

Nelson, 96 years old, is confined to a wheelchair. Because Nelson cannot cook for himself, every day a volunteer from Meals on Wheels brings him a hot meal. Nelson is extremely thankful for this service and praises the Lord for sending persons who care for him this way. Nelson has been receiving meals for two years. Before church volunteers worked with Meals on Wheels to start a route in Nelson's community, no one provided this service.

Meals on Wheels is an organized system that prepares and delivers hot meals each weekday to persons who cannot cook for themselves and have no one to cook for them. Recipients are the homebound, elderly, or disabled. The meals, which are prepared by a food-service company, are delivered to distribution sites throughout the country, where volunteers pick them up and deliver them to homes. Volunteers work in teams of two to deliver meals. Most volunteers deliver meals one day a month.

Your men's ministry can help by volunteering to fill vacancies on routes in your area. Substitutes are also needed. You can get involved in Meals on Wheels by following these steps.

1. Contact the Meals-on-Wheels office in your area and inquire about their needs. Meals on Wheels might want you to supplement an existing route or to start a new one. If you don't know whether your area has a Meals-on-Wheels program, call your county's Council on Aging or social-services department.
2. Recruit volunteers from your church. Note the days your volunteers are available and how often they are willing to deliver meals. Give this information to Meals on Wheels.

CONDUCT FAMILY-MINISTRY PROJECTS

Encourage your men to sponsor a Family-Ministry Week at your church. This is a week set aside to encourage families to minister in their neighborhoods. Listed below is a variety of projects families can choose from. Use each opportunity to share Christ.

- Make care packages for your mail carrier, your school-bus driver, or the persons who pick up your garbage. Let them know how much you appreciate the important jobs they do.
- Read your local newspaper to discover persons who have had tragic losses from fire, flooding, death, and so on. Determine ways your family can minister to these persons.
- Cook for the hungry. Check with the feeding locations in your area to learn whether you can help buy supplies, prepare meals, or clean up.
- Remove snow from the walks and driveways of the elderly and disabled.
- Cut a neighbor's lawn or shrubbery free of charge.
- Serve free refreshments for neighbors doing yard work.
- Offer to baby-sit so that a couple in your neighborhood can go out to eat.
- Give gifts to a neighbor who has had a baby.

START A FOOD-DISTRIBUTION MINISTRY

Ministering to human needs can unite the men of your church and greatly strengthen its witness for Christ. Christ, who identified with the poor, based His judgment of individuals on their ministries to the needy: " 'I was hungry and you fed me' " (Matt. 25:35, GNB). James 2:14-16 and 1 John 3:16-18 further underscore ministering to the needy as a sign of a believer's true faith and love.

A food-distribution ministry may take the form of a food pantry, a soup kitchen, or a voucher system for purchasing groceries.

The following general procedures may be used to start this ministry.

1. Begin with a man who senses a call and has a commitment to this type of ministry.
2. Coordinate your efforts with other ministry groups in the church, such as the church staff, mission council, or benevolence committee, to maximize your strengths and to avoid duplication.
3. Build a network of contacts with other churches and agencies in the area who provide food and other services to the needy. You may want to begin by assisting one of these entities rather than beginning your own ministry. By coordinating your efforts, you can help prevent the abuse of the system by a few, providing all needy people an equal opportunity to be served.
4. Discover community needs by establishing personal contacts with the food-stamp office; Aid to Families with Dependent Children (welfare); the county health department's Women, Infants, and Children (WIC) Supplemental Nutrition Program; senior-adult centers (Elderly Nutrition Program); and public schools.
5. Begin small and publicize to the community. For example, you may choose to distribute food only on a given Saturday of each month. Sunday is also a good time to provide a hot meal for the needy since most other agencies are closed.
6. Survey resources.
   - Involve Sunday School classes in recruiting volunteers and contributing food items.
   - The North American Mission Board and several state Baptist conventions have hunger funds. Funds may also be requested through your Baptist association.
   - Salvageable food can be purchased at food banks. Sometimes churches are needed to serve as distribution centers for surplus food commodities.
7. Establish policies for the days of operation, the number of times an individual or a family can be served, and referral procedures.
8. Develop a simple record-keeping system that allows you to register those seeking assistance and to maintain a list of items needed for special diets, such as infant formula or food for diabetics.
9. Secure storage space and stock the pantry. Provide groups a list of items needed.
10. Train your workers in how to share the gospel. Include gospel tracts in grocery sacks.

For guidance in starting and maintaining a food-distribution ministry, consult your state Baptist men's ministry department. Its staff can also advise you on how to develop a disaster-relief team. Additional information can be secured from your Baptist association's church and communities ministries director, the North American Mission Board, and the Ethics and Religious Liberty Committee (see "Resources," p. 103).

DEVELOP A MINISTRY TO PRISONERS

Your men's ministry can reach out to prisoners and their families and share Christ's love with them in a number of ways.

Prison worship services. This God-given opportunity holds great promise if the worship leader prepares with inmates' perspectives in mind. He should do appropriate research about inmates, interview prison officials, and talk with inmates to determine needs and approaches.

Be sure to have guests, handouts, and new materials approved by the chaplain or program director. Never announce anything until it has been approved. Provide ample time for music, because inmates love to sing. Also plan time for personal prayer needs and concerns.

Develop a balanced preaching ministry that includes discipleship as well as evangelism. Emphasize concepts like how to love and be loved, forgive and be forgiven, live ethically, and take responsibility for actions. Help inmates visualize ways to become useful members of God's family.

Use common language, stories, drawings, and objects to keep attention. Close the service with a question-answer time as appropriate. Have a strategy in place to follow up with inmates who make decisions for Christ. Be sure to obtain their names and identification numbers.[1]

Discipleship. Use the ideas in point 5B in this manual to disciple inmates by offering small groups, mentoring, and support groups.

Angel Tree. This popular ministry to offenders' families during Christmas was started by Prison Fellowship. The names, ages, and needs of inmates' children are placed in envelopes on a Christmas tree. Persons then take envelopes and purchase gifts for the children.

Your men's ministry can implement an Angel-Tree ministry by following these steps.

1. Select an Angel-Tree coordinator. Have the coordinator contact the Angel-Tree Ministry of Prison Fellowship (see "Resources," p. 103). Prison Fellowship provides training, the required forms, and a comprehensive how-to manual.
2. Recruit and train volunteers.
3. Your church coordinator will receive the forms listing each child's name and address and the guardian's phone number. The coordinator may choose to assign

volunteers by task: some to make initial calls, some to do follow-up calling, and some to deliver gifts. Or the coordinator may assign each volunteer a few families, and the volunteer is responsible for those families from the initial contact to the delivery of gifts. The church members who give gifts or the volunteers who deliver them are provided the imprisoned parent's name and address so that they can tell the inmate what gifts their child received.
4. When you deliver the Christmas presents, present a Bible and have a short prayer with the child's caregivers. Ask if they would like to visit your church.

Literacy. Approximately 40 percent of incarcerated Americans are unable to read above a fourth-grade level. Christians have a wonderful opportunity to reach persons with the gospel as they learn to read or improve their reading skills. Often, General Educational Development (GED) classes are offered in institutions. Inmates need literacy training before they can seriously hope to pass the GED exam. Volunteers can also tutor for the GED exam.

Literacy classes for offenders' families can also be offered. Tutoring individuals to develop reading skills could also be part of a literacy class. Specific training is available for persons wishing to be involved in literacy.

English as a Second Language (ESL) classes. ESL instruction meets a need of minorities inside or outside correctional facilities. Often, these classes need to precede GED studies or job training.

Recreation. Some volunteers find sharing Christ easier in informal settings, where friendships can lead to witnessing opportunities. If the prison in which you want to minister has a recreational facility but no program, consider offering organized recreational activities. If inmates can be transported with proper security to another facility or to your church, plan activities such as basketball, volleyball, and softball.[2]

For more guidance on ministering to prisoners, refer to *Leading Criminal Justice Ministry: Bringing Shalom* (see "Resources," p. 103).

OTHER IDEAS FOR EQUIPPING MEN FOR MINISTRY

1. Offer a course on discovering and using spiritual gifts.
2. Offer a weekly men's ministry prayer group.
3. Hold Pastor Appreciation Day.
4. Work in the church nursery or extended session.
5. Do automotive or lawn maintenance for senior adults.
6. Staff a community clothes closet.
7. Provide career counseling for job seekers.
8. Offer mission education for men and boys.
9. Assist with church-building-and-grounds maintenance.

10. Provide help for men in crisis because of homelessness, alcoholism, drug addiction, or other problems.
11. Provide help for single fathers, such as encouragement, fellowship, seminars, and emergency child care.
12. Provide clothing for indigent men seeking employment.
13. Prepare a free prayer breakfast once a week.
14. Offer a car-care-and-safety course for teens that includes a Christian testimony.
15. Provide visitation, spiritual help, and practical ministry for the homebound.
16. Provide lawn care for senior adults.
17. Provide transportation for senior adults.
18. Prepare and distribute baskets of food to needy families during holidays and at other times.
19. Provide a Christmas toy store for children whose parents cannot afford toys.
20. Provide free help with income-tax preparation at the church during specified hours.
21. Distribute donated furniture and other household items.
22. Provide church facilities in which homeless persons can sleep on cold or stormy nights.
23. Host an appreciation day for law-enforcement personnel and firefighters.
24. Give Bibles to groups such as college students, military personnel, firefighters, athletic teams, law-enforcement officers, and nurses.
25. Provide a free car wash, sharing that Christ's love is the reason for this service.
26. Organize a prayer team to support the pastor.[3]

✳ Use the one-year calendar on page 104 to schedule ministries for equipping men for ministry during the next year. Be sure to check the church's calendar so that you do not double book with any key church activities.

✳ Use the ministry timeline on page 105 to list each task needed to establish each ministry action. Also include a projected beginning date for each task.

✳ Step back and consider:
- Are your goals realistic? ❑ Yes ❑ No
- Are your goals measurable? ❑ Yes ❑ No
- Are your goals open to evaluation? ❑ Yes ❑ No
- Are your goals flexible? ❑ Yes ❑ No

Resources

Angel Tree, a Ministry of Prison Fellowship; P.O. Box 17500; Washington, DC 20041-0500; *www.prisonfellowship.org*; (800) 398-HOPE.
Ethics and Religious Liberty Commission of the Southern Baptist Convention; 901 Commerce Street; Suite 550; Nashville, TN 37203-3696; (615) 244-2495; *www.erlc.com*.
Graham, Franklin. *Living Beyond the Limits*. Nashville: Thomas Nelson, 1998.
Habitat for Humanity International; 121 Habitat Street; Americus, GA 31709; (800) HABITAT; *www.habitat.org*.
Hassler, Betty, comp. *Leading Criminal Justice Ministry: Bringing Shalom*. Nashville: LifeWay, 1998.
Hemphill, Ken. *Serving God: Discovering and Using Your Spiritual Gifts*. Nashville: LifeWay, 1995.
The North American Mission Board of the Southern Baptist Convention; 4200 North Point Parkway; Alpharetta, GA 30022-4176; (770) 410-6000; *www.namb.net*.
Roesel, Charles L., and Donald A. Atkinson. *Meeting Needs, Sharing Christ*. Nashville: LifeWay, 1995.
Wilkes, Gene. *Jesus on Leadership: Developing Servant Leaders*. Nashville: LifeWay, 1996.

Notes

[1]Neron Smith, unpublished training materials, n.d., n.p., n. pag.
[2]Adapted from Betty Hassler, comp., *Leading Criminal Justice Ministry: Bringing Shalom* (Nashville: LifeWay, 1998), 83–84.
[3]Selected ideas adapted from Charles L. Roesel and Donald A. Atkinson, *Meeting Needs, Sharing Christ* (Nashville: LifeWay, 1995), 159–68.

EQUIPPING MEN FOR MINISTRY:
ONE-YEAR CALENDAR

SEPTEMBER	OCTOBER	NOVEMBER
DECEMBER	JANUARY	FEBRUARY
MARCH	APRIL	MAY
JUNE	JULY	AUGUST

EQUIPPING MEN FOR MINISTRY:
MINISTRY TIMELINE

	Ministry	Tasks	Beginning Date	Date Completed
1.				
2.				
3.				
4.				

POINT 5D

◆

Provide Entry Points: Extend Men on Mission

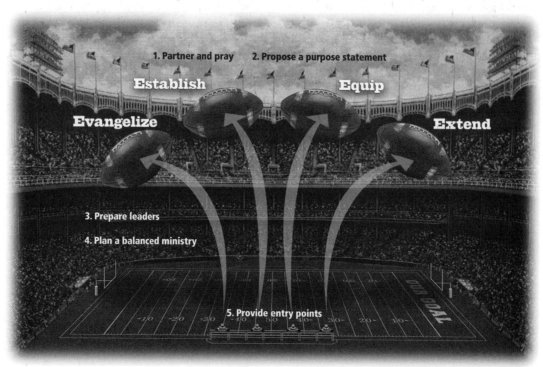

Point 5D offers a variety of ideas for extending men on mission. Prayerfully consider ways your men's ministry can use or adapt the ideas to involve your men in reaching the world for Christ. A calendar and a timeline are provided at the end of the point to assist the leader with planning.

PARTICIPATE IN A STATE-SPONSORED VOLUNTEER MISSION PROJECT

Magnolia had lived in the same farmhouse for all of her 86 years. But the years had taken a toll on her old homeplace. On a very limited income, Magnolia was hardly able to pay her monthly bills, let alone make many needed repairs. An elderly brother offered all the help he could, but year after year major repair needs went unheeded. Both the bathroom and kitchen floors were rotting, the result of a leaky water heater. Outside some siding needed to be replaced, and the whole house needed to be scraped and painted.

Some church members heard about Magnolia's need through their state Baptist convention. Working together with the local Baptist association and the county's Council on Aging, the church members began working to fix Magnolia's home, including providing the materials needed to repair it. Young and old alike

> *"Open your eyes and look at the fields! They are ripe for harvest."*
>
> John 4:35, NIV

pitched in. Five days later, Magnolia's house had been transformed, complete with repairs and a new paint job.

Like Magnolia, many people are barely surviving on a fixed income while their homes are falling down around them. Many churches are filled with people who have the skills needed to help—contractors, roofers, carpenters, plumbers, electricians, and other building professionals. Some may be willing to work with other church members to accomplish the needed repairs.

Your men's ministry can get involved in an in-state mission project by following these steps.

1. Contact your state Baptist convention to learn about possible mission projects.
2. Decide which project your men's group will adopt, taking into consideration the talents volunteered by church members. Discuss how your group will raise the necessary funds to do the work. Set a date for beginning the project.
3. Examine the site beforehand, meeting with the homeowner; a representative from the Baptist association; and perhaps a representative from a local support agency, such as the Council on Aging or a social-services department. You may want to bring someone to do an additional estimate.

4. Make arrangements with the local Baptist-association representative for lodging and meals during your stay. In many cases local Baptist churches act as host churches, providing lodging and meals for volunteers. The associational representative may also be able to help you make contacts with local building-supply companies.

5. Arrange for building supplies to be delivered.

6. Arrive and do the work.

7. When the project is completed, present a Bible signed by team members. Pray with the homeowner.

PARTICIPATE IN A NATIONAL VOLUNTEER MISSION PROJECT

Listed below are national volunteer mission opportunities that are available through the North American Mission Board of the Southern Baptist Convention.

Construction. Individuals and groups construct between 300 and 350 new church buildings a year. All skills are needed, especially finish carpenters. Remodeling is also done in some mission centers and mission churches.

Nonconstruction. Individuals and groups do community surveys, Vacation Bible School/Backyard Bible Clubs, house parenting, resort work, and other ministries for mission areas. Most volunteers serve from one week to four months.

Mission Service Corps. Individuals serve for four months or more in a variety of volunteer mission assignments. MSC volunteers can start churches; strengthen churches; or serve on church, associational, or state staffs. These volunteers commit to serve at least 20 hours a week.

Disaster relief. Individuals are trained to help in times of disaster. The training is very specific and is coordinated through state disaster-relief directors. Ministries include mass care (feeding and cleanup), child care, damage assessment, long-term rebuilding, and others. Volunteers are deployed through the state disaster-relief director. Contact your state Baptist convention for information on how your men can get involved in disaster-relief ministry.

National Fellowship of Baptists in Missions. These affinity groups minister through their skills, interests, vocations, and avocations. Fellowships center on education, criminal justice, and construction.

Campers on Mission. This program involves persons who enjoy combining camping and missions. Volunteers help with all volunteer programs, including construction, disaster relief, fairs, and resort missions.

Volunteers for national mission projects pay all of their expenses. For information call the North American Mission Board of the Southern Baptist Convention (see "Resources," p. 109). Your state Baptist convention's men's ministry department can also provide assistance.

PARTICIPATE IN AN INTERNATIONAL VOLUNTEER MISSION PROJECT

The International Mission Board of the Southern Baptist Convention can help you involve your men in international missions. The board sends not only career missionaries but also volunteers throughout the world to build, preach, teach, heal, and love in Christ's name.

Your men can use their gifts for God's glory in literally hundreds of ways. Projects range from two weeks to four months and are available in the following areas.

Evangelism	Human Needs
• Partnership missions	• Community health
• Revivals	• Hunger relief
• Witnessing	• Water relief (well
• Sports	drillers)

Medical	Church Growth
• Physicians	• Discipleship
• Nurses	• Leadership conferences
• Dentists	• Church planting
• Paramedics	• Witness training

Education	Construction
• English teachers	• Church construction
• Math teachers	• Emergency repairs
• Pastor-training schools	

If your men feel that they have no skills, the greatest gifts they can offer are their love for people and their desire to share Christ.

It is not difficult to go on mission. If you or your men have never volunteered before, call your Baptist associational and state-convention offices. Ask them whether you can serve in a project they are coordinating with the International Mission Board.

If your association or state is not involved in a project when you call, contact the International Mission Board, which will send you a list of current needs. After you have reviewed the list and have sought the Holy Spirit's leadership in selecting a project, the International Mission Board will assist you in planning for this project by providing you with orientation material, country information, and guidance for spiritual preparation.

Examine the chart "International Mission Opportunities" on page 108 to discover some of the possibilities available to your men.

JOIN AN INTERNATIONAL PRAYER NETWORK

Mission researchers have identified more than two thousand unreached people groups that make up the Last Frontier of world evangelization. Reaching these peoples who live in spiritual darkness and do not have access to the gospel light is difficult and taxing but not impossible. It requires prayer and commitment, persis-

INTERNATIONAL MISSION OPPORTUNITIES

Opportunity	Action
1. Pray that God will cultivate in you a heart for His mission. Pray that God will send workers into the fields. 2. Pray for specific missionaries.	1. Contact the 24-hour prayer line at (800) 395-PRAY or CompassionNet, a worldwide prayer network, at *www.imb.org*. 2. Adopt missionaries by calling (800) 999-3113, extension 1470, or emailing *adoptamissy@imb.org*. Write encouraging letters to missionaries or pray for them. Request a missionary directory from the International Mission Board that gives missionaries' names, addresses, and birthdays.
3. Pray for specific people groups. 4. Give to missions.	3. Adopt a people group by calling (888) 462-7729. 4. Give through the Cooperative Program. Give to the Lottie Moon Christmas Offering.
5. Give to development projects.	5. Call (800) 362-1322 or see the list of strategic priority needs at *www.imb.org*.
6. Give to human-needs projects.	6. Order *Wonder Working Power 1998*, a publication of the International Mission Board, by calling (800) 866-3621.
7. Go as a career missionary.	7. Call (888) ICANGO1 or email *initial.contacts@imb.org* with questions about missionary service.
8. Go on a short-term assignment through the Journeyman program or International Service Corps.	8. Journeyman program: call (800) 789-GOYE, visit the Web site at *www.imb.org/go/jman*, or email *journeyman@imb.org*. International Service Corps: call (800) 789-GOYE, visit the Web site at *www.imb.org/go/isc*, or email *isc@imb.org*.
9. Go as a volunteer on a short-term project.	9. Call (800) 888-VOLS, visit the Web site at *www.imb.org*, or email *vimd@imb.org*.
10. Become a global priority church.	10. Call (877) 462-4721.

tence and involvement. And it will happen as Christians pray and obey.

PRAYERplus Partnerships allow Christians to be more directly involved in reaching the people of the Last Frontier. Local churches, as well as groups like men's ministries, can be linked with a specific Last Frontier people group to pray for and work with missionaries as they take the gospel to these people.

The PRAYERplus Covenant

A group of men commits to—
- PRAYER without ceasing for the opening and evangelizing of its people group;
- plus obedience to God in whatever He directs the group to do in coordinated effort with the International Mission Board to evangelize its group.

Steps to a PRAYERplus Partnership

1. Pray about participating.
2. Consult with the International Mission Board to identify a Last Frontier people group.
3. Commit to partner with this unreached people group.

To become involved in PRAYERplus, write to the International Prayer Strategy Office; the International Mission Board of the Southern Baptist Convention; P.O. Box 6767; Richmond, VA 23230-0767; call toll free (888) 462-7729; or email *PRAYERplus@imb.org*.

ORGANIZE A BAPTIST MEN ON MISSION UNIT

Baptist Men on Mission is a mission-education ministry for men ages 18 and older. The unit is the basic organizational grouping for the coordination of mission awareness, prayer, and mobilization of Christian men in the local church. This coordination can also be incorporated into existing men's enrichment or ministry experiences such as builders, witnessing or prayer teams, deacons, sports teams, and others. A unit may become involved in missions in the following ways.
- Sponsoring or planting new churches
- Becoming involved in mission education
- Providing regular opportunities for volunteer mission service
- Praying for missionaries and mission concerns
- Giving to mission causes

The unit may meet monthly or as often as needed.

The unit is church-based, which means that it is supported by, accountable to, and an integral part of a church's mission and ministry. Unit meetings, ranging from 45 minutes to 1½ hours, can meet in a home, church, restaurant, or outdoors. A fellowship meal or project can be incorporated to allow time for informal visiting, meeting visitors, and creating a bond of unity. The presence and participation of the pastor and related staff members can encourage men's mission education.

Resources that support regular unit meetings and other unit activities include *Missions in Motion*, which is a quarterly planning kit that contains a videotape with a leader guide, and pupil books (see "Resources" on this page). Leaders use the kit to promote the elements of awareness, prayer, and mobilization in a five-step process: invite, introduce, instruct, involve, and inform.

Each meeting provides opportunities for men to investigate, develop, practice, and implement an on-mission strategy for participating with God in reconciling the world to Himself. Baptist Men on Mission commits to pray for workers in the field as well as for participants' personal awakening to the needs of people around them. Unit activities present opportunities to implement strategies learned and to mobilize men to carry the gospel to their world. An additional resource for individual or unit on-mission growth is *On Mission*, a bimonthly magazine that shares examples of on-mission principles at work through individuals and strategies (see "Resources" on this page).

Here are ideas for starting Baptist Men on Mission.

1. Enlist a group of men to pray faithfully for the commitment of men to be on mission through Baptist Men on Mission.

2. Enlist a coordinator to work with other men to develop strategies in mission awareness, prayer, and mobilization.

3. Contact the North American Mission Board for a resource catalog and suggested resources for the unit meeting. Order *Missions in Motion* as the curriculum resource and *On Mission* magazine as a support resource for the unit meeting (see "Resources" on this page).

4. Schedule dates, times, and places for unit meetings.

5. Publicize the meetings, make announcements, and utilize personal contacts to communicate a specific meeting's content or the unit's purpose so that men will know why it is important to participate.

6. Gather men to plan the unit meeting and to pray for God's leadership to be experienced.

7. Start the meeting on time. Keep the meeting moving. Be sensitive to the Holy Spirit. Finish on time.

8. Involve men in the meeting through prayer groups, testimonies, announcements, and project participation.

9. Encourage men to pray for one another as they strive

to live godly lives, share the gospel, and plant churches.

✴ **Use the one-year calendar on page 110 to schedule ministries for extending men on mission during the next year. Be sure to check the church's calendar so that you do not double book with any key church activities.**

✴ **Use the ministry timeline on page 111 to list each task needed to establish each ministry action. Also include a projected beginning date for each task.**

✴ **Step back and consider:**
  • **Are your goals realistic?** ❑ **Yes** ❑ **No**
  • **Are your goals measurable?** ❑ **Yes** ❑ **No**
  • **Are your goals open to evaluation?** ❑ **Yes** ❑ **No**
  • **Are your goals flexible?** ❑ **Yes** ❑ **No**

Resources

The Commission (magazine). Richmond: The International Mission Board of the Southern Baptist Convention. Order by calling (800) 866-3621.

Dempsey, Margaret McCommon. *The On-Mission Team: Mobilizing Your Church for the Great Commission*. Alpharetta: The North American Mission Board of the Southern Baptist Convention, 1999.

Greenway, Roger S., and Timothy M. Monsma. *Cities: Missions' New Frontier*. Grand Rapids: Baker, 1989. Out of print.

The International Mission Board of the Southern Baptist Convention; P.O. Box 6767; Richmond, VA 23230-0767; (804) 219-1000; email *imb.org*; visit *www.imb.org*.

Missions in Motion. Alpharetta: The North American Mission Board of the Southern Baptist Convention. Order by calling (800) 233-1123 or by visiting *www.namb.net/catalog*.

Nix, William. *Transforming Your Workplace for Christ*. Nashville: Broadman & Holman, 1997.

The North American Mission Board of the Southern Baptist Convention; 4200 North Point Parkway; Alpharetta, GA 30022-4176; (770) 410-6000; fax (770) 410-6054; visit *www.namb.net*. For volunteer information call (800) 462-8657 or visit *www.namb.net/vols*.

On Mission (magazine). Alpharetta: The North American Mission Board of the Southern Baptist Convention. Order by calling (800) 233-1123 or by visiting *www.namb.net/catalog*.

On Mission with God (monthly video series). Richmond: The International Mission Board of the Southern Baptist Convention. Order by calling (800) 866-3621.

Perkins, John M. *Beyond Charity: The Call to Christian Community Development*. Grand Rapids: Baker, 1993.

Robinson, Darrell W. *People Sharing Jesus*. Nashville: Thomas Nelson, 1995.

Rogers, Mike, and Debi Rogers. *The Kingdom Agenda: Experiencing God in Your Workplace*. Nashville: LifeWay, 1997.

EXTENDING MEN ON MISSION:
ONE-YEAR CALENDAR

SEPTEMBER	OCTOBER	NOVEMBER
DECEMBER	JANUARY	FEBRUARY
MARCH	APRIL	MAY
JUNE	JULY	AUGUST

EXTENDING MEN ON MISSION:
MINISTRY TIMELINE

Ministry	Tasks	Beginning Date	Date Completed
1.			
2.			

Ministry	Tasks	Beginning Date	Date Completed
3.			
4.			

POINT 6

◆

Promote God's Victories and Kick Off New Ministries

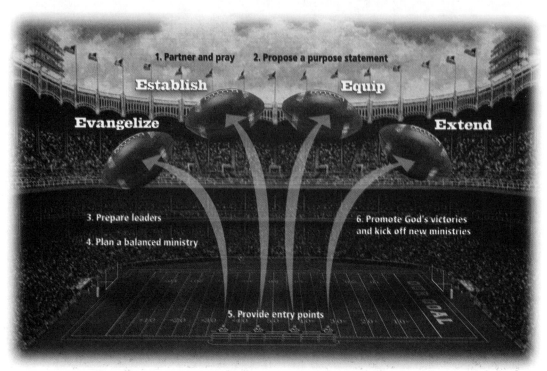

1. Partner and pray   2. Propose a purpose statement

Establish   **Equip**

Evangelize   **Extend**

3. Prepare leaders

4. Plan a balanced ministry

6. Promote God's victories and kick off new ministries

5. Provide entry points

Picture yourself in a football stadium filled with one hundred thousand screaming fans. Two teams playing for the conference championship are deadlocked. The final seconds are ticking off the clock when the home team breaks through to score the go-ahead touchdown. A celebration immediately breaks out. Enthusiastic fans cheer wildly, and total strangers exchange hugs and high-fives. The band plays the school song with gusto, and people join in with what remains of their voices. On the field the player who just scored the touchdown kneels in the end zone to express his thanks to God. He then stands and salutes the lineman who threw the block that cleared the way for him to cross the goal line. His teammates surround him, patting him on the helmet, shoulder pads, and … well, you get the picture. Soon the players along the sideline race onto the field to join the celebration.

Just as celebrating a victory with others is the ideal conclusion to a football game, celebrating the victories Jesus Christ has won in the lives of men is an important and necessary aspect of men's ministry. Men's ministry leaders will want to use every means available to give

> *O sing to the Lord a new song, for He has done wonderful things, His right hand and His holy arm have gained the victory for Him.*
>
> Psalm 98:1, NASB

God the glory for the lives He is touching and changing through the men's ministry. As you read point 6, you will understand the significance of gathering men together to promote God's victories and to kick off new ministries. It all starts with a winning game plan—one that carries out God's purposes for the men in your church and community. In developing your game plan, you will learn how to develop a comprehensive one-year calendar for your men's ministry. You will also examine other planning suggestions for developing a budget, advertising the ministry, and evaluating men's ministry activities. These responsibilities are carried out behind the scenes. But just as an off-season weight-training program and preseason conditioning determine a football team's readiness for a new season, these preparatory activities can significantly affect the results of your men's ministry during the coming year.

ADOPT A BIBLICAL MODEL

When the early church began to be persecuted in Jerusalem, many believers fled to other cities. As they dispersed, they carried the message of the gospel with them. Many in Antioch responded to the good news about Jesus Christ and received Him as their Savior (see Acts 11:19-30). This new church grew in strength and numbers and was used mightily by God. The reason this church became so influential for Christ was its devotion to God through prayer and fasting and its willingness to follow the Holy Spirit's leading. In one of their times of worship, the Spirit of God communicated that Barnabas and Saul were to be "set apart" for a special assignment (see Acts 13:2). Everyone agreed and showed their support. Notice that God led those involved in this ministry to kick off the new ministry together: "While they were worshiping the Lord and fasting, the Holy Spirit said, 'Set apart for me Barnabas and Saul for the work to which I have called them.' So after they had fasted and prayed, they placed their hands on them and sent them off" (Acts 13:2-3, NIV).

In the verses that follow that commissioning service, Luke described all God accomplished through Barnabas and Saul on their first missionary journey. These two men witnessed the power of the gospel changing lives by breaking down the walls that divided different ethnic, cultural, and religious groups. After they completed the work, Barnabas and Saul returned to Antioch to share with the church how God had worked through them to save many souls and establish several churches: "From Attalia they [Barnabas and Saul] sailed back to Antioch, where they had been committed to the grace of God for the work they had now completed. On arriving there, they gathered the church together and reported all that God had done through them" (Acts 14:26-27, NIV).

This model church, which was used so mightily by God to spread the gospel to the Gentiles, serves as an example for men's ministry today in at least three ways.
1. Men's ministry should seek God above the things of the world.
   • A God-centered men's ministry should practice biblical unity. Acts 11:23 says that Barnabas "saw the evidence of the grace of God" (NIV) in Antioch, which means that he saw Jewish and Gentile believers worshiping together. The gospel has the power to break down barriers that separate men.
   • Leaders need to devote themselves to seeking the Lord. Acts 13:2 says, "While they were worshiping the Lord and fasting" (NIV), the Holy Spirit communicated to them. As we saw in points 1–3 in this manual, from a right relationship with God comes clear direction for your ministry. All of your ministry plans and activities need to grow from God's revealed purposes.
2. It is important to kick off new ministries together. The entire body in Antioch was involved in praying for the safety and success of the mission. Acts 13:3 states that "after they had fasted and prayed, they placed their hands on them [Barnabas and Saul] and sent them off" (NIV).
3. Evaluate your ministry and report the results to the body. In other words, promote God's victories. Acts 14:27 tells us that Barnabas and Saul returned to Antioch and "reported all that God had done through them" (NIV).

✳ **One implication of the Bible passage you have studied is that from a right relationship with God comes clear direction for your ministry. This step is a prerequisite to anything else you do in your men's ministry. In point 2 of this manual you were urged to spend a day in spiritual preparation for planning your men's ministry. What direction did you receive during that time with God?**

_____

_____

✳ **In point 1 of this manual you were encouraged to establish ongoing prayer for your men's ministry. What direction has prayer provided for your men's ministry thus far?**

_____

_____

PRACTICE BIBLICAL UNITY

A Spirit-led men's ministry reflects the power of the gospel to change lives. In this kind of ministry Christ breaks down the barriers that separate men from one another, just as Barnabas witnessed Jews and Gentiles worshiping together (see Acts 11:23). Spirit-led men intentionally take steps to demonstrate their love and acceptance of others who are different. Jesus Christ moves them out of their comfort zones to embrace men of other races, denominations, and backgrounds.

No church vote or human effort can bring about biblical unity. Unity is the result of the Holy Spirit's work in men's hearts. That is why it is so important for your men's ministry to be intentional in its efforts to reach out to other races and denominations in your community. In Galatians 3:28 the apostle Paul stated that "there is neither Jew nor Greek, slave nor free, male nor female, for you are all one in Christ Jesus" (NIV). Paul's emphasis was on the power of the gospel to bring together different types of people.

Unity is important to Jesus. Shortly before His crucifixion, resurrection, and ascension into heaven, our Lord prayed that believers would " 'be one, Father, just as you are in me and I am in you. May they also be in us so that the world may believe that you have sent me. I have given them the glory that you gave me, that they may be one as we are one: I in them and you in me. May they be brought to complete unity' " (John 17: 21-23, NIV). Such unity does not come naturally to men. Left to their own agendas, men associate only with those who look and talk like themselves. In his pride the natural man sees himself as better than others. Therefore, men's ministry leaders must have a strategy for reaching out to other language/ethnic-culture groups and other denominational groups in their community. As God creates unity across racial and denominational lines, many lost men will yield to the source of unity, Jesus Christ, and will come to salvation in Him.

Men's ministry has the opportunity to demonstrate the power of the gospel to change lives. The following suggestions are offered to help men's ministry leaders develop a one-day emphasis on biblical unity. The leader may choose to spread these activities over the course of an entire year. Whether planning a one-day or year-long emphasis, begin with a prayer foundation. Also examine information about the demographics, human needs, and relationship needs in the community. This information can be obtained from the local Chamber of Commerce, school district, Baptist associational office, and/or a survey conducted by your church or men's ministry.

✳ From the information your men's ministry has gathered or from your knowledge of the community, what evidence indicates the need for unity among believers in your locale?

_____

_____

Contact other churches in your community to let them know of your concern for them. Invite them to share Christ's love with all people in the community by joining your men's group to pray for and proclaim biblical unity.

Pray for Biblical Unity
Encourage all who are to participate in the day's events to attend a one-hour prayer session. This can be a time to introduce others to your men's ministry prayer teams. The directed prayer time should include at least two elements.

Private confession. Read Scriptures like John 17:20-23 and Galatians 3:27-28 and challenge men to consider God's call to unity. Allow the Holy Spirit to guide men to confess pride, selfishness, and prejudice and to seek God. He alone can cleanse and purify their motives and thought processes and bring a fresh perspective to their efforts.

✳ **Read John 17:20-23. Check the basis of our unity as believers.**
❑ **Common church practices and a common creed**
❑ **A common relationship with God through Christ**
❑ **A common agreement**
Check your answer on page 127.

Corporate petition. The leader expresses thanks to God for bringing men to the day of reconciliation and asks for God's wisdom, blessing, and protection as they seek to demonstrate His Kingdom community in their locale.

Proclaim Biblical Unity
Prior planning for this component is essential. The time frame could include a mid-day or evening meal. If a church of one race or denomination served breakfast, ask a different group to provide lunch.

The rallying theme is "Getting to Know You." A lack of knowledge about one another is a significant hindrance to cultural understanding and acceptance. Allow from three to four hours for learning about others through interaction. The outcome depends on each man's efforts to share from his life. Activities can range from a simple, brief, one-to-one contact to the development of a network of service and support.

Each of the following activities can be completed in one day.
1. Two men and their families invite the members of a bicultural family or a family of another language/ethnic-culture group to spend the day together. The families should bring photos, videos, and other memorabilia to the gathering place. Each family should take turns sharing about themselves.
2. Enlist a Christian entertainer or a professional athlete to speak on the theme of reconciliation through Christ. Follow up with an open forum in which the goals of reconciliation are stated and discussed.
3. Hold an open forum in which men of different races and denominations form small groups to discuss the following questions.
   • Does our church have a role in empowering our community to become a caring and healing community?
   • What resources do we need to accomplish this goal, and what could we do to make it an important effort of our church?
   • To whom do we need to defend this idea? How?
Set a time to end the small-group discussions. Assure participants that they are not expected to solve all dilemmas of cross-cultural relationships and reconciliation. Inform group leaders that a representative from each table is to give a brief, personal reflection on the day's discussion or a statement the group considers valuable to the whole assembly.

4. Have men of different ethnic groups and churches observe the Lord's Supper in an intimate setting around small-group tables. Each table should be supplied with the necessary elements, which are prepared and covered in advance. At a signal by the pastor or presiding official, the elements are unveiled, and deacons, elders, or group leaders serve the Lord's Supper to the men at their tables. Use appropriate Scripture readings and hymns.

✳ **How does the Lord's Supper emphasize unity in Christ?**

_____

_____

The Lord's Supper reminds us that Christ died for all men, who are of equal value before God. By crucifying our prejudice, we can be reconciled with God and one another.

✳ **Check two ideas you would like to use to promote biblical unity through your men's ministry.**
  ❏ **Men and their families spend a day with families of a language/ethnic-culture group.**
  ❏ **Enlist a Christian entertainer or a professional athlete to speak on reconciliation.**
  ❏ **Hold an open forum to discuss reconciliation.**
  ❏ **Observe the Lord's Supper with men from other ethnic groups and churches.**
  ❏ **Other:** _____

DEVELOP A WINNING GAME PLAN

All successful football teams do a lot of off-the-field preparation. Before they play games, they recruit players, watch videos of their opponents, and formulate a game plan. In men's ministry you must also make important behind-the-scenes preparation to ensure a winning season. Three key planning steps are timelining, budgeting for, and advertising your ministry. These steps bring together all of the important preparation you have been making throughout this manual to implement a men's ministry that changes lives and honors God.

Timeline Your Ministry

In points 4 and 5 of this manual you examined the components of a balanced ministry: evangelizing men to salvation and church membership, establishing men to spiritual maturity, equipping men for ministry, and extending men on mission. But how do you put it all together in a balanced ministry? Timelining your ministry will enable you to plan exactly how to make it all happen. Plot your ministry on a calendar. Place everything in order according to the month on the calendar,

because some things can't happen until other things take place. This will also help you avoid overextending yourself, trying to do too much at the same time.

"Sample One-Year Calendar" on page 116 shows you how to bring together plans for men's ministry for an entire year. A blank calendar is provided on page 117 for timelining your men's ministry actions for one year. After you complete your calendar, distribute copies at the annual kickoff and promote monthly.

✳ **Look at the one-year calendars you completed for the four ministry areas in points 5A, 5B, 5C, and 5D (pp. 81, 96, 104, and 110). Transfer these actions to "Men's Ministry One-Year Calendar" on page 117. Is your ministry balanced, providing adequate opportunities to evangelize, establish, equip, and extend?** ❏ Yes ❏ No

If you answered no, don't feel badly. Remember:
1. Think long-term and go slowly. A well-rounded, full-blown ministry takes years to happen.
2. It is more important to do one ministry well than to do a lot of ministries poorly. When men sense that you are doing things with excellence and purpose, they will be drawn in and will involve others. Stay flexible and open to God's leading. Give God the freedom to change your plans.
3. What works in one church may not work in another. Although the principles of God's Word never change, the methods for implementing them may vary in accordance with the needs of the men in a given church or community.

Budget for Your Ministry

Another vital planning step is to develop a men's ministry budget for the year and then to make sure the money is used appropriately. A guiding budgeting principle for any God-centered ministry must be that God will support what He wants to sponsor. Follow His leadership and trust Him to provide the financial and human support needed to complete what He wants to do through your men's ministry.

Each church has a different budgeting process. Speak to the church-staff member or committee assigned to men's ministry to learn the specific budgeting process for your church. In many churches budget proposals must be presented in the early fall in order to be presented to the church for adoption and to go into effect beginning with each new calendar year. Regardless of when and how your church adopts its budget, be sure to work through the proper channels. Allow yourself enough preparation time that you can pray and plan without rushing to meet deadlines.

The suggested type of budget is a zero-based budget. In this type of budgeting your leadership team overviews

SAMPLE ONE-YEAR CALENDAR

Year: _____

Month	Extend	Equip	Establish	Evangelize
September	Men's state-mission project		Flag-football league	Annual kick-off—fish fry with sports speaker
October		Habitat for Humanity or Baptist Builders project		Witness training
November			Growing Disciples Weekend	
December		Angel Tree		
January	Men's Day	Men's Day	Men's Day / Small groups	Men's Day
February	Baptist Men on Mission units	Spiritual-gifts discovery group	Basketball league	Wild-game dinner
March			Legacy Builders retreat	
April	Disaster-relief training	Clothing ministry	Softball league	
May				Golf tournament
June		Home repairs		Father-child cookout and softball
July	Mission trip			
August	Adult mission-education leader training	Small-group leader training		Fall sports clinic

MEN'S MINISTRY ONE-YEAR CALENDAR   Year: _____

Extend	Equip	Establish	Evangelize	
				September
				October
				November
				December
				January
				February
				March
				April
				May
				June
				July
				August

the actions it has planned for the year and decides what every event and activity would cost. Try to make all of your activities and events self-sufficient so that most of your annual budget can be applied to training and promoting the ministry. This means that most expenses for men's events and discipleship are recovered through fees or offerings received from the men who participate.

Here are potential categories to consider when developing your annual budget.

- Printing—ministry brochure, newsletters, posters, letters, other printed literature
- Postage—monthly reminders, bulk mailings at the beginning of the year, committee meetings
- Leadership development—training seminars, books, tapes, meetings, appreciation dinner, retreat
- Ministry/missions—brochures, training materials, extra costs for projects

The budget will be much more realistic and helpful with adequate research and planning. Make each team leader responsible for preparing the budget for his assigned area of ministry.

You can get a visual picture of your budget by using a pie chart that reflects the percentage allocated to each ministry component. Examine the sample below.

SAMPLE MINISTRY BUDGET

Establish
Men's retreats and events like wild-game supper and fathering seminar. Includes speaker's honorarium and travel expenses

Equip
Resource support for leadership development, appreciation banquet for men's ministry prayer team and small-group facilitators

Postage, printing, office supplies

12%

10%

3%

25%

25%

25%

Promotion

Evangelize
Witness training
Sports outreach

Extend
Assistance for mission projects

✳ **Apply this idea to your men's ministry by developing a pie chart based on your ministry's projected expenses for the next year.**

Later you will need to develop a budget for a specific event you will sponsor. For example, you may want to hold a special event in the fall to create momentum for your ministry. Some areas for which you might need to budget are food, publicity, honorariums for speakers and musicians, materials, rent for a facility, and speakers' transportation and lodging. It is best to cover all costs with the registration fee.

You may want to charge participants a little extra to cover any unexpected expenses and to provide seed money for the same event next year. Keep accurate records and receipts to document everything for the church's financial secretary. Be sure that the person or committee that maintains the church budget understands that you plan to carry over a surplus from one year to the next and that it is to be designated for the men's ministry.

Advertise Your Ministry
After you have framed a program for men, raise the identity of the ministry and make sure men know what will take place. Here are ways you can get the word out about your ministry.

Ministry brochure. Create a brochure promoting the upcoming year's events and ministries. Mail copies to men in the fall and give copies to newcomers and visitors to your church.

Bulletin spots. Enlist a man to be responsible for submitting events for the church bulletin at least three weeks ahead of time.

Direct mailing. Two or three times a year send a cover letter and a brochure for an upcoming event to every man in the church.

Reminder cards. Send postcards to small groups of men to remind them of upcoming events. For example, send cards to men who have attended a Saturday breakfast fellowship to remind them of the next one.

Women's ministry. If you want men to come to an event, involve their wives. If your church has a women's ministry, regularly announce upcoming men's events and distribute registration forms during women's events and activities. The wives will usually tell their husbands.

Newsletter. A regular newsletter is a wonderful tool to share what has happened and what will happen in the ministry. Be aware, however, that newsletters require a great deal of ongoing work.

Testimonies. Ask your pastor if you can periodically have someone from your ministry share on Sunday morning what God is doing in his life as a result of your men's ministry. If you send a group of men to a national conference in the summer, for example, have a couple of men share when they get back.

Bulletin board/kiosk. Ask whether your ministry could have this full-time or could share one.

Fliers. Print fliers not just to give to the men already in your ministry but also to insert in the church bulletin or to distribute as people leave worship services.

Radio, television, and newspaper ads. If your budget allows, place ads that target men outside your church.

Word of mouth. This is the best form of advertisement. The key is to carry out your ministry with excellence. If men come to a well-orchestrated event or begin to see their lives change, they will tell other men about the ministry.

Publicity is necessary for a ministry to happen. Don't be afraid to spend energy and money on advertisement. The money you use to bring men to your activities puts them in a position to be changed by God—and that's what it's all about.

At the same time, realize that men will not attend your event merely because you do a good job publicizing it. Relationships are the key. You will reach men outside the church only if men inside the church invite them personally.

KICK OFF NEW MINISTRIES

Earlier we saw that the church in Antioch prayed for the safety and success of the mission. Then, "after they had fasted and prayed, they placed their hands on them [Barnabas and Saul] and sent them off" (Acts 13:3, NIV). It's no different in men's ministry. You have spent months praying, seeking God's direction for your ministry, and planning. Now it's time for the opening kickoff.

Key to planning ways to kick off new ministries is the concept of creating and sustaining momentum in your

men's ministry. It is tempting to offer one big event after another, like a retreat, sports banquet, father-son camp out, or national conference, without giving any thought to involving men in an ongoing process of spiritual development. Your challenge is to sustain the momentum God created through these events so that men are always aware of their goals and of the direction in which your ministry is taking them.

✳ **Men will come back and participate in your men's ministry over the long term because—**
❑ **you hold great events;**
❑ **you find a super speaker;**
❑ **you persistently invite them;**
❑ **they believe that you and the other men care about them personally;**
❑ **they feel that it offers hope for life change.**

The first three choices will get a man to come once, but only the last two will persuade a man to get involved long-term. These benefits can be offered only by men's ministries that develop a long-term approach to disciple making. Remember that Jesus mentored a small group of men for three years. He took a few men deep in their relationship with Him, because He knew that the depth of their relationship with Him would determine the breadth of their ministry.

A men's ministry must be more than just events; it must help men become mature in Christ. Almost always this will take place over a period of years in the context of significant relationships with other men. Any momentum created through an activity or event should be sustained by helping men grow in Christlikeness. Before planning an event, your leadership team should address the following questions.
- How can we help men attending the event become aware of their need to join a small group in order to grow as a disciple?
- Which studies and what types of ongoing ministry will offer the greatest variety to meet the varied needs of men?
- What concrete goals can we set for forming new small groups and becoming on-mission Christians?

Make a First Down
Special events are the easiest ways to make a first down—to create momentum for your men's ministry. Events are motivational. They create excitement, interest, and converts. They get the message out. They can give your ministry a quantum leap forward. In addition, special events are flexible. You can reshape almost anything you do—a retreat, barbecue, sports outing, or rally night—to serve a specific purpose in your ministry.

What do events accomplish?
Special events raise the identity of your ministry. If you

are starting your ministry, special large-group gatherings let men hear about the ministry and its plans.

Special events can be safe places for a new man to come or to bring another man. You can plan most special events as entry points into your ministry. A man can simply come and listen and not feel compelled to state his opinions or feelings.

Special events are opportunities for men to be gently encouraged to go deeper. When you sponsor special events, you know that new men will attend, so plan a testimony from someone who has participated in a small group. At the conclusion of the event give men the chance to take the next step beyond the large, relatively anonymous event and join a small group.

Special events develop leaders. Many key leaders in men's ministry began on a special-event committee. Activities pull men into service. Because these events have a defined start and finish and because men love activity, many men are open to getting involved.

Special events are a great way to kick off a new year. Special events give your leadership team a platform to promote the upcoming year and to register men for the activities. At your fall special events, set up publicity tables for all components of your ministry.

Good special events don't just happen. Here's what holds them together.

Specific purpose. Early in the planning process agree on the purpose of the event so that team members aren't trying to do different things. Every event you do cannot meet all of the men's needs. Be specific.

Shared responsibility. To hold an event without burning out an individual leader, build a team of men to work together. You will not only spare your sanity but will also give other men a chance to grow as leaders.

Enlist a coordinator or, better yet, co-coordinators. Having co-coordinators spreads the responsibility and builds accountability. These co-coordinators recruit the other team members. It's important when they recruit men for the team that they detail what each man will do. Men want to know what tasks they're responsible for and how long the job will take. They may not offer to help next time if they experience too many surprises.

Let's say you are planning a fall ministry kickoff at the church on a Saturday evening in late August or early September. The purposes of the get-together are to inform the men of your church about what will happen in men's ministry in the coming year and to give them an opportunity to worship, fellowship, and learn what it means to be a godly man. Team members needed for a kickoff include a chairman, publicity coordinator, budget manager, registration coordinator, facilities coordinator, hospitality coordinator, program coordinator, food coordinator, and prayer coordinator.

Timing. Plan your event with the whole church calendar in mind. Don't hinder other ministries by the tim-

ing of your event. For instance, don't plan a men's retreat the weekend after a couple's retreat or a men's event on Valentine's Day or Mother's Day.

Evaluation. If an event is worth doing, it is worth evaluating for next time. Give men time at the event to evaluate it and to make suggestions for the future.

Planning and preparation. After you have decided what you want to do and when you will do it, make a checklist for all you need to complete. Start one year in advance and list things that must be done at that time. Then move forward, listing what must be done each month. Move forward to the day of the event.

✳ **Examine "Event Planning Checklist" on page 121. Select an event you have planned for the coming year and, on a separate sheet of paper, adapt or add to the steps on the checklist to develop your own list of preparatory steps for your event.**

Ideas for special events include the following.

Retreats. Whether one or two nights, retreats provide opportunities for men to get away from life's distractions to fellowship, relax, receive good teaching, and be exposed to small groups. Many churches use retreats in the fall to kick off their programs for the year or in January or February to give a boost to the ministry.
Guidelines:
1. Decide on your purpose for the retreat.
2. Utilize facilities that will accommodate the men attending.
3. Plan your retreat one year in advance. You need time to secure a location and a speaker.
4. Leave plenty of time for the men to unwind and spend time with the Lord and with one another.

Golf outing. This one-day event is a great way to involve men outside your church and to provide fellowship for men in your church. Besides playing golf, you can have a meal together either before or after you play to share the vision of the ministry. You might want to consider having a speaker before or after golf.
Guidelines:
1. Make plans for the golf course well in advance.
2. Decide on the reason you are conducting the event. Communicate the purpose to all of the men.
3. Stay on schedule if lunch is provided.
4. Place on the carts ahead of time the rules for the game you will play. The club pro can assist.

Barbecue. This event provides an evening of food, fellowship, and fun. It could include a pig, steak, or chicken roast; music; and a short program. This event allows uninvolved men to catch a glimpse of what your ministry is about as well as a chance to spend time with other men.

Sporting event. This event provides an opportunity for a group of men to go to a sporting event together, like a

EVENT PLANNING CHECKLIST

–1 year	❑ Secure main speaker. ❑ Determine expenses for speaker. ❑ Put everything in writing. ❑ Get written confirmation from speaker.
–6 months	❑ Secure location.
–10 weeks	❑ Inspect facility—room size, seating arrangement, sound system, etc.
–6 weeks	❑ Select leaders for follow-up strategy. ❑ Plan follow-up logistics. ❑ Design promotional plan—business-card invitations, posters, bulletin inserts, promotional video (if applicable), newspaper, radio. ❑ Decide on purpose and style of music. Secure musicians.
–5 weeks	❑ Implement promotional plan: Get men to invite men over lunch, using business-card invitations. Target men outside church. Gather a team to call every man in church. Distribute bulletin inserts. Display posters. Announce from pulpit. ❑ Gather prayer team to pray daily. ❑ Begin registration and/or ticket sales. ❑ Confirm travel and details with speaker. Arrange for lodging.
–4 weeks	❑ Order books or training materials.
–3 weeks	❑ Plan refreshments/meals. ❑ Secure volunteers—greeters, registration table, book tables (if applicable), food, cleanup.
–2 weeks	❑ If desired, create retreat agenda to give to attendees. ❑ Confirm agenda with speaker. ❑ Reimburse speaker's travel (if not done). ❑ Plan airport pickup and return. ❑ Decide on emcee and review his role. Give speaker's bio to him.
At event	❑ Seminar administrator verifies props, setup of book tables, sound system, and so forth. ❑ Form groups to implement short-term follow-up strategy. ❑ Distribute comment cards. ❑ Give honorarium check to speaker. ❑ Provide an opportunity for men to enroll in small groups.
After event	❑ Provide supervision to ensure success of follow-up strategy. ❑ Meet financial obligations.
+1 week	❑ Implement plan to sustain momentum by forming small groups.

basketball, football, baseball, hockey, or soccer game. Sporting events build strong relationships.

Guidelines:

1. Purchase tickets early.
2. Decide ahead of time whether this event will be men only or will include families.

Fishing outing. This outing, a one-day or one-week event, provides a great opportunity to build relationships with other men.

Guidelines:

1. Provide a list of what to bring.
2. Make reservations far in advance.
3. Inform everyone about the type of fishing and the kind of gear needed.
4. Have someone responsible for devotionals.
5. If you use your own equipment, make sure everything works, especially if on a camping trip.

Men's rally. One of the best approaches for creating interest in men's ministry on the associational level is a Thursday-night or Saturday men's rally (not during football or deer season). Host the event at a church where you will have the enthusiastic support of a pastor who is actively involved in men's ministry and is well respected by fellow pastors. Provide inspirational music by a men's praise team or quartet and a message, followed by two 40-minute breakout conferences for men's ministry leaders. Provide a meal, perhaps prepared by a local or state disaster-relief team.

Consider bringing two or three associations together for the event. Organize a combined lay and ministerial advisory council to plan. Consider including other denominations. Be intentional in your strategy to include other races. Start by making them a part of the planning process.

Promoting through your associational and church newsletters can help get the word out, but the number one reason men attend these types of events is that a friend invited them and arranged to carpool with them. Attendance can be boosted by having an athlete, TV personality, and/or nationally known author or speaker give a Christian testimony or speak on men's issues.

Some ministries are using "The Man God Uses" as a theme. Another possibility is a biblical-unity theme, like "One Faith, One Brotherhood." Or you may want to use a Christian-legacy theme, creating an opportunity for men to spend time with their children. This focus, of course, would place limits on the length of the sessions and subject matter.

Other ideas for special events:

- Seminar on men's issues, money management, or time management
- A Christian professional athlete to speak on a Saturday morning
- Couples dinner with a speaker
- Outreach breakfast or lunch
- Barbecue
- Kickoff event
- Father-child breakfast
- Father-child bike trip
- Father-child canoe trip
- Financial weekend
- Regional men's rally
- Summer conference
- Sweetheart banquet
- Super Bowl or bowl-game party

Plan to hold an event not more than quarterly and not less than twice a year. Periodically host additional events to create fresh momentum and to build on what God has begun.

✳ **Review the ideas for events and name two to four you would like to consider during the coming year.**

1. _____

2. _____

3. _____

4. _____

Maintain variety in the atmosphere of your events. Tailor some of the events so that men who are not actively involved will feel as comfortable as possible. Make sure the only thing men stumble over is Jesus.

You may not want to have a strong evangelistic appeal at every event. Sometimes lost men just need an opportunity to build relationships with Christian men.

Create a warm, nonthreatening environment. Remember, men are uninvolved for a reason. Don't frighten them with religious jargon. Consider having a businessman from the congregation, rather than a pastor, serve as host or emcee.

Chill out and have a good time. Hang out with the men as Jesus did. Dismantle any holy huddles that don't result in loving, grateful service to God.

Be sure to implement each event with a high level of quality and sensitivity so that your men trust you enough to bring their friends. It may take a while to convince them that you really understand where their friends are coming from. You want them to walk away with the feeling that you genuinely care about them.

✳ **Select an event you have planned for the coming year and complete the information about it on "Event Planning Guide," page 123.**

Keep the Drive Alive

God can use a special event to create an enormous amount of momentum for your men's ministry. How

EVENT PLANNING GUIDE

Name and date of event				
How does this event help accomplish your purpose statement?	This event will … □ Evangelize □ Establish □ Equip □ Extend	This event will … □ Evangelize □ Establish □ Equip □ Extend	This event will … □ Evangelize □ Establish □ Equip □ Extend	This event will … □ Evangelize □ Establish □ Equip □ Extend
Which target group(s) will you reach?	□ Lost men □ Hurting men □ Spiritual child (beginning) □ Spiritual disciple (growing) □ Disciple maker (ministering) □ Colaborer in ministry (equipping) □ Other: ____	□ Lost men □ Hurting men □ Spiritual child (beginning) □ Spiritual disciple (growing) □ Disciple maker (ministering) □ Colaborer in ministry (equipping) □ Other: ____	□ Lost men □ Hurting men □ Spiritual child (beginning) □ Spiritual disciple (growing) □ Disciple maker (ministering) □ Colaborer in ministry (equipping) □ Other: ____	□ Lost men □ Hurting men □ Spiritual child (beginning) □ Spiritual disciple (growing) □ Disciple maker (ministering) □ Colaborer in ministry (equipping) □ Other: ____
Where will the event take place?	□ Church □ Homes □ Neutral turf □ Other:	□ Church □ Homes □ Neutral turf □ Other:	□ Church □ Homes □ Neutral turf □ Other:	□ Church □ Homes □ Neutral turf □ Other:
What advance steps need to be taken?				
What means of follow-through will sustain your momentum?				

can you sustain this momentum and keep the drive alive? Create a variety of opportunities for men to get better acquainted with Christ, since men will be motivated to know Him in many different ways. Each time you ask uninvolved men to take another step, some will drop by the wayside. That's OK. The parable of the sower (see Matt. 13:1-9) is always at work. Reach out to the men who want help. Entrust the others in prayer to our sovereign God. Even Jesus had dropouts, but some continued with Him (see John 6:66-68).

Most meaningful change takes place in the context of church-based relationships. One of the best ways to foster those relationships is to get men involved in small groups. Provide as many men's growth and discipleship opportunities as possible. The greater variety you offer, the more opportunities a man will have to find something that engages him in his walk with God. Suggestions for discipleship were offered in points 4B and 5B of this manual.

✳ **Recall what you learned in points 4B and 5B about establishing men to spiritual maturity. Name two ways you can sustain momentum by involving men in discipleship experiences.**

1. _____

2. _____

Another way to keep momentum going is through monthly or quarterly meetings. These meetings can be helpful for several reasons.
- They provide the next step after the big event.
- They create a place for new men in the church to get involved.
- They build a springboard for men to join small groups.
- They serve as a place for the purpose of the men's ministry to be shared.
- They provide a place where leadership can be developed.

To begin an ongoing large-group-meeting ministry, be sure to cover these bases.

Develop a planning team. Appoint co-coordinators to call the meetings, develop the team, and make sure every man on the committee is doing his job.
- Publicity—to place bulletin announcements, to submit articles for the church newsletter, to send reminders
- Cooking—to prepare the meal or refreshments
- Program—to enlist speakers, music, testimonies, emcee, multimedia
- Table talk—to recruit discussion leaders, to make sure the speaker has questions for discussions that relate to his talk

- Greeters—to meet the men when they arrive and give them name tags, to meet after the meeting to evaluate and discuss details for the next meeting

Develop a purpose statement. Your planning team needs to develop a purpose statement for the meeting. Allow the team time to think through and discuss why they want to meet and how the meeting fits the men's ministry's larger purpose.

Decide on a structure. What you want to do can be done in many different ways. Much depends on your church situation and when your men prefer to meet.

Enlist speakers. Schedule speakers as far in advance as possible. Some churches use outside speakers exclusively, while others like the consistency of one speaker. You might want to ask your pastor whether he would like to speak at these meetings. If you use outside speakers, provide an honorarium, lodging, and travel expenses.

Develop a theme for the year. A theme communicates to men that you are serious about these meetings and have thought about what you want to accomplish. Everything that occurs at the meetings should focus on that theme.

Use your meetings as a bridge. Incorporate elements in the meetings that provide men opportunities to take the next step. Announce new small groups or a service opportunity, for example. Continually ask yourself: *How can we use this to move men forward?*

Follow up on newcomers. Go where the Spirit leads. If a man attends for the first time, he did so for a reason. Maybe he wants fellowship, encouragement, or guidance. Have someone call him and ask how he liked it. This personal follow-up helps men feel cared for and counted on. It may open doors to ministry.

Plan your meetings carefully. When you plan your meetings, keep in mind the following criteria.
- Are there smooth transitions from one part of the meeting to the next? Does the meeting flow, or is it awkward and choppy?
- Are there breaks in the meeting so that men can stretch?
- Is there a chance for men to talk with other men? It is possible to overstructure the meeting so that the men can never meet this simple need.
- Do the components of the meeting fit together?
- If you have music, are the overhead cels or song sheets easy to read? New men will feel out of place if you sing songs without printed words.
- Are the seats comfortable enough to sit on for an extended time?
- Is a sound system necessary for the room you are using? Does it work properly?
- Is the message practical and relevant, meeting men where they are? Does it have points for men to apply? Is it biblically based?

Large-group meetings offer a variety of ways to minister to men. These may be all you choose to do during the first year of your ministry. Or you may choose to use other methods in your first year and add a large-group meeting later.

✳ **Describe a large-group meeting you would like to plan for the coming year.**

Subject: _____

_____

Outcome: _____

_____

Next step: _____

_____

PROMOTE GOD'S VICTORIES

When Barnabas and Saul returned to Antioch, they "reported all that God had done through them" (Acts 14:27, NIV). They celebrated God's victories! Spiritual leaders make praising and thanking the Lord a priority. Testifying to God's work in our lives is the natural and appropriate response to His gracious acts on our behalf. As a men's ministry leader, make sure you provide frequent opportunities to praise God for His work in men's lives. Regularly evaluating your ministry will reveal many reasons to celebrate.

Evaluate Your Ministry

One of the most overlooked aspects of building your ministry is evaluation. Just as a football coach continually evaluates his team's performance and scouts their opponents by watching videos of practices and games, the leadership team frequently needs to take time to evaluate the effectiveness of the men's ministry, as well as of specific events and activities. Such examination allows you to assess and celebrate ways God is working in men's lives. God can also use the evaluation process to alert you to adjustments you need to make to join His work. For men's ministry to be effective, it must determine how best to lead men into a love relationship with Jesus Christ and to develop men who are on mission with Him.

Men's ministries flounder and fail for any of the following reasons.
- The ministry was built on programs instead of prayer and love relationships with God and men.
- The pastor was not initially involved or was not informed and included.
- Leaders lacked understanding of the men

the ministry was proposed to reach.
- The ministry lacked a clearly defined purpose.
- No leader-training process was in place. As a result, too many ministries were launched without called, trained, godly leaders to direct them.
- The ministries launched were not interdependent and mutually supportive of one another and did not offer a variety of entry points to make it easy for men to get involved.

Evaluation can be done at least once a year at a planning meeting or as part of a planning retreat. The following questions can be useful in evaluation.
1. Is our purpose statement still relevant?
2. Is everything we are doing in line with our purpose statement?
3. Is our prayer team in place and praying?
4. Is our leadership team functioning properly? Where do we need help?
5. Is the pastor being informed at the level he desires?
6. Do we have a leader-training process in place?
7. Is the ministry balanced in the following areas?
   - *Evangelism.* Are men trained to witness? Are men building relationships with unchurched men? Are men leading others to Christ? Are we providing evangelistic events to supplement men's individual efforts?
   - *Establishment.* Do we have a mechanism to disciple new believers? Are the men trained to follow up with a new believer? Do we have small groups in place for ongoing growth?
   - *Equipping.* Do we have a means for men to discover, develop, and use their spiritual gifts? Are we getting men to serve in the church based on their gifts? Do we have a way to train men to be leaders in their homes, workplaces, church, and world?
   - *Extension.* Have we helped our men develop a vision for the harvest? Are we providing our men opportunities to serve across the street and around the world? Have we planned any international mission trips this year?
8. How many entry points do we have in the ministry (small groups, quarterly meetings, events, etc.)?
9. How easily can a new man enter the ministry through these entry points?
10. Do we allow for different levels of commitment?
11. Do we offer a variety of service opportunities?
12. Is our ministry progressive?
13. Is our ministry based on God's Word?
14. Do we have an intentional and effective way to get men into small groups?

✳ **The previous list of evaluation questions is not exhaustive. On a separate sheet of paper, list evaluation criteria appropriate for your ministry.**

In addition to evaluating your total ministry, it is helpful to evaluate individual activities and events throughout the year. If an event is worth doing, it is worth evaluating. Give men time at the event to indicate what they thought of it and to make suggestions for the future. Here are evaluation questions given to men who attended an evangelistic outreach luncheon.

1. Was the setting appropriate for our purpose?
2. Was the service good at your table?
3. Was the food hot when it reached your table?
4. Was the message clear?
5. Did the program allow for follow-up of the discussion on the way back to work?
6. What should we change the next time we have an event like this one?
7. What should we do the same way next time?
8. What other recommendations do you have for the planning committee?

Evaluations work best when done both by participants and by the men who organized and carried out the program. With participants' evaluations in hand, the working committee does its own evaluation. One week after the event, hold an evaluation meeting while everything is still fresh in everyone's mind. Review each aspect of the event and ask tough questions. For example, you would ask about publicity: Was the brochure out on time? Was the brochure clear to those who were invited and to those who invited others? Did we use every means possible to bring men to the event? What could we do differently next time?

The type of evaluation you do depends on the type of event being evaluated. Sometimes you need only a quick, 10-minute meeting after the event. Other events require a full evening of discussion. At times evaluation can be a grueling, even painful process. But it helps your men learn and prepare for next time—even if next time is a completely different program or event.

Provide Opportunities to Praise God

Those who give direction to men's ministry today are standing in a long line with Christian leaders of the past who directed others to join them in praising and thanking the Lord at the beginning, in the middle, and at the conclusion of God's work among His people. These praise times frequently included large numbers of people and were often intended solely to express thanks to God for His watchcare or to dedicate a project to His glory. By involving men in celebrations of God's victories, leaders help men see that God holds the world in the palm of His hand and that nothing is too difficult for Him (see Jer. 32:17). That's worth cheering about!

After the Lord brought Moses and the Israelites safely through the Red Sea, they stopped and sang a song of praise to their Deliverer. They exclaimed:

"I will sing to the Lord,
*   for he is highly exalted.*
The horse and its rider
*   he has hurled into the sea.*
The Lord is my strength and my song;
*   he has become my salvation"*
(Ex. 15:1-2, NIV).

When David dedicated the tent of meeting in Jerusalem, where the Ark of the Covenant would be placed, he "appointed some of the Levites to minister before the ark of the Lord, to make petition, to give thanks, and to praise the Lord, the God of Israel" (1 Chron. 16:4, NIV). David then directed Asaph and other men to lead the singing of a "psalm of thanks to the Lord" (1 Chron. 16:7, NIV) that all could hear (see 1 Chron. 16:7-36). The choir that sang when Nehemiah and his colaborers completed the rebuilding of the wall around Jerusalem sang so loudly that "the sound of rejoicing in Jerusalem could be heard far away" (Neh. 12:43, NIV). Even the powerful and wealthy king of Israel instructed the people to take their eyes off the earthly king and look upward to God, who "reigns" and is "exalted over all the nations" (Ps. 99:1-2, NIV).

In Psalm 98:1 the writer encouraged the people to

Sing to the Lord a new song,
for He has done wonderful things (NASB).

By using the word *new,* the psalmist called on others to testify about the new things the Lord was doing in their lives. God continues to answer prayers, open doors, and overcome obstacles in people's lives. Each experience provides an opportunity for someone to write a new song or tell a new story about God's ability to help in times of need. When the psalmist wrote,

His right hand and His holy arm have
gained the victory for Him (Ps. 98:1, NASB),

he was declaring that God works in events and lives to influence people to turn their eyes and their hearts toward Him. The Lord wants to raise up men today who can proclaim, "Look what God has done for us!" Each new song points men to the Lord Jesus Christ and directs others to find satisfaction and self-worth in a love relationship with Him.

By sharing real-life praise reports with men, you not only make God the central focus of your men's ministry but also help men realize that He is touching men in ways relevant to their daily lives. For example, men are inspired when they hear another man share how Jesus Christ has helped him become a better husband and father. God may use such a testimony to touch the heart of a man who wants to improve his relationships with his wife and children. He may then join a small group in which he can develop friendships with other men who will pray with and for him.

Men like to win, and they like to be part of something that has direction. A time of praise and thanksgiving gives leaders the opportunity to say to men, "Here's what we prayed about with you last year, and here's how God has answered our prayers in evangelism, discipleship, ministry, and missions." Show men ways their involvement in the ministry is making a difference in lives today and will impact their families and society in future generations. Sharing God's success stories communicates to men that they are taking part in something of eternal significance.

Men's gatherings are also times to communicate that Jesus has won the victory on our behalf (see 1 Cor. 15:57; 2 Cor. 5:21) and that those who are in Him and serve Him will not be disappointed when Christ returns (see 1 John 2:28; 3:2). The Holy Spirit can use the testimony of an ordinary man to build the faith of another man as he realizes that it is not wealth, education, or position but the presence of Jesus Christ in a man's life that determines whether a man is a success. First Corinthians 1:27-31 says, "God chose the foolish things of the world to shame the wise; God chose the weak things of the world to shame the strong. He chose the lowly things of this world and the despised things—and the things that are not—to nullify the things that are, so that no one may boast before him. It is because of him that you are in Christ Jesus, who has become for us wisdom from God—that is, our righteousness, holiness and redemption. Therefore, as it is written: 'Let him who boasts boast in the Lord' " (NIV).

Men grow in their faith as they see God working through their lives on the basis of who they are in Christ rather than on the basis of human effort. It is His mighty power at work in them, rather than human effort, that Christian men celebrate. Men are challenged to yield themselves to God as they behold Him at work in the lives of ordinary men who are broken vessels available for God's use (see 2 Cor. 12:9-10).

✳ **Check the benefits that result when your men celebrate God's victories.**
   ❑ **1. God is praised as the central focus of your ministry.**
   ❑ **2. Men receive rewards for the work they have done.**
   ❑ **3. Men realize that God is touching men in relevant ways.**
   ❑ **4. Men realize that their involvement is making a difference.**
   ❑ **5. Men look important in front of their families.**
   ❑ **6. Jesus is praised because He has won the victory on our behalf.**

Check your answers on this page.

✳ **Read 2 Corinthians 12:9-10. How do you feel when you realize that God can work through your weakness to accomplish His purposes? Write a prayer that expresses your willingness to let Him work through you to minister to men in your church and community. Then pray your prayer.**

_____

_____

_____

_____

_____

_____

At the beginning of this manual you were asked to visualize the kind of man you would like to see God develop through your men's ministry. Our world needs more men who, like Enoch, walk with God. Our families and our society need men who, like John the Baptist, are filled with the Holy Spirit and are calling fathers to turn their hearts back to their children. Our church and society need men who are used by God to turn the disobedient to righteousness and to prepare people for Christ's return.

Now as you approach the end of this manual, think about how you want to be remembered at the end of your life. No man is perfect in his own strength. It is Jesus Christ who alone is able to present us faultless before the throne of God (see 2 Cor. 5:21). Through Christ, then, let each of us faithfully serve God, fixing our eyes on Him who is "the author and perfecter of our faith" (Heb. 12:2, NIV). When we come to the end of life's journey, may it be said of us that we were men after God's own heart who did everything He wanted us to do, having served God's purpose in our own generation (see Acts 13:22,36).

Resources
A Bunch of Clip Art and Ways to Get People Involved in Discipleship. Nashville: LifeWay, 1998.

Hemphill, Ken. *The Antioch Effect: Eight Characteristics of Highly Effective Churches.* Nashville: Broadman & Holman, 1994.

Washington, Raleigh, Glen Kehrein, and Claude V. King. *Break Down the Walls: Experiencing Biblical Reconciliation and Unity in the Body of Christ.* Chicago: Moody, 1997.

Answers to Activities
Page 114: A common relationship with God through Christ
Page 127: You should have checked 1, 3, 4, and 6.

CHRISTIAN GROWTH STUDY PLAN

Preparing Christians to Serve

In the Christian Growth Study Plan (formerly the Church Study Course) this book, *Drawing Men to God: Men's Ministry Manual*, is the text for course LS-0034 in the Adult Leadership and Skill Development diploma plan. To receive credit, read the book; complete the learning activities; attend group sessions; show your work to your pastor, a staff member, or a church leader; then complete the following information. This page may be duplicated. Send the completed page to:

Christian Growth Study Plan, MSN 117
127 Ninth Avenue, North
Nashville, TN 37234-0117
Fax (615) 251-5067

For information about the Christian Growth Study Plan, refer to the current *Christian Growth Study Plan Catalog.* Your church office may have a copy. If not, request a free copy from the Christian Growth Study Plan office, (615) 251-2525.

DRAWING MEN TO GOD: MEN'S MINISTRY MANUAL
COURSE NUMBER: LS-0034

PARTICIPANT INFORMATION

Social Security Number (USA ONLY) | Personal CGSP Number* | Date of Birth (MONTH, DAY, YEAR)

Name (First, Middle, Last)   □ Mr. □ Miss □ Mrs. □ | Home Phone

Address (Street, Route, or P.O. Box) | City, State, or Province | Zip/Postal Code

CHURCH INFORMATION

Church Name

Address (Street, Route, or P.O. Box) | City, State, or Province | Zip/Postal Code

CHANGE REQUEST ONLY

□ Former Name

□ Former Address | City, State, or Province | Zip/Postal Code

□ Former Church | City, State, or Province | Zip/Postal Code

Signature of Pastor, Conference Leader, or Other Church Leader | Date

*New participants are requested but not required to give SS# and date of birth. Existing participants, please give CGSP# when using SS# for the first time. Thereafter, only one ID# is required. **Mail to:** Christian Growth Study Plan, 127 Ninth Ave., North, Nashville, TN 37234-0117. Fax: (615)251-5067